Political
Awakenings

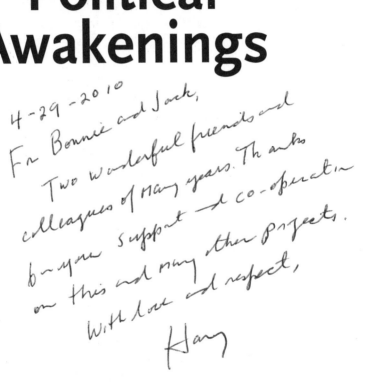

4-29-2010
Fr Bonnie and Jack,
    Two wonderful friends and
colleagues of many years. Thanks
for your support and co-operation
on this and many other projects.
    With love and respect,
            Harry

Political Awakenings

CONVERSATIONS WITH HISTORY

Interviews with Twenty of the
World's Most Influential
Writers, Thinkers, and Activists

Harry Kreisler

THE NEW PRESS

NEW YORK
LONDON

Requests for permission to reproduce selections from this book should be mailed to: Permissions Department, The New Press, 38 Greene Street, New York, NY 10013.

Published in the United States by The New Press, New York, 2010
Distributed by Perseus Distribution

LIBRARY OF CONGRESS CATALOGING-IN-PUBLICATION DATA

Political awakenings : conversations with history / Harry Kreisler.
    p.   m.
  History archive is maintained by the Institute of International Studies of the University of California, Berkeley—Preface.
  ISBN 978-1-59558-340-6 (pbk. : alk. paper)   1. World politics—1945–1989—Sources.   2. History, Modern—1945–1989—Sources. 3. World politics—1989—Sources.   4. History, Modern—1989—Sources.   5. Political activists—Interviews.   6. Politicians—Interviews. 7. Journalists—Interviews.   8. Oral History.   I. Kreisler, Harry. II. University of California, Berkeley. Institute of International Studies.
D839.3.P76 2010
920.02—dc22

                                                            2009036808

The New Press was established in 1990 as a not-for-profit alternative to the large, commercial publishing houses currently dominating the book publishing industry. The New Press operates in the public interest rather than for private gain, and is committed to publishing, in innovative ways, works of educational, cultural, and community value that are often deemed insufficiently profitable.

www.thenewpress.com

Composition by NK Graphics
This book was set in Scala

Printed in the United States of America

10   9   8   7   6   5   4   3   2   1

For Edie and Jeremy

CONTENTS

PREFACE

I. History of the Series

In 1982, as Executive Director of the Institute of International Studies at the University of California at Berkeley, I started Conversations with History, an archive of one-hour videotaped interviews. The idea was to expose students and the public to the reflections of the distinguished men and women who pass through Berkeley on a daily basis, sharing the university's distinction as a global forum for ideas with a larger audience. In the beginning, this material was placed in the Berkeley video library. Over the next two decades, as new technologies were developed, the archive became much more—it became a resource for many broadcast media, including cable, satellite television, the World Wide Web, YouTube video, and podcasting (http://globetrotter.berkeley.edu/conversations).

Our conversations would occur as the tape rolled, since editing was not within our budget. Over time, I learned to work with this limitation by preparing extensively. I would read and study whatever relevant material I could get hold of, including books, monographs, vitae, and newspaper articles. I was then positioned to be not only an on-camera host who was responsive to what was said but also a thoughtful and engaged guide to a unique intellectual journey. I allowed the conversation to be moved in unexpected directions. My interviewing style invited the guest to be frank and honest as he or she recounted ideas that were central to his or her own personal narrative, and my questions were intended to elicit very personal and human responses, which I hope resonated with the audience. As an informed guide, I became an ideal representative of the interests and concerns of an audience that wants to learn more about the world.

In my approach, I was influenced by two heroes from the 1950s. When I was growing up in Galveston, Texas, I regularly watched Edward R. Murrow's *Person to Person* and Walter Cronkite's *You Are There*. In the early years of television, Murrow took you into the homes of the movers and shakers in the arts and politics to explore their personalities. Cronkite took you back into history, where newsmen would interview actors playing historical figures. Both Cronkite and Murrow emphasized the importance of personality in shaping events.

My goal was to create a coherent sense of my guests so that the audience could understand who they were and how their unique mix of personality, intellect, and character came together to shape ideas that would affect the world. I explored the influence of parents, teachers, and events, the role of luck, and the consequences of setting. As these stories unfolded, I began to sense the strange mix of ingredients, often unplanned and unintended, that shaped these individuals and their distinctive contributions in fields as diverse as science, public policy, theory, art, journalism, political activism, and military affairs.

As a forum for these distinguished men and women to reflect on their past experiences, the Conversations with History program became, for the guest, a conversation with his or her own past. In this way, the conversation was enlightening as a case study in the formulation of ideas and how those ideas can shape our world.

Between 1982 and 2009, I conducted more than 475 interviews. Guests included diplomats, statesmen, and soldiers; economists and political analysts; scientists and historians; writers and foreign correspondents; activists and artists.

II. Political Awakenings

Political Awakenings contains twenty interviews from the larger archive. This set of interviews was selected to capture the diversity of the people who, by the power of their intellect and the strength of their character, make a difference in our ever-changing world. These interviewees came to see their world in a radically different way—with important implications for our world. They embraced ideas and actions that implied a different way of perceiving politics. Politics in this context means more than party affiliation; it refers to an understanding of power relations. The insights didn't just happen but were the consequences of life experiences that helped clarify the way things held together—moments of political awakening. Invariably, because of the interface between past and present, because of the limits and opportunities of their profession, or because of the interaction of different worlds, my guests were positioned to imagine alternatives to the conventional wisdom. A new way of seeing emerged in their thinking, in their writing, in their activism. With courage, perseverance, and determination, they took their ideas to a broader audience. In so doing, their world—and the politics of their world—were changed forever.

Harry Kriesler
Berkeley, California
November 2009

ACKNOWLEDGMENTS

I wish to thank The New Press, especially Marc Favreau for proposing this selection focused on political awakenings and Priyanka Jacob for help in shaping the manuscript. In addition, I wish to thank my wife, Edie Cottrell Kreisler, for her love and support. Her contribution to the Conversations with History project and to this volume is immeasurable.

PROTEST AND CHANGE

Citizens in the street can change the course of history. These first interviews speak to the transformative power of the labor movement and of the widespread acts of protest during the Vietnam War. Such historical moments can shake the foundations of society, altering our preconceived notions about politics, justice, and the legitimacy of power. At the core of such turning points is the realization by certain individuals of the larger picture—an acute awareness of social injustice. The transformative power of social movements is central to the political awakenings of both Noam Chomsky and Daniel Ellsberg.

Noam Chomsky

Noam Chomsky is Institute Professor and Professor Emeritus of Linguistics at the Massachusetts Institute of Technology. His prolific work in linguistics revolutionized the scientific study of language. Among his books in linguistics are *Logical Structure of Linguistic Theory*, *Aspects of the Theory of Syntax*, and *Language and Mind*. In addition, he has wide-ranging political interests that inform his major contribution to radical dissent. He was an early and outspoken critic of U.S. involvement in the Vietnam War and has written extensively on many political issues. Among his political writings are *American Power and the New Mandarins*, *Manufacturing Consent* (with E.S. Herman), *Rogue States*, and *9-11*.

Daniel Ellsberg

Daniel Ellsberg is an activist and strategic analyst. He was a major figure in the public protest to halt the Vietnam War. His leaking of the Pentagon Papers to the *New York Times* set in motion a series of events, including illegal actions by then-President Richard Nixon that led the president to resign his office rather than be impeached. Ellsberg is the author of *Secrets: A Memoir of Vietnam and the Pentagon Papers* and *Papers on the War.*

Noam Chomsky
March 22, 2002

How do you think your parents shaped your perspectives on the world?

Those are always very hard questions, because it's a combination
of influence and resistance, which is difficult to sort out. My parents were immigrants, and they happened to end up in Philadelphia, as part of what amounted to kind of a Hebrew ghetto,
Jewish ghetto, in Philadelphia. Not a physical ghetto—it was scat-
tered around the city—but a cultural ghetto.

When my father's family came over, for whatever reason,
they went to Baltimore, and my mother's family, from another
part of the Pale of Settlement, came to New York. The families
were totally different. The Baltimore family was ultra-orthodox.
In fact, my father told me that they had become more orthodox
when they got here than they even were in the shtetl in the
Ukraine where they came from. In general, there was a tendency
among some sectors of immigrants to intensify the cultural tradition, probably as a way of identifying themselves in a strange
environment, I suppose.

The other part of the family, my mother's, was mainly Jewish
working class—very radical. The Jewish element had disappeared.
This was the 1930s, so they were part of the ferment of radical
activism that was going on in all sorts of ways. Of all of them, the
one that actually did influence me a great deal was an uncle by
marriage who came into the family when I was about seven or
eight. He had grown up in a poor area of New York. In fact, he
himself never went past fourth grade—on the streets, and with a
criminal background, and all [the things that were] going on in

the underclass ghettos in New York. He happened to have a physical deformity, so he was able to get a newsstand under a compensation program that was run in the 1930s for people with disabilities. He had a newsstand on 72nd Street in New York and lived nearby in a little apartment. I spent a lot of time there.

That newsstand became an intellectual center for émigrés from Europe; lots of Germans and other émigrés were coming. He wasn't a very educated person, formally—like I said, he never went past fourth grade—but maybe the most educated person I've ever met. Self-educated. The newsstand itself was a very lively, intellectual center—professors of this and that arguing all night. And working at the newsstand was a lot of fun. I went for years thinking that there's a newspaper called *Newsinmira*. Because people came out of the subway station and raced past the newsstand; they would say "Newsinmira," and I gave them two tabloids, which I later discovered were the *News* and the *Mirror*. And I noticed that as soon as they picked up the "Newsinmira," the first thing they opened to was the sports page. So this is an eight-year-old's picture of the world. There were newspapers there, but that wasn't all there was—that was the background of the discussions that were going on.

Through my uncle and other influences, I got myself involved in the ongoing '30s radicalism, and was very much part of the Hebrew-based, Zionist-oriented—this is Palestine, pre-Israel—Palestine-oriented life. And that was a good part of my life. I became a Hebrew teacher like my parents, and a Zionist youth leader, combining it with the radical activism in various ways. Actually, that's the way I got into linguistics.

You actually wrote your first essay as a ten-year-old, on the Spanish Civil War.

Well, you know, like you said, I was ten years old. I'm sure I would not want to read it today. I remember what it was about because

I remember what struck me. This was right after the fall of Barcelona; the fascist forces had conquered Barcelona, and that was essentially the end of the Spanish Civil War. And the article was about the spread of fascism around Europe. So it started off by talking about Munich and Barcelona, and the spread of the Nazi power, fascist power, which was extremely frightening.

Just to add a little word of personal background, we happened to be, for most of my childhood, the only Jewish family in a mostly Irish and German Catholic neighborhood, sort of a lower middle-class neighborhood, which was very anti-Semitic, and quite pro-Nazi. It's obvious why the Irish would be: they hated the British; it's not surprising the Germans were [anti-Semitic]. I can remember beer parties when Paris fell. And the sense of the threat of this black cloud spreading over Europe was very frightening. I could pick up my mother's attitudes, particularly; she was terrified by it.

It was also in my personal life, because I saw the streets. Interesting—for some reason which I do not understand to this day, my brother and I never talked to our parents about it. I don't think they knew that we were living in an anti-Semitic neighborhood. But on the streets, you know, you go out and play ball with kids, or try to walk to the bus or something; it was a constant threat. It was just the kind of thing you knew for some reason not to talk to your parents about. To the day of their death they didn't know. But there was this combination of knowing that this cloud was spreading over the world and picking up, particularly, that my mother was very upset about it—my father too, but more constrained—and living it in the streets in my own daily life, that made it very real.

Anyhow, by the late '30s, I did become quite interested in Spanish anarchism and the Spanish Civil War, where all of this was being fought out at the time. Right before the World War broke out, a kind of microcosm was going on in Spain. By the time I was old enough to get on a train by myself, around ten or eleven, I would go to New York for a weekend and stay with my aunt and uncle, and hang around at anarchist bookstores down around Union Square and Fourth Avenue. There were little bookstores with émigrés, really interesting people. To my mind they looked about ninety; they were maybe in their forties or something, and they were very interested in young people. They wanted young people to come along, so they spent a lot of attention. Talking to these people was a real education.

These experiences we've described, you were saying they led you into linguistics, but also led you into your view of politics and of the world. You're a libertarian anarchist, and when one hears that, because of the way issues are framed in this country, there are many misperceptions. Help us understand what that means.

The United States is sort of out of the world on this topic. Here, the term "libertarian" means the opposite of what it always meant in history. Libertarian throughout modern European history meant socialist anarchist. It meant the anti-state element of the Workers' Movement and the Socialist Movement. Here it means ultra-conservative—Ayn Rand or Cato Institute or something like that. But that's a special U.S. usage. There are a lot of things quite special about the way the United States developed, and this is part of it. In Europe, it meant, and always meant to me, an anti-state branch of socialism, which meant a highly organized society, nothing to do with chaos, but based on democracy all the way through. That means democratic control of communities, of workplaces, of federal structures, built on systems of voluntary association, spreading internationally. That's traditional anarchism. You know, anybody can have the word if they like, but that's the mainstream of traditional anarchism.

And it has roots. Coming back to the United States, it has very strong roots in the American working-class movements. So if you go back to, say, the 1850s, the beginnings of the Industrial

Revolution, right around the area where I live, in Eastern Massachusetts, in the textile plants and so on, the people working on those plants were, in part, young women coming off the farm. They were called "factory girls," the women from the farms who worked in the textile plants. Some of them were Irish, immigrants in Boston and that group of people. They had an extremely rich and interesting culture. They're kind of like my uncle who never went past fourth grade—very educated, reading modern literature. They didn't bother with European radicalism; that had no effect on them, but they were very much a part of the general literary culture. And they developed their own conceptions of how the world ought to be organized.

They had their own newspapers. In fact, the period of the freest press in the United States was probably around the 1850s. In the 1850s, the scale of the popular press—meaning run by factory girls in Lowell and so on—was on the scale of the commercial press or even greater. These were independent newspapers that [arose] spontaneously, without any background. [The writers had] never heard of Marx or Bakunin or anyone else, yet they developed the same ideas. From their point of view, what they called "wage slavery," renting yourself to an owner, was not very different from the chattel slavery that they were fighting a civil war about. So the idea of renting yourself, meaning working for wages, was degrading. It was an attack on your personal integrity. They despised the industrial system that was developing, that was destroying their culture, destroying their independence, their individuality, constraining them to be subordinate to masters.

There was a tradition of what was called Republicanism in the United States. We're free people, you know, the first free people in the world. This was destroying and undermining that freedom. This was the core of the labor movement all over, and included in it was the assumption, just taken for granted, that those who work in the mills should own them.

In fact, one of their main slogans was a condemnation of what they called the "new spirit of the age: gain wealth, forgetting all but self." That new spirit, that you should only be interested in gaining wealth and forgetting about your relations to other people, they regarded it as a violation of fundamental human nature and a degrading idea.

That was a strong, rich American culture, which was crushed by violence. The United States has a very violent labor history, much more so than Europe. It was wiped out over a long period, with extreme violence. By the time it picked up again in the 1930s, that's when I personally came into the tail end of it. After the Second World War it was crushed. By now, it's forgotten. But it's very real. I don't really think it's forgotten; I think it's just below the surface in people's consciousness.

You examine in your work the extent to which histories and traditions are forgotten. To define a new position often means going back and finding those older traditions.

Things like this, they're forgotten in the intellectual culture, but my feeling is they're alive in the popular culture, in people's sentiments and attitudes and understanding and so on. I know when I talk to, say, working-class audiences today, and I talk about these ideas, they seem very natural to them. It's true, nobody talks about them, but when you bring up the idea that you have to rent yourself to somebody and follow their orders, and that they own and you work—you built it, but you don't own it—that's a highly unnatural notion. You don't have to study any complicated theories to see that this is an attack on human dignity.

So coming out of this tradition, being influenced by and continuing to believe in it, what is your notion of legitimate power? Under what circumstances is power legitimate?

The core of the anarchist tradition, as I understand it, is that power is always illegitimate, unless it proves itself to be legitimate. So the burden of proof is always on those who claim that some authoritarian hierarchic relation is legitimate. If they can't prove it, then it should be dismantled.

Can you ever prove it? Well, it's a heavy burden of proof to bear, but I think sometimes you can bear it. So to take an example, if I'm walking down the street with my four-year-old grand-daughter, and she starts to run into the street, and I grab her arm and pull her back, that's an exercise of power and authority, but I can give a justification for it, and it's obvious what the justification would be. And maybe there are other cases where you can justify it. But the question that always should be asked upper-most in our mind is, "Why should I accept it?" It's the responsi-bility of those who exercise power to show that somehow it's legitimate. It's not the responsibility of anyone else to show that it's illegitimate. It's illegitimate by assumption, if it's a relation of authority among human beings which places some above others. Unless you can give a strong argument to show that it's right, you've lost.

It's kind of like the use of violence, say, in international af-fairs. There's a very heavy burden of proof to be borne by anyone who calls for violence. Maybe it can be sometimes justified. Per-sonally, I'm not a committed pacifist, so I think that, yes, it can sometimes be justified. So I thought, in fact, in that article I wrote in fourth grade, I thought the West should be using force to try to stop Fascism, and I still think so. But now I know a lot more about it. I know that the West was actually supporting Fascism, supporting Franco, supporting Mussolini, and so on, and even Hitler. I didn't know that at the time. But I thought then and I think now that the use of force to stop that plague would have been legitimate, and finally was legitimate. But an argument has to be given for it.

You've said, "You can lie or distort the story of the French Revolution as long as you like and nothing will happen. Propose a false theory in chemistry and it will be refuted tomorrow." How does your approach to the world as a scientist affect and influence the way you approach politics?

Nature is tough. You can't fiddle with Mother Nature, she's a hard taskmistress. So you're forced to be honest in the natural sciences. In the soft fields, you're not forced to be honest. There are standards, of course; on the other hand, they're very weak. If what you propose is ideologically acceptable, that is, supportive of power systems, you can get away with a huge amount. In fact, the difference between the conditions that are imposed on dissident opinion and on mainstream opinion is radically different.

For example, I've written about terrorism, and I think you can show without much difficulty that terrorism pretty much corresponds to power. I don't think that's very surprising. The more powerful states are involved in more terrorism, by and large. The United States is the most powerful, so it's involved in massive terrorism, by its own definition of terrorism. Well, if I want to establish that, I'm required to give a huge amount of evidence. I think that's a good thing. I don't object to that. I think anyone who makes that claim should be held to very high standards. So, I do extensive documentation, from the internal secret records and historical record and so on. And if you ever find a comma misplaced, somebody ought to criticize you for it. So I think those standards are fine.

All right, now, let's suppose that you play the mainstream game. You can say anything you want because you support power, and nobody expects you to justify anything. For example, in the unimaginable circumstance that I was on, say, *Nightline*, and I was asked, "Do you think Kadhafi is a terrorist?" I could say, "Yeah, Kadhafi is a terrorist." I don't need any evidence. Suppose I said,

"George Bush is a terrorist." Well, then I would be expected to provide evidence—"Why would you say that?"

In fact, the structure of the news production system is, you can't produce evidence. There's even a name for it—I learned it from the producer of *Nightline*, Jeff Greenfield. It's called "concision." He was asked in an interview somewhere why they didn't have me on *Nightline*. First of all, he says, "Well, he talks Turkish, and nobody understands it." But the other answer was, "He lacks concision." Which is correct, I agree with him. The kinds of things that I would say on *Nightline*, you can't say in one sentence because they depart from standard religion. If you want to repeat the religion, you can get away with it between two commercials. If you want to say something that questions the religion, you're expected to give evidence, and that you can't do between two commercials. So therefore you lack concision, so therefore you can't talk.

I think that's a terrific technique of propaganda. To impose concision is a way of virtually guaranteeing that the party line gets repeated over and over again, and that nothing else is heard.

What is your advice for people who have the same concerns, who identify with the tradition that you come out of, and who want to be engaged in opposition?

The same as the factory girls in the Lowell textile plant 150 years ago: they joined with others. To do these things alone is extremely hard, especially when you're working fifty hours a week to put the food on the table. Join with others, and you can do a lot of things. It's got a big multiplier effect. That's why unions have always been in the lead of development of social and economic progress. They bring together poor people, working people, enable them to learn from one another, to have their own sources of information, and to act collectively. That's how everything is changed—the civil rights movement, the feminist movement, the solidarity movements, the workers' movements. The reason we don't live in a dungeon is because people have joined together to change things. And there's nothing different now from before. In fact, just in the last forty years, we've seen remarkable changes in this respect.

Go back to '62, there was no feminist movement, there was a very limited human rights movement. There was no environmental movement, meaning rights of our grandchildren. There were no Third World solidarity movements. There was no anti-apartheid movement. There was no anti–sweat shop movement. I mean, all of the things that we take for granted just weren't there. How did they get there? Was it a gift from an angel? No, they got there by struggle, common struggle by people who dedicated themselves with others, because you can't do it alone, and [their efforts] made it a much more civilized country. It was a long way to go, and that's not the first time it happened. And it will continue.

You believe that when we focus on heroes in the movement, that's a mistake, because it's really the unsung heroes, the unsung seamstresses or whatever in this movement, who actually make a difference.

Take, say, the civil rights movement. When you think of the civil rights movement, the first thing you think of is Martin Luther King Jr. King was an important figure. But he would have been the first to tell you, I'm sure, that he was riding the wave of activism, that people who were doing the work, who were in the lead in the civil rights movement, were young SNCC [Student Non-violent Coordinating Committee] workers, freedom riders, people out there in the streets every day getting beaten and sometimes killed, working constantly. They created the circumstances in which a Martin Luther King could come in and be a leader. His role was extremely important, I'm not denigrating it, it was very important to have done that. But the people who were really important are the ones whose names are forgotten. And that's true of every movement that ever existed.

Is it the case that by seeing so much you understand that very little sometimes can be accomplished, but that may be very important?

I don't think we should give up long-term visions. I agree with the factory girls in Lowell in 1850. I think wage slavery is an attack on fundamental human rights. I think those who work in the plants should own them. I think we should struggle against what was then the "new spirit of the age": gain wealth, forgetting everybody but yourself. Yes, that's all degrading and destructive, and in the long term—I don't know how long—it should be dismantled. But right now there are serious problems to deal with, like thirty million Americans who don't have enough to eat, or people elsewhere in the world who are far worse off, and who are, in fact, under our boot, we're grinding them into the dust. Those are short-term things that can be dealt with. There's nothing wrong with making small gains, like the gains that I was talking about before, from the '60s until today. They're extremely important for human lives. It doesn't mean that there are not a lot of mountain peaks to climb, there are. But you do what's within range.

The same in the sciences. You might like to solve the problems of, say, what causes human action, but the problems you work on are the ones that are right at the edge of your understanding. There's a famous joke about a drunk under a lamppost looking at the ground, and somebody comes up and asks him "What are you looking for?" He says, "I'm looking for a pencil that I dropped." They say, "Well, where did you drop it?" He says, "Oh, I dropped it across the street." "Well, why are looking here?" "This is where the light is." That's the way the sciences work. Maybe the problem you would like to solve is across the street, but you have to work where the light is. If you try to move it a little farther, maybe ultimately you'll get across the street.

Daniel Ellsberg
July 29, 1998

When did you first become involved with Vietnam?

I've really never discussed this before in public, but the fact is that I was there in 1961 in connection with a task force, a study group for the Kennedy Defense Department, on limited war research and development. I got a picture of Vietnam at that point that led me to decide to stay away from that problem, bureaucratically, for the rest of my career if I could. I came back and helped write a report for RAND, which incorporated what I had learned in that study group, and the advice was, basically: don't ask for research money for this, don't get involved, stay away from it, this is a total loser. Because it was already apparent in 1961, or earlier for that matter, that there was really no promise of Western efforts to subdue the movement for national independence and sovereignty in Vietnam, which was led by communists, who had beaten the French, who had very strong American financial support, materials and so forth. We were facing essentially the same people there, and the likelihood that we would do better than the French had done seemed very small.

During the Kennedy administration in 1961 and 1962, 1963, I really avoided getting into discussions of Vietnam. I didn't want to be drawn into it. I thought being tarred with that, essentially, would be like being associated with the Bay of Pigs, that perfect failure which had ruined the careers of nearly anybody who had touched it.

But then a few years later you actually went back to Vietnam?

No, I was assigned. . . . I was brought back in, somewhat reluc-
tantly, to Vietnam. And I wanted to see governmental decision-
making now from the inside, having studied it as a researcher
and a consultant for a number of years before that. The first day
I started involving myself in it, reading the cables, as they say,
which means immersing yourself in this huge flood of telegraph
messages that come from a particular region. Almost the first
cables I read had to do with an apparent attack on our destroyers
in the Tonkin Gulf. It was August 4, 1964. Now I was seeing very
urgent cables coming in, saying that destroyers were again under
attack, this time late at night. And their only knowledge of this
was by radar and sonar.

To leap ahead some years: it was clear in later years that there
had been no attack. They were fighting radar shadows and sonar
shadows in the water, firing at them. And there had been no tor-
pedoes in the water as they supposed.

But at the time, to begin with, they were told very clearly that
these boats were under attack. Then, at a certain point on that
very first day of my involvement, I read a cable that said, "Hold
everything." The commodore of that two-destroyer flotilla recom-
mended no action be taken until they had a chance to look at the
water surrounding them the next day in daylight and see if there
was wreckage or oil slicks or survivors in the water. Since they
thought they had actually destroyed some boats, there should be
some sign of it. There was very strong doubt as to how large the
attack had been or whether there was an attack at all. It was not
really possible to confirm. Nevertheless, the president had already
decided, by the time that cable was received, to start air operations against North Vietnam.

So here we were, launching sixty-four sorties against North
Vietnam. I was up all night in the Pentagon following these raids
and their aftermath, which were taking place on the other side of
the world, twelve time zones different, so it was daylight over
there and night for us.

And then over the next couple of days, the president got Congress to support almost unanimously what he was to regard as the functional equivalent of a declaration of war—the Tonkin Gulf resolution, which he felt gave him congressional support for a war, although that was not what Congress was led to understand they were voting for. And we were now off on the heavy U.S. combat phase of the Vietnam War.

At that time did you have doubts about what the president was asking the Congress for, based on what you were seeing?

Far beyond doubts. The president said to Congress and the public that the evidence for the attack on our ships was unequivocal. That was false. I knew that was a lie. Well before the attack got off, many, many doubts had been raised and it was clearly unclear [what was happening]. I think I would have said, and most people would have said "probably" with all this: "probably there was an attack." But that was not what the president told the public. He lied to the public.

Second, he said, assuming that there was an attack, it was clearly an unprovoked attack against destroyers on the high seas. That was a lie in the sense that the actual attack that had occurred two days earlier had followed covert, secret, denied attacks by the United States on North Vietnam just the night before. So there was just as much evidence that it had been provoked by us. McNamara, Rusk, Vance, all continued to conceal from the Congress that these U.S. attacks were taking place.

With the environment you were working with in the Pentagon, how did people deal with this incompatibility between what was being said publicly and what you and others knew inside the corridors of power?

Well, I had been consulting for the government for about six years at that point, since 1959, [for] Eisenhower, Kennedy, and now Johnson. And I had seen tens of thousands of pages of classified material by this time, and had been in a position to compare it with what was being said to the public. The public is lied to every day by the president, by his spokespeople, by his officers. If you can't handle the thought that the president lies to the public for all kinds of reasons, you can't stay at that government at that level, where you're made aware of it, every week.

I mention that because sometimes people speculate [as to] why I had given the Pentagon Papers to the *Times* with the expectation that I'd be sent to prison for it. As Harrison Salisbury of the *New York Times* said, "He couldn't stand the lying." Well, that's basically foolish. I was not going to prison for years simply to set the record straight. If you can't live with the idea that presidents lie, you can't work for presidents. The fact is, presidents rarely say the whole truth, essentially never say the whole truth of what they expect and what they're doing, what they believe and why they're doing it. They rarely refrain from lying, actually, about these matters. It's simply more convenient and more politically effective, they feel, for them to present matters to the public in a way that happens not to correspond to reality.

Subsequently you became more involved in the war. You actually went to Vietnam and worked there after this period.

Yes, by the summer of 1965, the president had decided on an open-ended escalation of that war. We had been bombing now since February and were heavily involved; we had over 100,000 troops in Vietnam by that time. We were at war. And I, as a former marine in peacetime, 1954–1957—marine platoon leader and company commander—I didn't like the idea of following the war from Washington. I volunteered to go to Vietnam to do liaison work at the embassy with the Vietnamese. I had a feeling that would give me a better chance to understand the war and perhaps avoid the worst kinds of outcomes.

Most of the time I was involved in Vietnam, it was quite clear that nothing lay ahead for us but frustration and stalemate and killing and dying. Very little hope of a favorable outcome or even an outcome that could be called acceptable, except for the possibility of postponing a defeat or shift in policy.

Presidents, I found from studying it later in the files, had never really faced much recommendation that held out a clear-cut hope of a successful outcome in Vietnam to them. But on the other hand, they had faced the possibility that they could postpone the kind of embarrassment or defeat that was involved in getting out of Vietnam and letting the Vietnamese determine their own politics—which would have meant, over time, almost surely communist hegemony. And their alternative to that was that they could put it off at increasingly higher costs to the U.S. and to the Vietnamese, in terms of lives and money and involvement. Each president chose to do that, and that's what Kennedy chose and that's what Johnson chose while he was in office. And that's what Nixon chose until he was removed from office.

Coming back to Washington and to RAND, you had access to what became known as the Pentagon Papers. Explain what those documents were.

I was in Vietnam for two years, from 1965–1967. I evaluated pacification there for most of that time, which took me to most of the provinces of Vietnam. I was in thirty-eight of the forty-three provinces. I used my former marine training, though I was a civilian, to work with troops part of that time, and I did actually experience significant combat for some periods. So I saw the war up very close, from the point, as a matter of fact, in an infantry company. And I got hepatitis, probably on one of those field expeditions, and came back to the U.S. and left the government and rejoined the RAND Corporation and was immediately assigned to a historical project that McNamara had organized in the Pentagon, which came to have the title "U.S. Decision Making in Vietnam, 1945–1968."

I was the only researcher, in or out of the government, who was given access to the entire forty-seven volumes of the study for the purposes of research. It was seven thousand pages, top secret. I had it in a top secret safe in my office, for the purpose of working on a study called "Lessons from Vietnam."

I was actually, oddly, the only person being paid by a U.S. government contract, or salary, to look at lessons from Vietnam, strangely enough. Most of the people who had worked on that had read only one volume of it, the one they worked on. For some time there were really only three of us in the country who had read that entire study and were able, in effect, to learn the lessons of the entire sweep of that period, that twenty-three year period from 1945 to 1968.

What was done in Vietnam was often not the most rational, but rather a reflection of a dynamic that was heavily influenced by politics. But for many years you lived with it.

By the way, from the president's point of view, that is the essence of rationality: staying in office, winning the election. He can always rationalize that in terms of larger interests by saying it's very important that my party and I bring our wisdom to bear on these decisions, rather than those other guys. For instance: it's terribly important that Goldwater not succeed. Rather than let Goldwater win, we had to do this and that. Just as, of course, the president's men said during Watergate, "Of course we did these things to prevent McGovern from being president; that would have been catastrophic." That was their rationale. So when you say, "It wasn't rational," what I'm saying is that the rationality had to do with domestic political power, staying in office, self-esteem, prestige of presidents, which presidents and the presidents' men very easily confound with the interests of the nation. They find it, in fact, very hard to distinguish between those two.

You remained for many years part of the government, part of the team, willing to live with the elements of this decision-making process. After much frustration with Vietnam, after reading the Pentagon Papers, you reached a different conclusion about what is acceptable and what is moral. Explain how that change in your thinking came about.

I learned in Vietnam nothing very new about the lack of good prospects for success. I went to Vietnam pretty much with that perspective already. But I did learn the faces of the Vietnamese. I learned to be concerned for what happened to Vietnamese people in a way that my colleagues back in Washington probably [weren't]. [The Vietnamese] had a reality for me. They weren't just numbers and they weren't just abstract ciphers of some kind, as they were for other people.

What I particularly learned, though, in 1969, and from the Pentagon Papers, was that Nixon, the fifth president in a row now, was choosing to prolong the war in vain hopes that he might get a better outcome than he could achieve if he'd just negotiated his way out and accepted, essentially, a defeat. He hoped to do much better than that. In fact, he hoped to hold on to control of Saigon and the major populated areas indefinitely for the United States—that these would be subject to our will and our policy and not be run by communists. And he hoped to do that, actually, in ways similar to the way Johnson had hoped—by threatening escalation of the war. He was making such threats, and he was prepared to carry them out.

I did not believe the threats would succeed, so I foresaw a larger war. The public would not, at that time, have supported a continuation of the war, let alone an expansion of the war. But he was successfully fooling the public, who didn't want to believe that any president could be so foolish and so narrow-minded in his own interests as to keep that war going after the Tet Offensive of 1968. So I saw once again a president making secret threats, almost sure to carry them out, and deceiving the public as to what he was doing.

By reading the Pentagon Papers, which I finished doing in the fall of 1969, I now had a historical sweep sufficient to reach a conclusion that I would have been very unlikely to reach without reading them—that there was very little hope of changing [the president's] mind from inside the executive branch—for example, by giving him good advice or by giving him realistic estimates of what was happening in Vietnam. Because what I saw by reading the earliest days of the Pentagon Papers was that every president had had such advice, as early as Truman. The fact now that Nixon was embarked on a new course held out very little hope that he would be more responsive to good advice about getting out than any of his predecessors had been.

That meant that if his decision was going to be changed— and because I cared about Vietnam and this country, I felt quite urgently that I wanted the United States to stop bombing and killing Vietnamese—the pressure would have to come from outside the executive branch. It required better information outside the executive branch, in Congress and in the public, about the past and about the present, than they had. If I had had documents on what Nixon was planning, I would have put those out to Congress to warn them of what was coming. I probably would not have bothered with the thousands of pages of history that involved the earlier presidents; I would have shown what Nixon was doing. But I didn't have those documents. And at that time, it was very hard to get the public to believe or to act on the possibility that a president was lying to them or deceiving them. That was not in the American consciousness, and it was a very unpopular notion even to put forward.

I once said in a courtroom, in defense of people who were on trial for resisting the draft, that the president had lied. This was in early 1971, before the Pentagon Papers had come out. The judge stopped the proceedings, called the lawyers up to the bench. "If you elicit testimony like that again," he said to the defense lawyer, "I will hold you in contempt. I will not have statements about the president lying in my courtroom." This was in a trial of people who were resisting the war nonviolently. And they weren't allowed to have witnesses who said that the president was lying. The Pentagon Papers changed that. Seven thousand pages of documents of presidential lying did establish forever—and they were confirmed of course by Watergate a couple of years later—that presidents all lie.

Were you also affected in your decision by the demonstrators and the moral positions that they advocated?

Less so by the demonstrators, actually, than by people that I'd met who were paying a much higher price in their lives to make a very strong message. People who would go to jail rather than go to the draft and Vietnam, or go to Canada, or become conscientious objectors, or go in the National Guard. They had a number of options to avoid combat in Vietnam, including being a conscientious objector. But they chose, actually, to make the strongest statement that you could that the war was wrong, that it should end, and that they would not cooperate with it in any way, even by accepting CO status. And they accepted prison as a result.

I met one in particular named Randall Keeler in late August of 1969, and when I understood to my amazement that he was about to be tried for draft resistance and expected to go to prison, where he did go for two years, it had a shattering effect on me to realize that we were in a situation where men as attractive in their intelligence and commitment as Randy Keeler found that the best thing they could do was to accept prison, to try to raise a moral issue to their countrymen. And I realized that was the best thing he could do. He was doing the right thing, and that defined the situation we were in. What a terrible situation! I felt that we were eating our young. Worse than cannibals: we were eating our own children. We were relying on them to pay the price for somehow getting us out of this war, sacrificing them like cannon fodder in the war itself. And they should be joined by people who were willing to do everything that one could, truthfully and nonviolently. These were Gandhians, in effect. And I had by this time, it so happens, been reading Gandhi and Martin Luther King, and now I was meeting people who had been living the life that I'd been reading about. And with the constraints, then, of truthfulness and nonviolence, I realized that, following their example, I was prepared to do anything I could, and that meant giving up a career and meant going to prison.

So I asked myself for the first time, what could I do to help end the war if I were willing to go to prison? I was trying to arrange that I could testify before Congress. I was trying to get hearings started. I was participating with others in writing letters from RAND. But I was also copying the Pentagon Papers in hopes of strengthening some of these other moves, such as my testimony to Congress, for what it might be worth. I didn't think, actually, that it had much chance of affecting events, but it had some chance. And I was ready to do anything I could, and that was one of the things I could do.

Any other factors that can help us understand the kind of inner strength it took? It was not the easiest choice to make for any individual.

Reading the Pentagon Papers burned out of me the desire to work for the president. I saw five presidents in a row who had been mistaken in this stubborn, selfish, foolish way for what was, at this point now, twenty-four years.

The idea that I'd had since I was a boy, and that most Americans had, was to get the opportunity to work for the president.

(We talk about growing up to be president but not many of us, other than Clinton, who is a rare example, had this seriously in his mind.) When I was a marine lieutenant, I already thought of myself as working for the president. I think, more than [the other armed forces], the marines tend to think of themselves as a fast reaction force at the president's disposal, kind of a presidential guard, and have that feeling of self-esteem that comes from identifying with the president. And in the executive branch everybody gets the habit of saying, "We did this, we did that"; it's a strong identification with being a president's man or president's woman.

And here I was in '69, I was the first RAND researcher who did work directly for the president's assistant for national security. I did staff work for Kissinger on Vietnam in the very beginning of the administration. And that was very prestigious and very exciting. Many, many people inside and out of the executive branch think that the opportunity to work in the executive branch is the highest calling that an American can have. You're working for the national security in the most powerful, effective way that you could possibly have. Nothing that you could do, write articles, write books, work for a congressman, be a congressman, none of that could compare with possibly informing and influencing the president. And that was true whether or not you had voted for that president or worked for his party. There was only one president at a time and the chance, whatever party he was, the chance to have some useful influence in informing him or shaping his policy seemed the most important thing you could do.

Reading the Pentagon Papers and reflecting on Vietnam revealed to me, first of all, that presidents could go terribly wrong despite the best advice they could get, and that, therefore, the best way of helping the country was not necessarily helping the president do what he wanted to do, because the best way might be keeping him from doing what he wanted to do. And that had to be done outside the executive branch, by Congress, by courts, by voters, by the public. So that, actually, you could do more for the country outside the executive branch.

And second, the aura of the president, the idea of identifying with him and working for him and being a president's man, a kind of feudal, chivalric relationship—that suddenly lost its aura. I no longer wanted to be a president's man. The idea of life outside the executive branch looked just as good or better than working for a president. And I don't think I've ever had a colleague who has ever reached that point in their lives. They can't imagine life outside the executive branch as being better. When their party gets out of office or if they're fired or if they move out for higher money or whatever, they nevertheless spend their lives waiting for the phone call, to be called back and give advice. No matter how painful the break was with the earlier president, they're ready to go back there. It's their highest calling, actually. Self-esteem, prestige, excitement, importance, and a sense of serving the country. That somehow was burned out of me by reading this seven-thousand-page record. And that made it possible for me to imagine doing something that would forever prevent me from working for any president again. No executive branch official would ever or could ever hire me again after I had done this. Most of my colleagues would not have been able to conceive of doing something that would keep future presidents from relying on them or trusting them or calling them in again. So that was crucial.

And finally, we come to the point that one of the things I was doing was, I thought, certain to put me in prison. How could I do that?

Actually, I'd been in the marine corps, I'd been in Vietnam, I'd been in combat. Three million men who went to Vietnam as soldiers exposed themselves to losing their legs, their bodies, their lives to a mine or to a sniper, or to a mortar round. And they were not regarded as heroes or crazy just because they accepted that role. Nobody did a psychiatric profile on them, as was done on me, to ask why did they do that? They were doing it for the

president or for the country. The president, however, was deciding very badly what was good for the country. But you did what
the president said, what he wanted you to do. And to do that is
sensible even if it involves your death, even if it involves your killing people, in what is in fact a bad cause. A bad cause by any
other standard but the fact that the president has endorsed it.
And this was a bad cause.

So dying, killing in a bad cause, all of that is regarded as very
reasonable. And I had done it. I had been over there. Even when
I didn't believe in the cause I served the president. And the point
was that what Randy Keeler revealed to me was that there were
other ways of being conscientious than serving the president.
There are other kinds of courage. And I had to ask myself, well,
if I was willing to be blown up in Vietnam or captured, as friends
of mine were, when I accepted the cause or supported it, should
I not be willing to go to prison or risk my freedom? And when I
faced that question, it was quickly answered.

When you ask me how could I be willing to face that, I was
the kind of guy who had been willing to go to Vietnam. That
didn't make me unique. It put me not with everybody in the
country but with a lot of people. The connection, however, that
not many of them had occasion to make was between doing that
sort of thing and making the same kind of commitment *against*
the president's will and policy, against what he wanted to do,
against what he was demanding. And to put yourself in the position of a dissenter, or of, let's say, a congressman who opposed
the war.

So, one shift was from the executive branch to helping the
Congress and working in the public. A major shift of identity
very, very difficult for an executive official to make. Another one,
of course, was a willingness actually to go to prison for what I
was doing. And that was because I made the connection with what
I myself had done in Vietnam or in the marines. But I wouldn't

have done that without the example of thousands of Americans. Actually, *Esquire* magazine called me just last month. They're doing an issue on heroes and they asked me if I would say if I had a hero that I wanted to name. And I mentioned Randy Keeler as a person who had changed my life by his example.

What then, briefly, is the responsibility of an individual in a democracy on matters of war and peace like we've been discussing?

I can say very briefly in terms of what I've just said about my own decision. I think that what I learned about what I ought to do applies not only to them at the time but to people in the future. First, that we are fortunate in this country, in our Constitution, in having not just an executive in charge of war and peace matters (as it likes to think that it is in charge), but actually a Congress which has the constitutional responsibility both to declare war and to finance, to control the budget, and has many, many methods for actually opposing executive policy on a matter of war and peace. Any of those executive officials could think of informing Congress, with or without the approval of the president. There are many ways they could do this with no legal liability. In fact, to the contrary, it often involves simply telling the truth instead of committing perjury, which is what they actually *do* do. So it involves obeying the law rather than violating the law, and obeying the Constitution. In short, work with Congress to change the situation. But it's in a way that they hardly think of doing because it involves crossing the man who appointed them. But, as I say, there is life outside the executive branch.

Second, they really could conceive of taking risks with their own career that are comparable to the risks they routinely ask of draftees and volunteers that they are sending to war. They could contemplate, in other words, paying a price in their own lives by telling the truth, by informing the public, by acting conscientiously, in a committed way, outside the executive branch to tell the truth, to inform the public. Again, at great cost to their future careers but a cost that they should be willing to pay. In short, they would find that they had much more power as individuals than they imagine they have if they were willing to pay a price in their own lives.

LISTENING TO
THE PEOPLE

Leaders can lay the groundwork for change by listening to people's stories and learning about the conditions that shape their anxieties, hopes, and aspirations. Indeed, democracy is an open-ended invitation for realizing this possibility. In the following interviews, Elizabeth Warren tells of directing her research to the realities of people's lives and hearing, to her own surprise, a very different narrative of the country's financial problems. As a member of a congressional commission, she was able to use those insights to expose failed policies, corruption, and fraud. Ron Dellums shares stories of community organizing and electoral campaigns that propelled his own political career. In these public forums, people can speak out, leaders emerge, small contributions can be made, and, over time, the organizational muscle of movements can be created and nurtured. Both interviews show how legislation can respond to the people's complaints, if leaders are willing to overcome institutional obstacles and entrenched political interests. In the process of their political awakenings, Ron Dellums and Elizabeth Warren took their observations and analysis to the citadels of power, with major societal impact.

Elizabeth Warren

Elizabeth Warren is the Leo Gottlieb Professor of Law at Harvard University. In addition to her legal publications, she has written two books, *The Two-Income Trap* and *All Your Worth*, both co-authored by Amelia Warren Tyagi. Her legal publications include major contributions to the study of bankruptcy and credit. In 2007, she first developed the idea to create a new Consumer Financial Protection Agency. In the wake of the 2008–9 financial crisis, she became the chair of the Congressional Oversight Panel to oversee the Troubled Assets Relief Program, the government's bank bailout.

Ron Dellums

For more than twenty-seven years, Ron Dellums was a congressman from California's Ninth Congressional District. In representing his district, Congressman Dellums not only brought to Washington the spirit and ideas of the '60s movements but at the same time earned the admiration and respect of his Washington colleagues. Perceived upon his arrival as a gadfly, an outsider from "Berzerkeley," he left the Congress after rising through the ranks and serving as chairman of the powerful Armed Services Committee. Upon his departure he received the Defense Department's Medal of Distinguished Public Service, the Pentagon's highest civilian award, and the Lifetime Achievement Award from Peace Action, the nation's largest organization promoting disarmament. In 2006, he was elected mayor of Oakland, California. He is the author of several books, including an autobiography, *Lying Down with the Lions: A Public Life from the Streets of Oakland to the Halls of Power*, as well as *Defense Sense: The Search for a Rational Military Policy*.

Elizabeth Warren
March 8, 2007

Where were you born and raised?

Born and raised in Oklahoma.

Looking back, how do you think your parents shaped your thinking about the world?

Well, my parents were from Depression-era, dust-bowl Oklahoma, and that shapes your life growing up. I was the last of four children—I have three much older brothers—and by the time I came along I was really kind of the second family for my parents. They hadn't recovered from the Depression, and I guess in many ways they never did. Those were the stories that permeated my childhood: what it was like to have seven years of drought, what it was like when nobody had any money, what it was like when all your neighbors left to go to California or someplace where they thought there might be jobs. My parents hung on, they stayed, and my father worked a series of different jobs. He was a maintenance man in an apartment house—it was his last job—but they always saw themselves as middle-class people. For them the distinction was that they used good English and they didn't say "ain't." Those were important indicia of middle-classness for my folks. They believed in education and were very proud of this little daughter they had.

Around the dinner table was there a discussion of politics, of law, or did that all come to you later?

Oh, no. Not around the dinner table. Mostly around the dinner table it was discussion of cars, or rodeos and dogs and cows and horses, and a little discussion of worry about others in the family. There was always a big sense of trying to look out for each other, but nobody in the family really had much of anything.

A theme that you pursue in your work is what's happening to the family. From what you're saying now I get the sense that the family was very important as a last resort for survival in the context of those very harsh times.

That's exactly right. People who didn't have family or people who broke from their family—they were the true poor, they were the ones with nothing. As long as you had family, you had people who would make sure that you got fed one way or another. Family was about canning peaches, and canning peaches was about making sure that there'd at least be something come next November, when it was cold outside and there were no more crops coming in. Family is the heart of what it's about.

When you were young, did you have any teachers as a young person who shaped your thinking about the kind of career you might take?

I'm of that generation where there were only two things that a woman could do, if she wanted to do something other than stay home: she could become a nurse, or she could become a teacher. And so, there were some amazing women who taught me from grade school on, and what they opened me up to was the possibility that I, too, could be a teacher. When I went off to college, that's what I wanted to do. I just didn't quite know what kind of teacher I would end up becoming.

At college what did you major in, and what was the focus of your interest?

I was sixteen years old when I graduated from high school, and I got a full scholarship in debate that was room, board, tuition, books, and a little spending money. It was a fabulous scholarship at George Washington University, if I would debate for them. It was sort of the equivalent of an athletic scholarship, only this was one that actually a girl could get, even though there weren't very many girls in debate either. I got my degree in speech pathology and audiology, which meant that I would be able to work with children who had head trauma and other kinds of brain injuries. And that's what I did.

I was married at nineteen while I was still in college. My first year post-graduation I worked in a public school system with children with disabilities. I didn't have the education courses and was on an "emergency certificate," so I went back to graduate school and took a couple of courses in education and said, "I don't think this is going to work out for me." I was pregnant with my first baby, so I had a baby and stayed home for a couple of years, and I was really casting about, thinking, "What am I going to do?" My husband's view of it was, "Stay home. We have children, we'll have more children, you'll love this." And I was very restless about it.

By this point we were living in New Jersey because of his job, so I went back home to Oklahoma for Christmas and saw a bunch of the boys from high school debate. They'd all gone on to law school, and they said, "You should go to law school. You'll love it." I said, "You really think so?" And they said, "Of all of us, you should have gone to law school. You're the one who should've gone to law school." So, I took the tests, applied to law school, and the day my daughter, who later became my co-author, turned two, I started law school at Rutgers Law School in New Jersey.

At that point, I'd never met a lawyer. I mean, I'd never—I didn't travel in those circles, but I took to law school like a pig takes to mud. I loved law school. And then in my third, final year in law school, I got pregnant again, and I didn't take a job. Alex was born

about three weeks after I graduated, and it was the hardest moment in my life, because I thought, this world that had opened
up to me, this world of ideas, and law was a tool you could use to
make things happen—and I thought, because I didn't take a job
right out of law school, it was all over. I just kissed it all good-bye.
I'd stepped off the train and would never have a chance to get
back on it. But I took the bar, hung out a shingle in northern
Jersey, did real estate closings and little incorporations and law-
suits, all on the civil side, and raised my two babies.

And then Rutgers called and said, "Somebody didn't show up
to teach a class. Would you like to come and teach it, and start
Thursday?" And I said, "Sure! How hard could it be?" And so, I
started teaching.

*What do you see in your background that made you able to seize
these opportunities?*

Partly my mother always said that I was just contrary, that some
kids are just born that way. Families tell stories, and those stories
both reflect what the children are and shape what the children
become. The story that was always told is that when I was about
two and a half I would be allowed to play in the front yard but my
mother would tell me, "Don't go into the street." And I would look
at her and wait until she turned her back and step right on the
street, and I would just stand in the street, just a little bit, just near
the curb, but I would stand in the street. And my mother was big
on switches. She'd pull a switch off a tree and just switch the
backs of my legs. And I'd cry, but I'd step right back in the street.
Finally my mother realized I was going to go in the street anyway,
so she said, "Okay, here are the rules. You look this way and you
look that way, and this is how you safely go in the street." She
gave me all the rules for the street, and I was perfectly happy.

I think partly that I always had my neck bowed, I was always
going to do something else. When we were able to pick an elec-

tive in junior high school and all the girls picked drama, I, of course, had to pick debate. I said I was going to take physics, you know, just because. So, there was a little bit of the "just because," and it was a moment when Gloria Steinem was out there talking. Did I think I was going to be one of those "women's libbers"? Heavens, no. I wanted children, I wanted a family, and I somehow thought those were either/or choices. And yet, I also wanted to do things.

I once was at a friend's house and I saw that they had wallpaper in their bathroom, and I thought it was the coolest thing I'd ever seen. So, I went to Sears and saw this brochure on how to do wallpaper, and I took my babysitting money and bought enough to wallpaper our bathroom. Two weeks later when it came, I announced at the dinner table, "I've bought wallpaper so we can wallpaper the bathroom." And my daddy said—because it was always a family thing—"Nobody in our family knows how to wallpaper. What are you doing?" I said, "How hard could it be? People dumber than us do it every day." So, I've thought that way—you know, you get out there and try it. The worst that happens is you make a mess out of it and have to throw it away.

You started in commercial law, but then you moved to the public realm. How did that transition come about?

I did my very first empirical study looking at the families who were going into bankruptcy back in the early '80s, and I'll tell you, I set out to prove they were all a bunch of cheaters. I was going to expose these people who were taking advantage of the rest of us by hauling off to bankruptcy and just charging off debts that they really could repay, or who'd been irresponsible in running up debts.

I did the research, and the data took me to a totally different place. These were hardworking middle-class families who by and large had lost jobs, gotten sick, had family breakups, and that's what was driving them over the edge financially. Most of them were in complete economic collapse when they filed for bankruptcy. They would never pay these debts off. Realizing this changed my vision. But it certainly didn't make me want to talk about it in any public sense, until, in 1994, Congress passed a law saying they were going to have a commission on bankruptcy, and I was recruited to work on it. And that's when I waded into the thick of it and started taking much of my research and translating it much more into public policy.

Without this public policy component, the work would have been so sterile by comparison with what it turned out to be. Oh, yeah, I'd have had great ideas for how 11 USC 1326(b)(2) should be modified in order to achieve a more harmonious result, but, oddly enough, the political part ultimately enriched my understanding of the scope of the problems. It took me far beyond bankruptcy and much more into questions about what's happening to the middle class. Often, it was other people who would ask me the big questions. "Why are families in so much debt?" "Who are these people who are filing for bankruptcy?" Or sometimes it would simply be their allegations of fact. "Well, we know it's just the poor and the profligate." That would cause me to say, "Oh, I've got to go back and study this some more." And so, it enriched and in many ways transformed the work that interested me as a scholar.

You mentioned that your initial attitude about these people who had gone bankrupt was that it was their fault, that they had failed, that they had been spenders, that they had been whatever negative values we associate with them. Do you think it serves a political purpose to believe those kinds of statements?

Absolutely. I began to see that there were a lot of people who really just didn't care one way or another who was in bankruptcy. The banks and credit card companies wanted this new legislation. In a democratically elected Congress how on earth are you going to pass legislation to benefit two dozen already powerful multibillion-dollar corporations at the expense of all the families filing for bankruptcy every year? This was straight wealth transfer.

So, policy makers and the media would make assertions about who these people were, and at first I believed these were assertions made out of ignorance. And so, I'd come in with the data and say, "Well, actually, let me show you how this works," and, "Here's a random sample of 1,250 families and here's how they were chosen and here's what we know about them, and look at what happened to them." And people just didn't want to hear it.

Finally, it was senators themselves who said, "Professor, you don't understand. So-and-so over here has taken $300,000 from credit card companies over the last so many years and this is something that industry wants; I see two lobbyists in here a day from the financial services industry to make this happen." The credit card companies wanted a piece of legislation to cut their losses and boost their profits. And so, the reality of these families' lives had to be reshaped to tell a politically acceptable story: that this is the fault of these families who are in financial trouble. But you know, the data are just overwhelming on this question, and that is just simply not the truth.

This is part of a larger story. For example, "We don't have to provide health insurance for folks, because decent people who worked hard and got an education and therefore got good jobs already have health insurance." There's an undertone that those who don't have it have made other bad life choices that caused them to be in a place where they don't get it.

Bankruptcy is a case in which literally, the lobbyists wrote the bill. I'm not being metaphoric here. The lobbyists wrote the bill, the credit industry paid for it, the campaign contributions then paved the highway for the bill to get passed, and ordinary families just lost out.

We reached a point in America a few years ago where more people went through bankruptcy than graduated from college in a single year! More people filed for bankruptcy than had a heart attack. More children lived in homes that were filing for bankruptcy than in homes that were filing for divorce.

To step beyond bankruptcy, we're on target now to see 1.4 million families thrown out of their houses this year [2007] in mortgage foreclosures. One in every seven Americans, right now, is dealing with a debt collector. We hear the word from [the Bush administration], "Oh, it's all about personal responsibility," over and over and over, but at some point the families themselves start to say, "Uh-uh, no good. This answer doesn't work." Indeed, I should point out, some of the family-oriented groups that have aligned themselves politically with conservatives have backed off and said on bankruptcy issues, on credit card issues, on payday loan issues, on home mortgage issues, Congress has got to go a different way. The cracks in the dominant story are starting to appear.

Let's go back and talk about this bigger picture where the middle class finds itself, both from your own personal experience and from what you were experiencing as a lawyer/academic studying these issues. What we're witnessing beginning in the seventies is a major economic transition in this country affecting the family, and everybody's running to catch up. Talk a little about it. Give us that big picture.

Starting in about 1970 a fully employed male's wages completely flattened out, and in fact, a fully employed male today, on average, earns about $800 less than his dad earned a generation ago. Unlike the first seventy years of the twentieth century when wages grew as the economy grew, now the family does better only if they can put two people in the workforce. Millions of mothers poured back into the workforce, and the norm switched from a one-earner family to a two-earner family, for those who are lucky enough to have it. Expenses in the same thirty-year period far outstripped what families were spending, and I'm not talking about consumer price index.

Start with the consumption. This is what everyone in the popular media [supposes] is the reason for people getting in trouble: too many GameBoys, too many iPods, too many $200 sneakers. In fact, families today, adjusted for inflation, spend less on clothing, less on food (including eating out), less on furniture, and less on appliances than they spent a generation ago. Where they spend more is for the three-bedroom, one-bath house. The median family is spending 80 percent more on mortgage payments, adjusted for inflation, than they spent a generation ago. They're spending about 75 percent more for health insurance than they spent a generation ago. Because today they need two cars instead of one, they're spending about 60 percent more on cars. They're paying for child care, which, of course, they didn't a generation ago, because the mother was home.

Today the median two-income family is spending 75 percent of their income on those five basic expenses, and with two people in the workforce they actually have fewer dollars left over than their one-income parents had a generation ago to cover everything. So, what we have today is two people working full-time, flat-out, hard-bore, and they actually have less money to spend than one person working full-time just one generation ago.

Today's family is already running full out. They've got both people in the workforce full-time, and that creates its own vulnerabilities. They have double the risk someone will get laid off or that somebody will get too sick to go to work. Today if a child gets sick, or if Grandma falls and breaks a hip, someone's got to take off work to be with them. A generation ago, you already had someone at home to be able to fill that other role. Today someone's got to take off, and for most jobs that means they lose income.

People are more likely to lose jobs than they were before; jobs are going abroad. When they lose jobs, statistically the odds that they'll get a new one that pays as well as the job they lost has gone down, compared with a generation ago. These are families that are losing health insurance, losing retirement, so what we're really watching here is a family unit that's getting more and more economically vulnerable. They're working harder than ever, they've got two people in the workforce, they're trying to do homework at night with the kids and hold it all together, and yet economically every part of the game is loaded against them.

You point out in this book [The Two-Income Trap] and in your writings that the focus on the family, the concern about education of one's children, impacts this very vulnerable situation to a greater extent over time, and it's all about "I want my kids to have the best education."

"I want my kids to have a shot of making it in the middle class." This is what it's about for parents. And so, what does that mean in America today, because of our peculiar way of financing education? It means you've got to get to the right zip code, because the right zip code will determine the school assignment for your child. But the prices have shifted upward for those zip codes.

Families with children have seen a 100 percent increase in housing costs since 1983. Why? Not because families with children have a bigger need for granite countertops or spa bathrooms, but because housing is the substitute way to buy into a decent school system. This is white families, African American families, Hispanic families, Asian families, it's across every spectrum. Families with children are tightening the belt one more notch, are working extra hours, are sending both people into the workforce, to try to get into the best possible school district for their children. Families are in financial trouble not because they're irresponsible but because they're too responsible. They're trying to do it for the kids.

All the literature in comparative politics, writings about democracy, democratization, point to the importance of the middle class as the foundation of a working democratic system. What are the long-term implications of what you're saying?

A strong middle class gives us a strong democracy and a strong economy; it's what makes us flexible and able to compete in the world; it's what makes us who we are. Here's what I fear. I think these data point toward a somewhat larger upper class, with the rest as just one big underclass. The old middle class is now comprised of families who are living paycheck to paycheck, who are dealing this week with debt collectors and next week with late fees and 29 percent interest on the credit card, who are on a treadmill that they can never get out of debt, never put anything aside in the way of savings. They have better moments and worse moments, but the differentiation between the poor and the middle class is no longer so clear. Now the differentiation is between the upper class and everybody else, because everybody else lives on a financial cliff. Some are getting pushed off, and some are just going to hang on the edge of the cliff. I fear we are moving toward a two-tier society and that government policies have pushed us in that direction, encouraged that division, and made it more comfortable for those who are well-to-do and much more dangerous for those who are part of the growing underclass in America.

Ron Dellums
February 10, 2000

How did your parents shape your character?

Let me start with my mother.

My mother is a person without letters. She dropped out of high school; I came into the world; then she went back and finished high school. She has a tremendous thirst for knowledge, and she is a very broad visionary human being who, in many ways, lived out her dreams of education through her children, as did my father.

My mother gave me a sense of who I was as a human being. I remember an incident when I had been challenged, and the name-calling was, "You dirty black African." I struck back at this person with anger. But my mother's point was that if calling you "dirty" was important enough to rise up, than that should have been the only justification, not because you're black or not because he called you African—because you're both. There are many adjectives that describe who you are as a human being, and two of them are that you are black and of African descent. And wherever you go for the rest of your life, you should be able to stand very tall and very proud as a human being and, when asked, when challenged as a black and an African—"Yes I am, and I'm very proud of it." So at that point my mother reinforced my humanity, my sense of myself, my own sense of pride, and her desire to see me fully educated.

My father, a person with a photographic memory, loved to debate, loved to challenge the order of things. When I talked to him about what I learned in school he would say, "Never accept at face value. Always be willing to question. Be open to ideas. Search. Probe. Don't just be a robot." And so both of them together were, I think, very much interested in the pursuit of educational excellence and, on the other hand, very proud people, race-conscious people, who allowed me to develop a sense of myself as a proud human being. They told me early on in my life that being black and being African was a good thing, so I was not burdened by that. I've never seen myself as a victim. I saw myself as fighting people who attempted to challenge me as a victim. So they gave me a very strong sense of myself and, at the center of it, education and learning and evolving are very important factors.

How did these influences affect you growing up in Oakland when you did?

Well, you know it was fascinating, because many of my friends internalized the same notions about my parents that I did. So whenever my friends were about to go off into adventures, sometimes on the edge, they would send me home. "Go home, man!" They would call me Sundown Ronny, because my friends knew that when sundown came, I had to be home. I had to be there for meals, I had to be there to do my homework. And so in one sense, many of my friends saw me as a special person, living with a special group of people who wanted very much to see me pursue my education, and I think, in many ways, they were very protective of me. You know: "You're one of the guys who are going to make it out of here." And that was significant in reinforcing who I was.

I was born in 1935, West Oakland. There were many white ethnics who lived in West Oakland as a working-class community. When World War II began, West Oakland became the major point of entry for black people coming in from the South, who came in to take advantage of the opportunities of the war economy, as it were. As a result of that, suddenly West Oakland overnight becomes a small Southern town. And here's this kid who

was going to St. Patrick's Catholic School, who spoke a little differently, who talked about different things, and many of these
older persons from the South, who had very little if any education, were fascinated by this young guy. "Where did you learn
these things?" The old folks would say, "Sit a while, because I
want to hear what this kid has to say." Then I would hear people
say, "That kid sure can talk! He's going to be a preacher or a lawyer some day." Well, as a kid, those are very positive reinforce-
ments, and I think that had some significant import in shaping
my life. I certainly wasn't a perfect guy. I dropped the ball many
times along the way.

Your uncle was also an influence on you. Tell us a little about him.

C.L. Dellums joined with A. Philip Randolph, and they were the
old left-wing guys of the '20s. They came together and organized
the first African American trade union in the history of America,
the Brotherhood of Sleeping Car Porters. These were guys who
placed a great premium on the spoken word as a way of organizing, and there was a need to be impressive when they challenged
people. You know, people thought these guys were Harvard grad-
uates, because they developed an affect that challenged the system to deal with them intellectually, at an eyeball-to-eyeball level.

Well, my uncle: here's this beautiful, erudite, incredibly well-
groomed, impeccable person with extraordinary articulation who
had an office over the pool hall on Seventh Street. I immediately
began to realize that C.L. was the man and that he commanded
respect across the broad spectrum of people in the Bay Area. And
going to his office: he had a staff person, he had an office, he
smoked a pipe, he dressed elegantly. He was a fighter, he was
strong, he was courageous. So this success model was very important in shaping my life, because here I knew that you could
succeed—you did not have to be intimidated—and that you
could be respected by people. The politics of that community came

through him: union activity, civil rights activity, et cetera. He was just this incredible, larger-than-life person who continued to push me to pursue my education.

To quote from your book Lying Down with the Lions, *people used to say about you, "Now that boy understands what we were saying." You learned to be a listener as a young person, didn't you?*

Yes. Sometimes I didn't understand. But I knew that I wouldn't understand if I didn't listen.

So I did learn how to listen. I was around adults a great deal and that became important: the ability to hear the other person, to try to fully understand what the other person is trying to say. My mother and my father and my grandmother instilled that in me. Listen to hear. And when they realized that I was listening and that, at some point, I could engage them seriously, they said, this guy is understanding. So that again was a positive reinforcement.

Any books that you read as a young person, or later when you matured into adulthood, that stand out now, that affected you?

You know, I've read a lot of books along the way. When kids would go out for the summer, I couldn't go out to play until I had read a certain number of books all the time, so that was a constant reinforcement, the reading and the use of the library. But there was one book that stood out, as a young adult having come out of the university. I had met this wonderful African American who was the first PhD that I met. He handed me a book one day and he said, "I want you to read this book." And the title of the book was *The Shoes of the Fisherman*. Very briefly, it's a story about a Catholic cardinal imprisoned in the Soviet Union, freed, goes back to the Vatican by a strange set of circumstances. He becomes the Pope, and it's the story of how this guy escapes the

Vatican to go out and touch people and continue to feel life in a real way. And he said, "When you finish the book, come talk with me." Later, he asked, "Why do you think I gave you this book?" I had no real idea. He said, "Because it's a story about the loneliness of leadership and the need to continue to fight isolation as a leader. I see you as a young leader, and you need to prepare yourself for leadership." Overwhelming! Made me go back and read the book a second time with different eyes and a different view.

You were also very much affected by the message of Martin Luther King Jr. when he came here and spoke at Berkeley. Tell us a little about that.

Martin Luther King Jr. had assumed an incredible role. He had mounted the podium at Riverside Church in New York and made a historic speech. He stood up and opposed America's involvement in Vietnam and had the audacity and the vision to raise his voice in the name of peace. After that speech he was criticized by whites and blacks—blacks thinking he had detracted from the civil rights movement; many whites thinking, you know, the audacity of this man to challenge American foreign policy. It's un-American! Well, he came to the University of California to speak to his critics. There were twenty-five or thirty thousand people who came to Sproul Hall. I was just a young guy near the back of the crowd, but with so much pride that tears came to my eyes just to see this extraordinary person command twenty-five thousand people with his eloquence, his courage, and his vision.

Whenever he spoke I used to get a notebook and write his statements down. One of the statements he made there was that there are two kinds of leaders, one who waits until the consensus is formed and then runs swiftly in front of the consensus to be the leader. And the second is the one who has the audacity to go out and mold and shape the consensus. And he said, I am from the latter. And that impressed me very much. The second point that he made, that just made sense out of all the movements to me, was that peace is more than simply the absence of war: it is the presence of justice. And those two comments together were significant in shaping the philosophical basis of my politics and the way I had to approach the politics of my life.

I want to quote you here on what you say in your book about King, an additional point. "King understood that if communities could step beyond the confines of their own pain and see how that pain manifested itself in other communities, larger political forces could be spawned. In order to achieve this objective he understood that a leader had to assume the responsibility for the knowledge he or she possesses. One part of that responsibility is to pass it on, to be an educator and to explain how pain is transcendent of color or race. The other part of the responsibility is to take risks in trying to bring people to this understanding."

I just thought that that was his magnificence, his eloquence. First of all, he understood the sophistication of coalition politics and the need to move beyond it.

That point—peace is more than the absence of war, it's the presence of justice—it meant that everybody's movement, that every effort to challenge injustice was a significant effort, and that if you brought people together challenging injustice, that could allow you to develop the kind of broad-based power that could bend the political will toward justice and toward your objective.

Assuming the responsibility for the knowledge you have once you see injustice, once you understand pain, you cannot walk away from that responsibility. Once you see the harm that's being done, you no longer can have the excuse of ignorance. And once you know, it seems to me that you then have to assume the responsibility of that knowledge. I believe that the overarching responsibility of a leader and a person in political leadership is to be part of the educative process, to bring people along with you.

The demagogues don't change the world; it's educators who are willing to contribute to the discourse, to attempt to inspire a broader range of people to participate and to be involved. And when [King] said that the other kind of leader is the leader that's willing to go out to shape the consensus, what he was saying is you have to be willing to risk. You've got to be willing to walk out there. You can't play it safe, you can't wait until the consensus is formed and say, hey folks, I'm leading. To be a leader means to be willing to take the risks of controversy.

I would go even further. When you take those risks to step out there to articulate an unpopular idea or an unpopular cause, if you help people understand why it's there, sometimes the hot light of controversy is focused upon you. My view is that when the hot light of attention is focused upon you, those are the moments when large numbers of people tend to focus, because people focus on controversy. Those are the moments when you have to step forward and be part of the educative process, take the risk. You can't be afraid of controversy; you have to figure out how to use controversy in a positive way to advance the ideas that you're talking about, to further educate human beings, to further respect the fact that if people are confronted with information, then at the end of the day more often than not, people will arrive at the appropriate place. But you've got to get people on the same page with a shared sense of knowledge. If you and I don't share a base of knowledge it's very difficult for us to find places where we can come together.

I get the sense from your growing up years, from your family, from your mentors, that you understood the importance of the dignity of the individual. And as I read your beautiful memoirs, I'm left with the sense that that empowered you to understand the dignity of ideas.

I think at the beginning of the day it starts with you as the individual, your sense of your own comfort, your own confidence. If you're comfortable with who you are, then you can look out and see someone else's humanity. And, by virtue of my family reinforcing my humanity, I was able to see other people's dignity as human beings, as people of worth and value. That's how I grew up. From there, at some point along the way I recognized, in King's contribution and other people's contributions, that at the end of the day it really doesn't have anything to do with personalities. It is the magnificence of ideas. Individuals come and go, but it's ideas that ultimately must prevail, ideas that ultimately must transcend.

I used to say to people that in my travels through life I've met some wonderful human beings, but I've never met a perfect person. But I have embraced what I've perceived to be perfect ideas. And ultimately, that's what we have to grapple with. All of us, at one level or another, have feet of clay. All of us. There are no perfect human beings. We all have our moments of courage. We also have our moments of cowardice and fear. It's not about that. So I don't believe in the cult of personality, although I respect human beings and respect people. That's the nature of life, engaging with other people. But it's ideas that must ultimately bring us together. People come and go. People have strengths and weaknesses. We're disappointed or not disappointed. But ultimately it's ideas that can allow us to continue to move forward. And that's what I think was the beauty of my family, that was the beauty of Martin Luther King. It was the power of ideas that propelled me forward.

Even in the movement, when I talk about the generation of young people in the '60s, I was inspired. Other people heard a strident sound, but I heard a chorus, I heard music, I heard brilliance and nobility and principles in the ideas of peace and justice and equality and fair play and all these things. So I didn't get caught up in the stridency; I tried to get caught up in the ideas. I said, "Wow! Who could fight these ideas?" No matter how stridently they're being articulated, the ideas are overarching, transcendent. So at times when I felt weak, at times when I felt discomfort, at times when I searched and questioned, "Why am I doing this? Can I really survive this? Can I really live through this? Am I big enough for it?" In those moments when I was scared to death, "Am I doing the right thing?" I grabbed hold to the idea and just kept walking forward because I said, "This idea is perfect, and if I stay true to this idea I can get through this moment."

You were caught up by the movement and were chosen by the movement to be its voice, really.

Yes. And it wasn't what I wanted to do with my life. I was a psychiatric social worker, and when I came home at 3:00 in the morning from a meeting where I had been drafted to be a candidate for the Berkeley City Council, for the next week I literally stayed in a fetal position, called into my job deathly ill. Because I was overwhelmed by this idea that people wanted me to be in public life. I agonized over this. And then I finally went to my friend and I said, "Look, I love you, and I love you guys, but this is what you want for me, this is not what I want for me. I want my life back. I don't want to be in public life."

"It's too late, man!" he said. "There's no way, you're the guy. It's done. That process can never be put back together. Everybody's expecting you to go out there and run."

So I had to suck it up and say, "Well, let me give it my best and then pray we lose." Well, I ended up putting thirty-one years of my life into an odyssey in public life that was not something that I really chose to do.

I didn't want to be the guy out front raising hell. I wanted to be the guy in the back room when people said, "Well, how are we going to address the problems of poverty?" I wanted to be the guy writing the policy ideas. I had never had any idea that I would be the guy out front that would end up spending thirty-some years of my life in public life. It may seem romantic now in the twenty-first century, but in the '60s it was a compelling idea to respond to the responsibility of the call to serve.

Did the skills that you acquired in social work become useful as you went to Washington to do politics?

Absolutely. The whole premise of social work is to hear, to listen, to understand, to totally focus, to block everything else out and to listen, to hear people. That was an important skill, listening to people in the community, in town meetings, in the streets. It was also important to sit there as a subcommittee chairman or full committee chairman and block out all of my other frustrations and worries and totally focus on what's being said, totally focus on what's going on. It almost gave me a leg up. And many of my colleagues, many of whom didn't necessarily agree with me, would come up and say, "You know, the one thing that I place a great value on, why I respect you?" And I said, "What?" They said, "You're the one person in these chambers that, if nobody else is listening, you're listening." Because in that training, in transcending from listening as a social worker to listening as an elected official, and in the discourse and the debate in the Congress, I figured out that the highest accolade that I could pay my adversary was to give that person my undivided attention. Many of my colleagues would have staff people write speeches for them. I rarely had that, I said, because my adversary will always give me my best speech if I'm willing to listen.

The other thing about social work is about being non-judgmental, so it allowed me to be in the process, to judge ideas rather than to judge other people. And the notion of the dignity of the human being: even people who are in the most impoverished of circumstances or in the most psychotic of episodes are still dignified human beings. And that is very important. I happen to think that social work training is an amazing baseline for people going into public life, because I don't believe that you can be a reactionary social worker.

When you were elected, the then–vice president, Spiro Agnew, attacked you as some horrendous radical from Berkeley, and you used the attack, in your own words, to define yourself. "If it is radical to oppose the insanity and the cruelty of the Vietnam War, if it is radical to oppose racism" and so on. So that you turned his words around to an affirmative definition of what you stood for and not what he said you stood for. A similar incident happened later on in your career when Ted Koppel called you anti-military.

It's important for you to define who you are, rather than to allow other people to define you. We tend to use words in this society without ever saying what those words mean. So for Vice President Agnew to say, "This is a radical who needs to be purged from American politics"—now, I don't even know what he meant by that. I needed to step up and use that moment to be educative. That allowed me not to defend myself from Agnew's attack, but to define myself to millions of people who wanted to know, "What is this Ron Dellums? Who is this 'radical' guy?" It allowed me to say, "Well, if it's radical to do this, thus and so." And then people said, "Well, okay. If that's radical, that's cool. Maybe I'm a radical as well."

We just use these labels and people start ducking from the labels. I say, what am I ducking about? I am equal to you intellectually; I am equal to you as a human being. I have to have the right to step up and define who I am. And if we're going to deal with each other in a free and open society with a legitimate exchange of ideas in the marketplace, then I cannot put myself in a second-class role to you to allow you to assume the capacity to even think that you could judge me. So if I'm not going to judge you and you don't judge me, now there are two equals in discourse. So I don't accept the labels that you place upon me. And if there are other people out there who are wondering what all these labels are about, let me tell you who I am. I'm not allowing this guy to define me. You can sit here for a hundred years, and you will never hear me characterize the other guy, because I don't believe in that kind of politics.

Now you come to Congress, the radical from "Berzerkeley," to quote what was said. You believed that respect and dignity had to be applied to your adversaries in Congress, even on the conservative side of the aisle, and that in showing them that you could respect them they would come to respect you, and then you could argue about the issues. But part of what was involved was learning the process, learning the details, the rules of the institution. Tell us a little about that.

I come to Congress with this incredible mantle, this tremendous burden—"Afro-topped, bell-bottomed, radical black dude from Berkeley wins election." I said, if I allow this process to marginalize me as a gadfly, five hundred thousand people who are counting on me to make significant and important, often life-and-death, decisions that affect them, their children, and their children's children into the future, will be diminished. So I cannot allow myself to be marginalized, otherwise I'm allowing half a million people to be marginalized. I'm allowing movement and beauty and nobility and principle to be trivialized. If I'm carrying this responsibility, the weight of controversial ideas, I've got to figure out how to not be a controversial person. Because a controversial person carrying controversial ideas is a double strain. So let me get myself out from under this. If people begin to see my personhood, that I'm a multidimensional human being, that I'm prepared to deal with them substantively, then we take Ron Dellums off the table, because Ron Dellums is irrelevant. It's the power of ideas. Now let's you and I talk about these ideas.

Secondly, I was a pretty good jumping-up-and-down community activist. Well, did people just send me to Washington to change the venue of my jumping up and down? Or did they send me to Washington to become the best progressive representative that I could possibly be? And I said, they put me in the national legislature, I've got to try to learn how to become the best legislator I can. I could have kept carrying protest signs back in Berkeley, but they sent me twenty-five hundred miles away to do something different. So I sat there hour after hour to listen, to learn how to handle myself on the floor, to take notes about which members of Congress, when they stepped into the well, could command the attention of my colleagues, what were their characteristics, what made them able to command attention? How did this process really work on a formal level and on an informal level? I became both a participant and a student.

There were times when I had to stay up to three and four and five in the morning reading briefing books because I said I have to try to become the best that I can be, because if I allow these people to pat me on the head and see me as simply a rhetorical human being who is without substance and without depth, then they could put me on the wall and that's where I'd be for the next twenty years. And I said no, I've got to try to bring dignity to the movements that I'm representing and to the constituency that I'm dealing with. And if that meant that I had to work harder than everybody else, then it was important.

Not an ego trip, it's just that I have to do that in order to make sure that, coming from the left and coming from a progressive perspective, and coming from Berkeley and Oakland, was not a recipe for disaster, nor was it a definition of a shallow and superficial human being with superficial ideas. So I did have to learn how to master the process, and I did have to learn how to master the arguments.

I remember one day I came off the floor, and I had given a speech about human priorities. And one of my colleagues walked up to me and said, "You speak brilliantly about the human priorities," he said, "but Mr. Dellums, you're very naïve." And he patted me on the back. And I said, "What do you mean?" He said, "You don't understand the Soviet threat. You don't understand the communist menace. You don't understand the national security problems we have." And when he walked away I went home and I said, no one will ever be able to do that again.

And so I got in bed with the books, with the missiles and the bombs and the force structure and the national security, so I'd learn, so I could walk on the floor of Congress and say, "Would the gentleman yield?" And the people would say, "Wow, you don't want to debate this guy, because he's ready." I realized somewhere along the way that I became in that institution the personification of these movements and the struggles from the '60s that were emanating from this community, and that I had a solemn responsibility to carry that forward to the maximum extent that I could.

There were many times when I would sit in my office late at night after being shouted down on the floor, sitting there in the dark just saying, whatever power that's larger than me, please give me strength to survive, because I don't know if I can handle all of this. Just to get up and go back out and keep my head up, when there was a tremendous effort to knock all the starch out of me as a human being. I said, I've got to figure out how to get beyond the limitations of my own personhood to survive this, because people are counting on me.

Often when you step forward to advocate, the first thing people ask is, "Do you think this will work? Do you think you have a snowball's chance in whatever to win?" And I never tried to answer that question, because I said I would leave that to others and to history. At the end of the day we cannot control events.

But I always believe that there are two factors over which we all have control: our fidelity, our faithfulness to our ideas. And the second thing you can control is whether you will show up for the fight.

If you're going to be there, be willing to pose the alternative, put it all out there. You have no idea what may happen. But if you're not faithful and you don't show up, there's one thing that you can guarantee—that your ideas will never see the light of day, that there's never any possibility of winning. That's why I don't believe in cynicism. At the end of the day it's not cynics that change the world. You have to be hopeful and optimistic and up-beat. And you have to believe that you have a responsibility to step up, put your ideas on the table, and see where they go.

What lessons would you hope that young people might draw from the life of Ron Dellums and the extraordinary work he's done?

I would think that I would say to young people, do not get caught up in the cynicism of this moment. You have to believe, in the very essence of your being, that your active involvement with other human beings can change the course of events. Don't buy into this overstated notion of cynicism that things can't change, that politicians are corrupt, frustrating human beings. People com-promise, people sell out, people are corrupt because they choose to be—that's not inherent in the process. And your active involve-ment and participation in it, I always believe, can be a cleansing process; it can inform the decision. The extent to which you opt out of the process, the extent to which you become an armchair spectator, the extent to which you allow your cynicism to deny your need to grapple with, and your sense that you can change the nature of, your circumstances—it's in overcoming all of that that you can do anything.

I'm not a celebrity. This is not Hollywood. This is not New York. This is Washington, D.C. I'm your representative. I'm here to grapple with you eyeball to eyeball. Don't look up to see the celebrity, look straight at me to see the person that is responsible for helping to make decisions that affect your lives on a daily basis. The only difference between us is age and area of responsibility, but we're all equals in this. This is a democracy.

The second point I want to make to you is that your engagement, your involvement, your participation, can change things. Don't ever think that just because somebody went inside the process, that that going inside in some way is a corrupting factor. If there's anything that this life is trying to tell you it's that you can go in, you can fight the good fight, maintain the fidelity of your ideas, be willing to step up to the fight and engage. And you never know, you may just change the world.

SCIENCE, FOOD, AND THE ENVIRONMENT: MOVEMENTS FOR JUSTICE

Though science and technology have the potential to benefit society broadly, corporate power and political interests can disproportionately reap the benefits to the detriment of the public good. When the rape of the land and the pollution of the environment become apparent, people become increasingly concerned with exploitation and injustice and begin to seek alternatives. Movements for justice are born. Science and technology can then become tools for organized efforts to right the balance. Science writer Michael Pollan recounts how he came to understand the politics of food; Oronto Douglas, an environmental lawyer, fights to save the natural abundance of his hometown in the Nigerian Delta; and Eva Harris, a molecular biologist, implements a program to distribute DNA technology to third-world clinics for aiding the war against disease.

Michael Pollan

Michael Pollan is the John S. and James L. Knight Professor of Journalism at the University of California, Berkeley's Graduate School of Journalism, and the director of the Knight Program in Science and Environmental Journalism. For the past twenty years, Pollan has been writing books and articles about the places where the human and natural worlds intersect: food, agriculture, gardens, drugs, and architecture. He is the author, most recently, of

In Defense of Food: An Eater's Manifesto. His previous book, *The Omnivore's Dilemma: A Natural History of Four Meals*, was named one of the ten best books of 2006 by the *New York Times* and the *Washington Post*. He has been a contributing writer to the *New York Times Magazine* since 1987, and his writing has received numerous awards.

Eva Harris

Eva Harris is a professor in the Infectious Diseases Division of the School of Public Health at the University of California, Berkeley, where she does research and teaching on molecular virology, pathogenesis, and epidemiology of dengue. She is the initiator and director of the Applied Molecular Biology/Appropriate Technology Transfer Program (AMB/ATT) and organizer and instructor of eleven of its workshops. Professor Harris is the president of the Sustainable Science Institute, a nonprofit organization based in San Francisco and dedicated to helping scientists in developing countries gain access to the resources needed to address local problems related to infectious diseases. A recipient of the MacArthur "Genius" Award, she is the author of numerous scientific papers and a book, *A Low-Cost Approach to PCR: Appropriate Transfer of Biomolecular Techniques*.

Oronto Douglas

Oronto Douglas is a leading human rights attorney in Nigeria. Douglas co-founded Africa's foremost environmental movement, the Environmental Rights Action/Friends of the Earth. He is the author of several works, including the groundbreaking *Where Vultures Feast: Shell, Human Rights, and Oil in the Niger Delta*, which he co-authored with Ike Okonta. Oronto Douglas served as one of the lawyers on the defense team for the Ogoni leader Ken Saro Wiwa, who was executed by Nigeria's military rulers in 1995.

Michael Pollan
December 16, 2008

Where were you born and raised?

I was born on Long Island in the town of Hempstead and grew up the first five years in Farmingdale, on the South Shore, and then in a town called Woodbury on the North Shore.

And looking back, how do you think your parents shaped your thinking about the world?

Oh, in many ways, my parents and my grandparents. I got very serious about gardening as a young boy. I had a grandfather who had been in the produce business, and he was a passionate gardener—this is the late '60s—and he was very kind of reactionary, and there was not too much we connected on except plants. I put in a garden at our house, too, in imitation of his garden, but I didn't call it a garden. I called it a farm stand, and every time I could get six strawberries together in a Dixie cup, I'd sell them to my mother. She was the only customer.

   That was one thread. Another was that I have a mom who's a terrific cook and very aware of food. My grandparents still cooked very traditional Jewish food, used duck fat, goose fat, or chicken fat to cook with. I remember stuffed cabbage, big deal special holiday food, and blintzes, and a whole range of Eastern European Jewish cooking. My mother did not cook that way. She fashioned herself more of a cosmopolitan, and she cooked every different ethnic food—sometimes French, Chinese, Italian—it was the '60s, it was that moment, you know, the World's Fair. You wanted to cook in every different kind of cuisine, and she was very good at all of them. And she doesn't cook the way my grandparents did; I don't cook that way now. So, one of the things that has struck me, writing about food, is how little stability we have in our food culture in this country, that we haven't held on to the immigrant traditions. Certain ethnic groups have more than others, but Jews? I don't think to such a great extent.

It's part of the homogenization that comes with American culture.

Homogenization and demonization in the case of traditional Jewish food. Everybody assumes that's lethal, to cook with all that animal fat, that that was too much meat, too much fat. It's all mythical, but the surgeon general didn't approve of a traditional Jewish diet for many, many years. So, I think that's part of it.

Let's talk about being a writer and being a science writer. What are the skills involved here, do you think?

I would argue that you could know too much about science to be a successful science writer. In other words, I don't have a deep background in science, and I have learned what I need to learn, article by article, book by book. I'm not far ahead of my reader. I don't take anything for granted. The jargon is weird to me, too; it's deeply unfamiliar, so I think I can write about it in a way that isn't so daunting. In one sense, science journalism is no different than any other kind of journalism. You find people who know the story, you interview them, you watch as much as you can, and you tell the story. A lot of journalists are intimidated because science seems so much more mystifying than politics, but it's no more mystifying than politics.

So, being able to do research is important . . .

Oh, absolutely, and history in particular. I think if there's a failing of American journalism, and there are many, one is a disregard for history—very often in the origins of a phenomenon you discover the meaning of a phenomenon. And so, it's a perspective I always cover. I'm always very interested in digging back to find the history of whatever I'm writing about. So, even if it's a scientific subject, it's really important to understand the history behind it.

For instance, history can make us aware that the way we get our food today really goes back to the early '70s, and that the appointment of Secretary of Agriculture Earl Butz was a pivotal turning point.

Well, that's a great example. We all know that subsidies are part of the problem and a waste of money. And then you dig back and you realize: oh, we changed everything in the 1970s; we changed our agricultural policies. And there is a real turning point in the history of American agriculture and food, and that is when Earl Butz was appointed by President Nixon with the explicit mandate of forcing down the price of food, because we'd had this bout of food inflation. Americans took to the streets because food got so expensive in 1973. Nixon hired Earl Butz, who was very skillful in agricultural economics, and he kind of redesigned the whole system of crop support in this country in a way that stimulated farmers. We used to hold up prices, basically, and he moved from that system to subsidizing crops and encouraging farmers to overproduce, to produce as much as possible. He was the guy who said: get bigger, get out, plant fence row to fence row, move toward monocultures, just crank out that corn and soy, and he redesigned the structure of the subsidies to encourage that.

And you can date the obesity epidemic and so many problems of the American food system to those policies—they are inadvertent consequences of what was a very popular thing, which was driving down food prices. Which he did. Americans only spend 9.5 percent of our income on food today. That's less than anybody in the history of civilization, and we have Earl Butz to thank.

In understanding food and agribusiness, politics is very important.

We're not aware of it, but food, like everything, is political. It is the biggest industry in the country; it's the most essential thing. We've had the luxury of not having to think about it for the last thirty years, thanks to Earl Butz and having all this cheap food around. But you know, if we as a society have to live without gasoline, which is unimaginable, we will figure out how to do it. We did it for millions of years. We've never lived without food. Food is really essential, and when you have anything that's essential, there're enormous political and economic forces that contend about how it will be organized.

In the last thirty years, we have had this kind of agriculture industrial complex, which by some measures has worked quite well. It's kept the price of food low; it's kept the food industry healthy; it's given us a lot of power overseas—we're big food exporters—but what we're getting in touch with, I think, is that the by-products of that system, or the unintended consequences and costs, are catching up—everything from obesity to diabetes. Because that was a system that specifically encouraged the consumption of cheap corn sweeteners, high fructose corn syrup, hydrogenated oils from soy, processed foods of all kinds, a lot of cheap meat. So, there's been a public health impact that's dramatic. That is what's bankrupting the healthcare system: the fact that half of us suffer from chronic diseases linked to the diet. There are $250 billion a year in costs tied to that. So, that's one set of problems.

The other set, of course, is environmental. The food system contributes more greenhouse gases than anything else, any other industry, and that happens at every level. It happens at the field, the way we fertilize crops, in the amount of energy that goes to produce that fertilizer, the way we use machinery on the farms, the way we process the food, the amount of animals, and the methane we release. It's about a third of greenhouse gases [that] come from the food system, and transporting the food all around the world, not to mention the agricultural pollution. Feed lots are the biggest source of pollution we have.

I mean, it's quite an accomplishment that you can go to a restaurant, eat a fast food meal, a big chunk of meat, French fries, large soda, for less than the minimum wage. In the history of humankind, that's quite an achievement, but it's come at a very high cost, and that cost, I think, is what we're getting in touch with right now.

You've suggested that part of the problem is that industrial capitalism and agro-capitalism essentially take a discovery and then find the best way to make the most money as soon as possible . . .

With incomplete information.

Right.

Well, genetically modified crops is another great example. We figured out something about genes, and we understand some connection between a gene, a protein, and a trait, and so we figured out a couple crops where we could introduce new genes from other crops. It works, but we overlook a whole lot of complexity, which we just dismiss as static. Why is it that when we introduce this gene, 90 percent of the time you get a freak plant? Well, we don't really know; it has something to do with gene expression; it has something to do with junk DNA. Look, reductive science is very powerful, but it's always important to understand that you're missing some of the complexity. When you apply that reductive science you can get into trouble because you're mistaking what you know for all there is to know. So, there's a lack of humility involved, and there is a tendency to apply these things long before we know what's working and what's not working.

A key turning point here is the Haber-Bosch process, which you've written about. Talk a little about that because it is a major turning point in seeing synthetic fertilizer as the be-all and end-all of everything.

The great crisis of 1900 was there's not enough nitrogen to feed everybody. Before then, all the nitrogen that was used in agriculture came from bacteria in the soil fixing it. That was proving to be inadequate; crops were failing. The Haber-Bosch process is basically the fixing of nitrogen, synthetic nitrogen, and it was a great invention; by some estimates 40 percent of the people on earth are here because of that process. However, it's a great example of a powerful technology that's had a lot of negative effects. Synthetic nitrogen, when it oxidizes in the soil, becomes nitrous oxide, which is a very potent greenhouse gas. Nitrogen fertilizer became so cheap and is used so profligately that it runs down the Mississippi River and into the Gulf of Mexico, where it has created this dead zone. And over time we have found that using too much synthetic nitrogen ruins the structure of the soil; it becomes too salty and basically nothing will grow. And you have the declining yield curve that we've seen all through the green revolution countries because of too much nitrogen in the fertilizer. The green revolution, for example, is the application of these technologies to the developing world: hybrid seed, fertilizer, ammonium nitrate fertilizer, and irrigation techniques, and growing in monocultures. There're a lot of very good intentions. There was a serious goal of feeding the world, but over the long term, it's been a disaster.

So, a lot of these technologies are double-edged swords. They're wonderful and powerful, and they're horrible and disastrous.

And what happens, it seems, is a loss of checks and balances, that we don't continue to monitor the process and, as more information comes along, think about what the implications are. Is journalism at fault here, because we have no language to address the problems?

Journalism could play a more aggressive role in assessing these things, but, in the end, journalism reflects the political culture of a country. One of the reasons we didn't have a debate about genetically modified crops before we introduced them in this country is because both the Republicans and the Democrats supported Monsanto and GMO technology, and when both political parties are on the same side, there's no space for journalists to operate. When you're introducing technologies, you need a public discussion, and you need to think through what are the benefits and what are the risks. And that must be decided publicly, not privately.

I think a lot of our problem is that we assume all technologies are innocent until proven guilty, in this country especially. We're technological utopians, and we think you're a party pooper if you raise questions about genetically modified crops. There's a lot of money and potential in it, a lot of interesting intellectual property for a lot of people, and you're a Luddite if you raise any kinds of questions. And then forty, fifty years later we deal with the possible impacts. It's not to say that synthetic fertilizer was something we should not have done, but had we applied more of a precautionary science to it, we might have anticipated some of the problems and been able to mitigate them before they got too serious. So, I think it's a society problem.

You've written about nutritionism as a kind of ideology that purports to be a science—tell us more about that.

We've adopted the reductive language of nutrition from the scientists: we all talk about saturated fats, high fructose corn syrup. It's fascinating to listen to Americans talk about food today. They sound like a bunch of amateur scientists. They don't talk about foods; they talk about nutrients. It's bizarre when you think about it, and it's been a fascinating phenomenon to watch.

"Nutritionism" is an ideology about food that's become general, and it's got four basic principles. The first is: foods don't matter, nutrients do. A food is essentially the sum of its nutrient parts, and a food, like steak, is a vehicle for carrying protein and saturated fat, because that's what matters.

The next premise is that you can divide the world into good and bad nutrients. There's always an evil nutrient that we're trying to rid from the food supply—trans fats, high fructose corn syrup, or saturated fat—and, on the other side is a blessed nutrient: if you could just get enough of that you'll be fine, you'll live forever. And that, of course, was fiber for a long time; now it's antioxidants or omega-3 fatty acids.

A third principle is if the important thing in food is a nutrient, and nutrients are invisible to normal people, then you need experts to tell you how to eat.

And the fourth premise of nutritionism is that the whole point of eating is health. You're either ruining your health or you're improving your health with every meal. And that's a kind of bizarre view of food. I mean, people eat for a great many other reasons.

So, I think we've lost our sense of food; we've lost our sense of eating as a complex social, as well as biological, phenomenon, involving community and identity and pleasure. All these categories have vanished under this regime of nutritionism. My last book is kind of a manifesto against nutritionism and in favor of returning food to the center of our discussion about food and making health a by-product of a happy relationship to food, rather than the goal of eating.

And that takes you back to the culture of food that you might have found at your grandparents' table, I think.

You're right. We've essentially displaced culture as a guide in telling us what to eat and put science in its place. We think cultural wisdom about food is just old wives' tales; if your grandmother thought it was true—I mean, what did she know? We have scientists now who can tell us all about antioxidants.

Yet the grandmothers were right about a lot of things. I was on a call-in show in Australia recently and a woman called and said, "My grandmother used to always say, eat your colors." Now that's a very interesting rule. We now know that the important plant chemicals all have a different color, and indeed, eating different colored foods is a guarantee that you are getting the diversity of antioxidants and phytochemicals you need to be healthy. How did that grandmother know that? This was before we knew what an antioxidant was.

So, my premise in this book is that culture still has a lot to teach us about food, and indeed, it is still wiser about food than science. I have enormous respect for nutrition science, and I hope that someday they'll figure it out, but they haven't yet. Nutrition science is approximately where surgery was in the year 1650.

We would do well to tune down that whole debate about fats and carbs that you read in the media, and not put so much stock in the latest nutritional finding, because it will be contradicted by the next nutritional finding, and to return to the cultural wisdom about how to eat, which guided people very well for a very long time.

You write about creating your own garden, [which] is a source for you not only of the subjects of interest but also of the values that drive your perception of the world. In that discussion, you also make a distinction between a gardener and a naturalist. Talk a little about that, because you seem to be suggesting that to see things whole, you have to be whole yourself, and gardening is a way to get there.

I think that's right. Look, a lot of my work grows out of my experience in the garden. My first book, called *Second Nature: A Gardener's Education,* was really an attempt to use what I was doing and experiencing in the garden as a place to explore our relationship to the natural world.

Traditionally in America, if you wanted to explore your relationship to nature you'd go to the wilderness, you'd do the Thoreau thing, the Emerson thing, the Melville thing. You have your confrontation with wild nature, and that's essential and authentic and a beautiful discussion, and it's given us things like the wilderness park, an American cultural invention, the idea of preserving a wild place that for most of history was regarded as wastelands and ugly landscapes. We learned how to appreciate them, and we've elevated them, and we've saved them.

But that whole discussion—and that worship of wilderness—doesn't help you with many other questions, or with the 92 percent of the American landscape you can't lock up. There are so many places where we need to engage with nature without destroying it, but we also can't just leave it alone. And the garden, in a way, is the great symbol of that place.

It's a place where we mix ourselves up with nature, where we are in this reciprocal relationship with other species affecting us, and we're affecting them, and it's a beautiful place, ideally. There is conflict, though; there are weeds; there are bugs. You can't get away from that, but merely sitting back and worshiping it will give you a disastrous garden and no crop to eat.

So, I began then, with that very first book, getting interested in that messy place between the human world and the wild, and trying to figure out how to behave in that world in a way that I could get what I wanted while also not destroying or diminishing nature. Food is another one of those messy places. I think that the garden is a really important model and that if we would let the garden guide us in our dealings with the natural world— and by that, I mean agriculture, architecture, design—I think we would be better off.

How has agribusiness failed to consider this?

Basically it's pushed too hard on the culture side of that dialectic and not appreciated that nature can't be bent to our will completely. Agribusiness essentially conceives of a farm or a garden as a factory: you put in these inputs—fertilizer, irrigation water, hybrid seed, pesticide—and you get out those outputs, and nature is just the factory floor.

That doesn't work because nature has its own interests. Nature pushes back. Nature is an obstacle to certain things we want to do, so that you need to think more like a gardener than a factory manager. When you do that, you find that there are ways to grow food of incredible quality, beauty, and healthfulness, while nature goes about getting what she needs. And that's really the challenge of good farming, figuring out a non–zero sum way. Most of our farming is like mining: we extract from the earth, we extract nutrients from the soil, we diminish the land the longer we farm it. So, is there a way we can get what we want from nature and leave nature not just undiminished but actually improved?

The garden shows that yes, that's possible. You have to know a lot; you have to know about ecology, entomology, soil science, but we have models. I've been on farms that are doing that right now. So, that's really the challenge—to bring the wisdom of the gardener to these larger arenas like the farm.

And you say, I think, at one point that a gardener is a citizen, a producer, and a consumer. You're suggesting that a food movement can bring a new kind of politics that might change this whole system.

So much of the agriculture and food system we have is the result of policy. Fast food, as Eric Schlosser brilliantly showed in his book, is not just the result of the free market doing its thing, it's the result of specific policies, sometimes well intentioned, sometimes not. We have this monoculture diet that's based heavily on corn and soy processed into all these different products; that's the result of a set of agricultural policies.

So, it stands to reason that another set of agricultural policies could give you a different kind of diet, different kinds of health outcomes as well. That's really the challenge before this food movement, to come up with policy ideas that will stimulate another kind of agriculture and also rebuild these local food economies which have so many virtues.

So, the food movement has many faces to it: there're people who are working on school lunch, people working on community food security in the inner city, and people working on changing the farm, and farm to hospital movements. It's a very big, inchoate movement that is just starting to gel and be felt, I think, at the national level. It's kind of where environmentalism was in the '60s, around the time of Earth Day, where there was this incredible sense of the importance of this issue, people in the streets, people very excited about it, yet it was not that well organized. Thirty years later, there are cadres of policy makers and lawyers that are ready, under the new administration, to go into the EPA, go into the Interior Department, and they know what to do with those levers of power. We're not quite there with the food movement yet, but we'll be there and it won't take thirty years.

How do you answer the contention that the food movement is for the affluent and not for the rest?

Well, the criticism that it's elitist is a serious criticism, and I think that there are ways in which the food movement has been guilty of that. It is true that healthy, fresh, seasonal, nutritious food is more expensive than conventional food and, therefore, has tended to be enjoyed by the affluent more than others, but you have to look at why that is. One reason is that we, of course, subsidize the other kind of food. The cheap food in the market tends to be industrial food. It doesn't have to be that way. It just happens to be that way because of policy.

There're large segments of the movement as well that have focused on the inner city: the community food security movement, the school lunch movement, the kind of work that Alice Waters is doing in the schools in Berkeley. If you've ever been in a Berkeley public school, you know that's a highly diversified society; it's not affluent. And reaching people at lunchtime, you're reaching everybody; that's not an elitist politics, to be reforming school lunch. So, it's definitely an issue, and the movement needs to do a better job of addressing it, but we're very aware of it.

You wrote in the New York Times Magazine *a memo to the First Farmer, President Obama—before he was elected—suggesting that the present financial crisis presents an opportunity and a challenge for action. You laid out an agenda demonstrating the interconnection between the energy and health problems that he clearly wants to address, and what you see as the agribusiness problems, which aren't as widely perceived. What has to be done and what can be done in this present situation where there're just so many crises?*

Well, these crises are linked, and I think that that's important. I wrote this article during the campaign, when nobody was talking about food. My point was that whoever is elected president, if they are serious about addressing climate change and about addressing healthcare costs, they will find themselves dealing with the food issue, because food is the shadow issue over all those other issues, and energy independence as well. Our food system is heavily reliant on fossil fuel. The genius of industrial agriculture has been to replace human labor in the fields, and in the processing of food, with fossil fuel, with the result that a fifth of our fuel consumption goes to agriculture and the food system. As I said earlier, a third of the greenhouse gases come out of this system. So, you're not going to deal with climate change unless you deal with agriculture. You could get the transportation system green, the power grid green, but if you're still growing food the same way, you're going to have a tremendous problem with climate change.

And you could nationalize healthcare, but the cost will bankrupt the system unless you get a handle on chronic disease—which is to say unless you deal with the catastrophe that is the American diet, and that diet is linked to that agriculture. If you can fix the American food system, you will have so many benefits: you will cut down on healthcare costs, you will cut down on greenhouse gases. I think connecting the food issue to those other issues has raised its visibility in the debate. I sense that it's being taken more seriously in the media, more seriously in the councils of government, and that's a good thing. Whether President Obama is ready to go to war with agribusiness—I don't see much sign of that, and it's probably premature to expect him to do that, but there's a lot he can do, and there's a lot we can do, too.

We need to build this movement and make it bigger and create those cadres of policy makers and politicos to really drive change, because, make no mistake, the agribusiness industrial complex is very powerful. Harry Reid said recently that the two best organized lobbies on the Hill are insurance and the commodity groups, by which he means the corn and soy people and the grain traders, that whole group. They're really well organized. They don't have large numbers of people, but they have got a lot of power. And you don't hear about them much.

I offered in this article changes at all different levels. I think you have to change the general incentives that are codified in the subsidies to encourage farmers to use less fossil fuel and more solar energy, and you do that through diversification. I talked about decentralizing the farm and the food economy, but I also talked about the bully pulpit. These are things the President can do without any approval from Congress, such as putting a garden on the White House lawn. This can be an eloquent statement of the fact that, look, the sun still shines, there is abundance. Imagine a White House that was actually feeding the poor of Washington, as well as feeding itself. It would send a very important signal. So, I don't think that those things are trivial. I think that how the White House organizes its own household around food, the kind of food choices that are made in the White House, can set the tone, elevate the issue, because the more the public pays attention to this issue of food, the less tolerable the current policies will be.

How would you advise the next generation to prepare for this kind of food culture that we've been talking about? Obviously, start a garden . . .

Well, that's not a bad thing. I mean, you learn a lot in a garden. You grow a lot of food, and you can economize with a well-run garden, but you also learn habits of mind that are going to be really important in the future, which is to say self-reliance, basically, that we may not be able to count on the society fulfilling all our needs when the oil runs out. We're going to have to do a lot more for ourselves, and in the garden you learn that hey, I can do that; I can feed myself in a pinch. Very, very important lesson.

Get out of the supermarket, shop at the farmers' market, vote with your fork essentially. We get three votes a day when it comes to food, and those votes, we have seen, have an enormous impact on the world. How you choose to spend your food dollars is a very important vote that you have, and so think about how you cast it and realize that, yeah, you may spend a few extra pennies or dollars for that local food, but you're accomplishing a lot. You're keeping farmers in your community, farmland open in your area, you're building redundancy into the food system, not to mention you're getting the healthiest, tastiest, freshest food you can get. And cook. That is one other very important thing. Learn how to cook because when you cook, you will be supporting local food and you'll be a lot healthier, too.

Eva Harris
May 5, 2001

Tell us a little about your background. Where were you born and raised?

I was born in New York City and raised between New York and Paris, actually, so maybe that was right in the middle of the ocean! I grew up and did high school in New York, but went back and forth between the two cultures.

How did your parents shape your character, do you feel, in retrospect?

I would say my parents and also all of their friends . . . I am an only child, and it was a really wonderful group of people who were their core friends in Europe, which is why we spent a lot of time there. So, for instance, one of the women who helped raise me fought in the Russian Revolution, as well as people who had been in the French Resistance and in the German workers' movement. I was very struck by their hearts of gold. People had given everything and risked their lives for other people. That made a big impression.

My parents believed in me and let me do everything I wanted. I was an overachiever on my own, so they joked that they hoped I would fail at something once in a while. I grew up without a TV, and so I read like a maniac. And that was just wonderful.

As a young person, did you do a lot of tinkering around the house?

As an only child, I did a lot of reading and a lot of crafts. So I wasn't really tinkering mechanically, but I made tons of things. I think

the element that you're referring to is really just trying to demys-
tify and break down complicated technologies and make them
accessible. So the motor behind that is to make things accessible
to low-resource communities. And yes, I like to make things.

Were either of your parents scientists?

Both are, to a certain extent, but not in the biological sciences.
My father is an applied mathematician and linguist. He actually
founded the field of linguistics in this country in the thirties and
forties at the University of Pennsylvania. He is truly a generalist,
as we are talking about that. It was just really wonderful. I spent a
lot of time conversing with him about many, many diverse topics.

My mother is a computer scientist and linguist, and has
worked on natural language processing and applications in med-
ical informatics, and has broken through in her own way.

*So what were the politics that you grew up with that made you sensi-
tive to ideas of equality and redistribution and so on?*

Basically, very progressive, left, radical, but very nondogmatic.
It was, essentially, the Workers' Council movement. Some of the
early movements that [believed that] the idea of a worker-run,
rational, humane society could somehow be possible.

Going into science, when did that magic moment happen?

One of the things that really moved me or drew me to science
was the way the cell works. For me, it's an absolutely beautiful
system that I see as a model for human society. Because if you
understand how all the molecules work, [you see that] there is an
incredible energy conservation. There is a feedback loop that actually functions. All the elements work together for the greater
good of the whole. All of these really beautiful principles are

played out, and that's how we—and all organisms—are able to exist. There are so many motives that we dream about in a just human world, [which] are actually being played out every instant in our own bodies. So I was really drawn to the beauty and the harmony of molecular and cellular biology.

So the dichotomy between research and activism is not inevitable; it's what you see and the way you act on it?

What I just described to you is kind of a vision. But then, I was stuck with the reality of science and the lab, and I was an activist in college. It was the 1980s—Central America—and I was at Harvard during the divestment issue—South Africa. My [science and activism] were very separate. There was my work in the lab, and then the work in the streets.

But my dream was somehow to bring them together, to bring my politics into my work. For a long time I talked about it as "science for [infectious disease] research in developing countries." Anyone who wanted to read between the lines for political content could read between the lines. And if not, it was just, "Isn't this nice, bringing science to the people," in a very generic way.

What does it take to be a biological scientist? It sounds like you have to be inventive. It sounds like you have to persevere. What other characteristics, virtues, are part of the endeavor?

Well, my path is quite unusual. Really, in academic science, it's pretty narrow, and you have to be incredibly good in your field and be politically savvy and go to the right meetings and talk to the right people and make the right connections and all that. But I hate to look at things that way. I just can't. It seems too utilitarian. I choose to ignore it, possibly to my own detriment.

I need to see a value system and a motivation that's beyond my own career. Not to put other people down, but generally, people are successful because they are interested in the science and also their egos to a certain extent. So the most successful people are the people who know how to work the system *and* who are good. I mean, you have to be good to succeed. How specialized one can be is what is selected by the system.

Of course, I like to be good at what I do, but I see it much more as an interdisciplinary approach to life and to science, which is difficult, because one has to be successfully multidisciplinary. People bandy that word about, but what it means is being excellent in a number of fields. And if you can't do that, then you have to know with whom to collaborate.

As you got into the biological sciences, there was a revolution going on in science with regard to DNA, and the key to this was PCR [polymerase chain reaction]. Explain to us what that is.

PCR was invented in this country in approximately 1987, and it's a method for amplifying, or multiplying, a single copy of DNA billions of times, so that you can visualize it and then work with it. There are myriad examples for its use in the basic sciences. It is also very useful for detection in what we call diagnostics, as well as for characterizing organisms—anything that has a DNA or RNA genome. So it's an incredibly versatile technique. And I saw PCR as an opportunity to put into practice my philosophy of technology transfer, and therefore used it as such in the field of infectious diseases.

You developed your own program, which is a technology transfer program in which PCR is brought to the world. How did that come about? Was it just natural for you to make this major leap as a lowly graduate student?

It's funny, because now I can look back—hindsight is great—and I can say, "Oh, look at this nice story," and I can make it seem as if I knew what I was doing. In fact, most of the time I was just going forward blindly, following a vision. I loved lab work, and as I mentioned before, I loved molecular and cellular biology. But then, I graduated from Harvard with a degree in biochemical sciences, and I thought, "What does this mean in the world?" I had a vision, but I wanted to have my hands in the world, in the real world. "How do I bring science to real-world problems?" It was completely unclear at that time how to do this.

There is international health. You become a doctor, and you have skills that are useful in the rest of the world, in developing countries. But when you're a scientist, what do you do? I wanted to create what I call "international science."[1] And so what happened was that I took a year off. Even though I had had been awarded several fellowships and had been accepted at a number of universities for graduate school, I decided to stop and take a year off. I was naïve; all I knew was that I wanted to try and do something with science somewhere where it mattered. I had done a lot of traveling in my life but never in the developing world. I didn't want to go as a tourist; I wanted to go to work. I had organized enough demonstrations that I felt like, "Okay, the next step is for me to go somewhere and put my money where my mouth is." And so it all kind of came together—I went to Nicaragua, where at the time one was able to volunteer—and I worked there for a while.

So you could make the transition from the salon to the labs very easily, by rolling up your sleeves and remembering what you learned.

Absolutely. But that [transition to the developing world] was a real eye-opener. I was moved by the urgency of the issues there, and so when I came back and started graduate school, all I knew was that there was so much research, knowledge, and resources

---

[1] Now often referred to as "global health."

here and so little there, I had to be involved, somehow, in sharing it. So that was the vision. It was completely unformed.

I stated to my future mentors that I was going to keep doing this work, period, and I would join their lab if they were fine with it, and I wouldn't if they weren't. And they agreed. So while I was in graduate school, earning a PhD investigating yeast genetics, I was going down and learning about infectious diseases and trying to support what my colleagues were doing in the Ministry of Health [in Nicaragua]. Then PCR was invented right at that time. And, all of a sudden . . . essentially, it all came together.

It turned out that my Nicaraguan colleagues didn't want me to just support what they were already doing; they wanted to learn molecular biology. I said, "Well, that's great. But, you know, there's barely running water here." And this produced a philosophical dilemma: if someone doesn't have the ability to do something, can you just say, "Well, you shouldn't learn about it?" Or do you say, "Okay, I'll teach you, but you can't implement?" At that point, PCR was simple enough that we thought, "Wow! Maybe we could actually do this here. And maybe there's an application of this technology to local problems," which was detecting microorganisms, infectious pathogens.

And so we tried it. The first time was just an incredible experience, where we were able, without much running water and with intermittent electricity, to manually amplify and observe a band of DNA representing detection of the parasite *Leishmania*. It was a moment that will live in my mind forever. Very exciting.

There was a big hubbub, and everyone was so excited, jostling each other to look through the goggles and see the DNA illuminated by ultraviolet light. Suddenly it became clear that "This is possible!" It was what I call a "Eureka" moment. And all the Nicaraguan scientists in the course loved it. So I continued organizing little workshops [in molecular biology].

But then I finished my PhD, and I was supposed to go on to do a postdoctoral fellowship at Dr. Stanley Falcow's lab at Stanford.

He is an incredible scientist, the father of microbial pathogenesis. I thought, "This is so beautiful, and I can use the genetics I learned in yeast, but applied to infectious disease problems." But I decided to take a year off, because by then, I had given talks at many international conferences, and there were a number of other countries clamoring to learn molecular biology and apply PCR in their own country. And I thought, "Well, I can't just go on with my career and ignore all the excitement that we've engendered, so I'll take a year and make good on my promises, and then go back to my scientific life."

After a year of investing in this program and conducting another set of workshops in Ecuador, it just snowballed. The work was written up in *Science* magazine, and hundreds of people wrote me, from everywhere. It got completely out of control. It was so urgent and exciting and gripping that I just canceled my postdoc and went with this new program.

I was really lucky to have someone supporting me at University of California, San Francisco, who said, "Why don't you just do this in a coherent fashion—create a program of technology transfer that incorporates the kind of sustainability and vision that you see fit?"

So I did just that—working in total collaboration with all my Latin American colleagues—and came up with the AMB/ATT [Applied Molecular Biology/Appropriate Technology Transfer] program, which is completely virtual.[2] It was just me and hordes of volunteers from here, from there, from many countries. We had a wonderful thing going, but no money for ten years. And then, right when we were really running out of resources and I didn't know how I was going to pay the rent, I got a call on my way to the airport, going to Bolivia to teach another workshop, that I had gotten the MacArthur award. That was just an incredible moment.

---

[2] Now the nonprofit organization Sustainable Sciences Institute, founded in 1998.

But as you're describing this, I'm reminded of your description earlier of what you saw when you were exposed to the world of cells and the beauty of that world. Now in the technology transfer work, you're actually creating an equally beautiful world in international society.

Yes, you're right. And by addressing public health issues where there's not a lot of funding, you essentially self-select for people who have a value system and really care about people and are willing to work hard not for their own profit. It was just beautiful because I collaborated with the best people, la crème de la crème, people who were dedicated to bettering humankind in whatever country, whether it was here, because they wanted to help, or there, because they were willing to devote themselves to projects over and above their own work to further infectious disease work in their own country to deal with pressing problems. It was wonderful, and I loved it, and I wished that it could go on forever, but you need resources. And so I knew during the whole time that I had to eventually pick a pathogen and start a whole basic research program at a university.

Which was the lucky pathogen that your research focused on?

Dengue virus, which was an issue, because, honestly, my training was in yeast and then parasites. I thought I would continue research with [parasites]; but dengue virus is exploding in Latin America, and there is very little work being done on it.

Dengue is a devastating, acute disease. It is caused by a virus that is transmitted by mosquitoes, and 2.5 billion people are at risk for this disease because of the distribution of the mosquito . . . including the whole southeast of the United States, I might add. There are approximately 50 million cases of dengue fever annually, which is a very debilitating, although self-limited, disease. There is a worse flavor of this same disease called dengue hemorrhagic fever and dengue shock syndrome, which can be fatal if untreated, and at the moment only supportive treatment is available. We don't understand why some people get this devastating disease and others don't. Very little research has been done because it is not a U.S. problem for the most part.

Let's talk a little about human rights, which can be thought of in terms of guaranteeing social rights, like the right to health, which is clearly your work in infectious disease, as well as ensuring civil rights and political rights.

There is a broader human rights aspect to this, which is transferring knowledge and empowering people, developing scientific capabilities so the local scientific communities can address relevant issues. Infectious disease is a human rights issue because of economic and political factors that create infectious disease problems for the poor end of the spectrum. So it is important to be able to deal with major infectious diseases locally and to address economic and social issues. Dealing with infectious diseases is addressing human rights issues in a broad sense.

It seems like it's important to you to retain the integrity of the scientific work, while also appreciating the complexity of the social and political reality. You're interested in bringing that scientific truth into the social and political realm.

Yes, that's true. For instance, in one's particular realm and one's discipline, one has to be objective and have a solid scientific base to stand on. But I also think it is very important for scientists and academics to step out of the ivory tower. We are in a community. We're in a domestic community. We're in a global community. I can't stand the idea that the world ends at the gates of the university, which is the way many academicians approach the world. I think that is dangerous. I think we have a commitment to society. We are getting tax dollars for our research, and we need to give something back to this country and to this world. We are incredibly privileged to have the life that we do and to be able to do interesting work. We complain about it in our various little ways, but we are incredibly lucky, and we owe it to the world to give something back. Most people don't see that, but I think this is a really important framework. That's the general aspect.

But also with our own science, people have to take a stand. DNA is being patented in the most abhorrent way. I mean, you can't patent DNA just because you sequenced it! And you can't block diagnostics being available at low cost to the rest of the world because you own the patent on a piece of DNA that you didn't invent. It's disgusting. And it's happening. There are many ramifications of patenting DNA, in the international arena, on the TRIPS (Trade-Related Aspects of Intellectual Property Rights) agreements, and very few scientists understand what is going on. It's terrifying. So something I try to do with my classes is to make the students aware of what's going on, in terms of patenting biologicals, and agriculture, and these kinds of issues. It's far from what I'm actually doing in the lab, of course, but it's something that I think scientists need to do—to move into the ethical realm to a larger extent.

We're going back to your theme of access, and one of the keys to access is public understanding of the issues. It seems that your work and your journey, thus far, raise a lot of interesting questions about science and about international cooperation. What insights would you like others to draw from your work?

[I give] a lot of outreach talks entitled "Science Across Borders." Frontiers—not just geographical frontiers, but gender issues, economic issues. Science is a great way to break down boundaries. We do science in an international community, and we have to continue fostering that spirit. And it's great—scientific papers have authors with interesting names from all over the world. Even basic research is an international endeavor, to a large extent, in terms of not having boundaries. It's an exciting area for a number of reasons, and I think that people need to bring the social context to science. Of course, young people coming into the field can carry that with them more than the people who are already set in their ways.

The hope of this movement from science to the society is to change society for the better.

Yes. Certainly, even in the most narrow definition, to control and prevent disease is a huge contribution in and of itself. And then, of course, there are all the other kinds of bonds, the international collaborations that can be made, the empowerment. And not just internationally. Right here in Oakland, for instance. We can start right here in our own backyard. There are a lot of positive messages that can come through this.

I'm left with a sense that there is a way to bridge the search for scientific truth and a value-driven concern about what the world is and what it can become.

Yes. What I would say is hold on to your values and follow your passion. If you believe in something and you have a vision, just go for it. I could never have said exactly what I was going to do, but I knew that this vision was important, and I was not going to let it go. There are a lot of people who feel things are important. You have to be good [at what you do], but if you believe in something, follow your passion. I think that that's the most important thing. And don't let go of values because that's what matters in the long term. If you can hold on to good values and make a positive impact on the world, then everybody else is going to benefit.

Oronto Douglas
May 5, 2001

Where were you born and raised?

I was born in 1966 and raised in a village called Okoroba, in the central axis of the Niger Delta, south from Niger in West Africa.

The region where I come from, the Niger Delta, is a very beautiful place. It is, of course, a tropical belt: rain forest, mango forest, wetlands. A really beautiful place—cascading streams, lots of wildlife—the kind of things that make life tick in terms of the unity between nature, humanity, and the totality of the environment. Growing up, it was natural that the first thing you learn to do is to be able to swim and be able to fish because that is our lifestyle: we fish and farm. I enjoyed doing that. I grew up in that kind of an environment before moving off to another part of the country.

You were born to the Ijaw people. Tell us a little about that group.

I am from the Ijaw ethnic nationality, a very ancient ethnic nationality. It is believed by historians to be perhaps one of the oldest nations to inhabit that part of the world. The Ijaws are fishermen, mostly, and farmers. They have been able to conquer the seas by being close to the seas. They go out in waves underwater. So the Ijaws are essentially fishermen and farmers, and we are very agrarian and rural in our living styles.

How do you think this environment shaped your character and the choices that you later made in your life?

When I was growing up, I came to realize the harmony [of nature] and where I grew up in that section [of the country] had an impact on me. I grew up not seeing gas flares, at least immediately around me. I noticed the fact that you can just walk to the bank of the river and get fish if you want, for your mother to be able to cook the next meal. You don't have to travel four or five hours. You can go into the forest and be able to observe monkeys frolicking in the wild. You could see crocodiles just by the river because the local people, the Ijaw people, don't kill crocodiles. They don't kill certain [other] types of animals as well, because they believe that they are deities, they are part of us.

Living in that kind of environment, going into the southwestern part of Nigeria, Abeokuta in the Ogun State, and returning back to the Delta for my university education, I realized that conditions are no longer what they were. The river had been polluted, the forest desecrated. There had been an assault on the totality of the ecology where I came from. I felt there was a need to stop that, to return back to our pristine [environment], to that tropical [paradise] that it used to be. So it really shaped [me] to be able to move beyond what I am seeing today.

Let's talk a little about your parents. How did they shape your character?

My father happens to be a fisherman. He is not one who wanted everything—he just wanted to live, he wanted us to go to school, he wanted us to love the environment where we come from, our culture, our tradition. My mom, on the other hand, was a traditional midwife, helping to deliver babies and children. She was one person who everybody knows. She was very active politically, at least in community politics and in the wider regional politics. So I grew up in that kind of setting, where your parents shape your perspective on life, in terms of nature, your upbringing, and so on.

Who were the other mentors in the course of your education who also shaped your way of thinking about the world?

When I was at the university, we read a lot about lawyers, like Gani Fawehinmi in Nigeria [and] Olesabakoba, also in Nigeria. I read about Nelson Mandela, another lawyer who was involved in political activism in South Africa, and other lawyers in other parts of the world, who are taking on the issues that concern the forward march of humanity. And this helped to be able to say, "Look, I am one that's not alone. There are people who are out there, who are concerned about changes." And there is a way to bring a new perspective, perhaps, standing on a different platform. You know, rather than just human rights, political life—in law, they all dovetail. But I felt that the survival question was important here, the environment upon which we are living, our day-to-day lifestyle, in terms of what we eat, where we go to, what are the other components of our life—the animals, the plants, the trees. These are also very important. And I felt I can also make a contribution along those lines.

You talked about going away and coming back. And the key here is that, in the '60s, the oil companies, especially Shell Oil, came to this area. On the one hand, you have this rural, agrarian, pristine setting; and on the other, there were a lot of resources under the ground that different corporations wanted. Tell us about that, the oil capacity there, and what the consequences were.

Yes. I started getting a feeling that things were not the same when my uncle, who I was living with in Abeokuta and who regularly traveled home about 600 kilometers away, came back to report to us. . . . I was in high school then. My uncle came back and was telling us about what was going on at home, that things were no longer the way I used to know, and that when I go back, it is possible that I will not recognize the community because I left while I was young, shortly after primary school. And he warned me about this. But what I saw when I came back was more dramatic than I could imagine.

We are talking here about 1986–87. When I came back, Shell was everywhere. They had taken over the land. They had established kingdoms in all the areas that they operate in. Chevron, as well. Mobil. Exxon. Texaco. Conoco. All the big oil companies, you name them, they had taken possession of our land. Shell struck oil in a community not too far from mine, called Oluebury, in 1956. That was the beginning. They did the thunderous explosion of the boils of planet Earth. The exploration activities of Shell led to the realization that underneath was the black gold. And that community of Oluebury, not too far away from my village, became a rallying point for the extraction of fossil fuel in my community, in the region where I come from.

The impact of that first strike was dramatic. There was a huge spill, which, according to the old men and women who witnessed that spill, leveled every plant, every animal, took over the whole survival intricacies and mechanisms of nature, and rendered life impossible for months. And it took time. They never had cleanup mechanisms at that time. This was in the '50s. And the oil companies continued the attack on nature—constant spillage and pollution and explosions from 1956 through the '90s. And they still continue now. A few days ago, there was a major explosion in Ogoni, where a lot of oil from Shell, this time again, was spewed into the surrounding environment.

The impact is largely on the local people. We are a largely agrarian community. We do not have the industries that the American or the European world depends on. We depend on land; we are from the ground. We plant our crops; we've been going to the river to fish. And when oil is now used as a mechanism to deny us our survival strategies, it is absolutely unjust. And that is what is going on in the Niger Delta today.

You started off as a lawyer, and one of your first cases was to be part of the team that defended Ken Saro-Wiwa. Tell us a little about him, what he stood for, and what happened to him.

I was actually a junior counsel in that case. I was called into the case by the senior counsel, who felt that I would be useful because I was from the area, and I knew Ken from 1989, while I was a student union leader. I had gone to see him in his office to profile him on what he'd been doing. Ken Saro-Wiwa was a writer, a playwright, an activist, an environmentalist, a public commentator, a businessman. He told us that his vision is for the younger ones to be able not to go through what he and the elders are going through, and that he is currently trying to design a program that will help to bring change. A year later, he started up the movement for the survival of the Ogoni people—that was in 1990—essentially aimed at mobilizing the Ogoni people, a very small ethnic minority in the Niger Delta, who over the years have been marginalized, like all other ethnic nationalities in the region. Ken Saro-Wiwa decided to change all that, first starting with the Ogoni people. But, unfortunately, the government, the military dictatorship at that time, in collaboration with the oil industry, decided that he has to be stopped before he goes beyond Ogoni. And there was a kangaroo court set up. He was brought before that kangaroo military court and charged with murder. A very fake charge, a charge that cannot be sustained in any court—any court that is manned by persons of justice. He was charged, and we had to go there to defend him. Unfortunately, the military dictatorship had made up its mind; the oil company was convinced that the best way to resolve the Ogoni issue was to stop the leadership. So Saro-Wiwa, along with eight others, was hanged on the 10th of November, 1995.

How did that verdict affect you and your movement?

It actually triggered us into taking in cognizance that the struggle is not over. That, in fact, it is just beginning. It fired a lot of us, who believe that we've got to do much more than we are doing now. We've got to internalize the issue. We have got to reach out to people of conscience around the world. We have got to organize. We have got to mobilize. We have got to act in a way so that generations yet unborn do not have to come out and face what we are facing now. So it was a major trigger that helped us to realize that the battle for environment protection, social justice, equity, and peaceful coexistence around the world, especially in our community in relationship with others, is a major work, and we've got to move on.

Is it fair to say you're more of an activist and less of a lawyer now, or do you remain both?

I will say I am more of an environmental rights activist. Once in a while I do go to court, for very serious cases of political significance, the type that probably the ordinary lawyer may not want to take on because of the danger. Today [May 5, 2001] Nigeria is still like a totalitarian state. In civilized society, if you commit a crime, you go out, fish out those youth, and send them to court and have them punished for crimes that they have committed. But in the Niger Delta, because oil is involved and because there is a pathological hit rate for the people, the strategy that was used was to teach these people a lesson: "Let's wipe out that community."

Help us understand the broader implications of the presence of the oil company. We talked about the degradation of the environment, but an additional problem is that because sufficient resources or a just amount of resources are not being returned to the community, there is a greater social dislocation—a lot of crime, a social chaos that leads to a lot of youth violence, and so on. Talk a little bit about that

*degradation of the human community, as opposed to the environ-
mental setting.*

Yes, the human resources. No nation, no people that really wants
to make progress will disregard the protection of the human beings in their particular environmental setting. We believe, in the
organization that we co-founded [the Environmental Rights Action Group], that [within] the environment, the human person is
central to existence. We believe that human beings should decide
the fate of the environment. Now, in the Niger Delta where I
come from, there has not been an attempt to protect the human
person in that part of the world. The oil companies and the government are conspiratorially in this. They attempt to prevent the
human being from standing, from moving forward. So what has
happened over the years is that because the region is rich, because the people are poor, they are a minority. The elite, who
likely hold the country in their pockets, in collaboration with the
oil industry, think that they can do anything and get away with
it. This had led to the degradation of the environment, and the
impoverishment of the human person—impoverishment, in the
sense that the mental capacity, the physical capacity of the people
to stand and be in a position to protect what they have, is now
gradually waning.

Now, the result of all this is that there is a desperate attempt to fight for survival, either individually or communally or
ethnic-wide.

You must realize that in the Niger Delta, people have been on
a long, long road towards freedom. Right from the days before
colonialism, in fact, before then, there was an attempt by outsiders to take the resources from the people. Palm oil was very central in the economy of Europe and other parts of the world, and
the Niger Delta was a central area where these resources could be
gotten. And companies like the Royal Niger Company that became
interested in these oil resources used violence to take these re-

sources forcefully to Europe. And the people resisted. Their resistance, of course, was crushed with superior firepower. And then,
of course, the attempt by Ken Saro-Wiwa, using the environment
and the nationality of Ogoni and human rights to provide another
platform to mobilize the people, became also another vista for our
forward march towards achieving our objective as a people.

We have seen all these phases of attempts to change the situation. We feel that our strategy should continue to be that which
will ennoble humanity, using peaceful, nonviolent strategy to
mobilize our people, to raise consciousness, to organize at the
village level or even at the hamlet level, town level, city level, family level. First, to convince ourselves and inform ourselves that,
"Look, the situation we are in now can be reversed, and we have
the capacity to do it if we are organized." It is only when we organize that we can achieve the victory that we so aspire to. And so
the organization of these various processes is on. It rises up once
in a while, and goes down again, and because the oppressive
mechanism that has been put in place at every point in time sup-
presses them, and because the people have designed strategies
which are peaceful, which are ennobling, which the oil companies and the oppressive internal colonialists find very abhorrent,
they push down to crush those [people.] Or we continue to remain hopeful that the rest of the world will wake up one day and
say, "Look, there's injustice here. Let us move in there and help
this poor, voiceless, defenseless people."

*In an age of globalization—on the one hand, you have these compa-
nies moving all over the world, extracting resources here, selling the
product elsewhere—but there is also a kind of an international civil
society. What are the strategies for calling the attention of this international civil society to this particular predicament?*

First of all, we discovered that what we were going through in the
Niger Delta was not unique to us. I have been in the States now

for two years, and I have had the privilege, or misfortune, of visiting communities that oil companies, big industries, target their polluting activities on. I have visited "Cancer Alley," Richmond in California. And then in Louisiana, that whole belt from New Orleans right down to Baton Rouge and all those areas. You will find that pollution has been targeted on these people. And they're usually poor, voiceless, and defenseless. They are also in the minority. We are not alone, we realized. These connections have been made with a view to building a common consensus, so that we can globalize our existence against injustice and oppression, whether in California or in the larger United States, whether in the Niger Delta or in the larger Nigeria and Africa, that we can build consensus to stop these injustices. The movement is on, and I'm very happy to say that we are making progress. The linkage is clear. We all live on one planet. If humanity does not protect planet Earth, and he or she thinks they will escape to space to escape from the pollution tendency here, then I think that we will just be going around in circles. Because when you get there, the same lifestyle, the same kind of activities, that same part of the universe that people are trying to escape to in the next thirty or one hundred years will become polluted. It's like a "not in my backyard" kind of situation: we can pollute the Niger Delta, but don't pollute the United States. And right now, it's becoming clear that they are also polluting the United States in communities of color, African American communities, in communities where people do not have political voice. We must make linkages, because the culprits are one and the same, those that are interested in profit and in power. They are united; they are organized in polluting, in taking away these resources for themselves and not for everyone. These are the challenges that we face. That is a major part in achieving our common goals, seeing the connections, identifying your life with the lives of others, and seeing the relationships that affect our common objectives.

The United States and its people have a central role to play in the resolution of the polluting nightmare that humanity is being presented with, and which we face today. The good news is that within the United States, there are good people; there are people of conscience. There are people who are willing to stand up and say no. We read beautiful things about what happened in Seattle, when the youth of the United States stood up to say, "We are saying no to WTO [World Trade Organization]." We are tired of pollution. We are tired of environmental degradation. We are tired of policies that do not ennoble humanity and provide an opportunity for humanity to reinvent itself for the years ahead. We are too short-term in our approach to the survival question and to the future of human progress.

Will the oil companies, over time, initiate these efforts to co-opt and defang the opposition?

They have a capacity of metamorphosis. They will change course where the profit is. We are saying now that the oil industry is not sustainable. We are saying that the way and manner it is being carried out does not take into cognizance our future. Now, when the voice of reason prevails, when ideas for the protection of the environment and human rights become holistic, I think that the oil companies will be on the defensive if they know they cannot win. And if that happens, they will then begin to reinvent themselves. They will begin to search for a new means of becoming relevant. We must be on the lookout, though, that in their present manifestation, that chameleonic manifestation, they must not change to more monstrous apparitions that we may not be able to control.

Reflecting on your own life, what are your motivations and inner strengths, and where do they come from in your particular case?

I am motivated, essentially, by the fact that every human being ought to make a contribution towards human progress. We are not just on this planet to eat, to sleep, and then we die. I think we came because we have a contribution to make. My little contribution in the area of environmental human rights is to further the whole debate about our progress.

It is absolutely important for us to understand that the dynamics of change could come from any quarter, whether through law, through lecturing, through activism, but they all come together. It could bring a lot of pain—for example, you have been arrested for campaigning on the environment; you are being hanged, or you have had to go for months and years having to own more than one passport, for example, so that you can be able to sneak out of a dictatorial setting as we had in Nigeria. Activism comes with a lot of pain, a lot of frustration, a lot of discomfort. But I think that at the end of the day, you will realize that progress has been made.

SEEKING TRUTH

During times of unquestioned government authority, journalists become increasingly essential to preserving freedom and accountability. Amira Hass, an Israeli correspondent for *Haaretz*, and Jane Mayer, a staff writer for the *New Yorker*, share what they discovered by probing the reality behind the accepted government rationales for anti-terrorism policies. Through meticulous research and by going to the source, these courageous journalists unearth disturbing truths and, through their writing, are able to establish a counter-narrative. Hass lives among the Palestinians and comes to understand the human costs of Israel's pass laws and the origins of terrorism among the Palestinians. Mayer reveals the consequences of America's post-9/11 torture policies by listening to military lawyers and interrogators who believe torture contradicts American law and values. Political awakening for both Hass and Mayer involves recognizing the contradiction between government action and the long-standing values of the community.

Amira Hass

Amira Hass is a correspondent for *Haaretz*, the Israeli newspaper. Her publications include *Drinking the Sea at Gaza* and a collection of articles titled *Reporting from Ramallah: An Israeli Journalist in Occupied Land*. She is a recipient of numerous human rights and journalism awards, including the Bruno Kreisky Human Rights Award, the UNESCO Press Freedom Award, the inaugural award from the Anna Lindh Memorial Fund, and the Hrant Dink Memorial Award.

Jane Mayer

Jane Mayer is a staff writer for the *New Yorker*. Prior to joining the *New Yorker*, Mayer was for twelve years a reporter at the *Wall Street Journal* and, in 1984, became the *Journal*'s first female White House correspondent. Mayer is the author of the best-selling 2008 book *The Dark Side: The Inside Story of How the War on Terror Turned into a War on American Ideals*, which was chosen as one of the ten best books of the year by the *New York Times* and as one of the best books of the year by *The Economist*, *Salon*, *Slate*, and Bloomberg. She is also the co-author of two other best-selling books: *Strange Justice*, written with Jill Abramson and published in 1994, which was a finalist for the 1994 National Book Award for nonfiction; and her first book, *Landslide: The Unmaking of the President, 1984–1988*, co-authored by Doyle McManus, an acclaimed account of the Reagan White House's involvement in the Iran-Contra affair.

Amira Hass
October 24, 2003

Where were you born and raised?

Jerusalem, Israel.

And looking back, how do you think your parents shaped your thinking about the world?

They were Jewish Holocaust survivors, members of the Israeli Communist Party. My mother had joined the partisans, but then she was deported to a concentration camp. My father was in a ghetto. I think I was raised by their personal attempt, an ideological attempt, to compensate for the terrible emotional and ideological vacuum and family vacuum created after the Second World War, with the loss of most of their family and friends, history and life—to compensate for this with the hope that you can work for a better world, where the principle of equality is recognized as a basic for human life.

In the introduction to your book, Drinking the Sea at Gaza, *I get the sense of both a legacy of loss, of looking back, but also of resistance.*

Yes, only that the loss is not that you look back and you feel the loss. The loss is always there. You don't have to look back to feel the loss. It's in everyday life. If your brothers and sisters and other beloved ones have all been murdered by the Nazi system, then the loss is ever-present.

Your mother [Hanna Levy Hass] was a writer.

That's right. She wrote a diary in the concentration camp [republished in English by Haymarket Books as *Diary of Bergen Belsen*], which already merited a death penalty if she had been found writing it. Her friends or the other inmates in the barracks were covering for her when she was writing. She wrote on pieces of paper that she found who-knows-where, and she described the life there. She didn't talk so much about herself. She made a kind of analysis of what was happening to people around her. She was also teaching children. It was another forbidden activity for inmates in this concentration camp. She taught children because she felt that they needed to be taken care of in this hell. To her it was a way of fighting, for sure, to have these most forbidden activities.

You've been involved in human rights work as well as journalism?

When I was already working for *Haaretz* as a text editor, I needed something for my *neshamah*, as you say in Hebrew, for my soul. So I volunteered. It was in the middle of the first Intifada. I volunteered in a group called Workers Hotline. We assisted Palestinian workers, mainly, whose rights were violated by Israeli employers. They were not represented properly by Israeli trade unions. So we started this advocacy group, and also offered active assistance by approaching the employers either through lawyers or directly in order to get for these people what they deserved.

Is this where you first developed your consciousness of the plight of the Palestinians, years ago?

No, no. I grew up in a political family and a political surrounding. I was active in the Israeli left wing for years. I always thought that our activity should be in the Israeli street with Israelis, and to explain to them and to try and promote the understanding that occupation is wrong. For this I didn't need to go and meet with or experience the Israeli Occupation. But there was a change with the first Intifada, and I felt that all this kind of political activism led nowhere.

My activism with Workers Hotline introduced me to Gaza, especially, and it was like discovering a new world. I didn't have prejudice, I think, but I didn't have much knowledge about ordinary life there; mostly I had theoretical knowledge. So it was an opportunity to have more detailed knowledge. I was fascinated by people in this society. I found it a very warm society, a very welcoming society, a very resilient society.

You, in your work, have gone to live in the communities that you write about. Tell us about that choice as a journalist.

I think this is a basic principle of journalism. But also, I have this research curiosity which I could satisfy by living there because it was ongoing research. So I'm very lucky; I discover a new society, and I discover all kinds of facets of this society by living in it, but still by being some sort of an observer and not part of the society in the real sense of the word. Of course, you become part of it to an extent, but I'm always in this position of an observer while living in the society.

Some have compared my work with anthropological work—maybe more progressive anthropological work. That, for me, has also been very important, personally. I do have an obsession with getting the taste or the flavor of things from inside. When I was twenty, I lived for four or five months in Romania. It was under Ceauşescu. I felt kind of a philosophical responsibility, I will tell you, because I came from a communist family. I didn't have any illusions about the regimes in Eastern Europe. But because I come from such a family and from such an ideological background, I have a philosophical responsibility to taste life in the mutation or in this terrible dictatorship that evolved in Eastern Europe.

What is the relation of theory to observation and facts in your work? Clearly, you've headed toward [an understanding] of the real situation, what people's lives are really like. But how do you think about theory in the back of your mind?

I always see the class conflict. I don't even have to theorize about it. It's all self-evident. That's why I was, very early on, very critical of the Palestinian Authority, because I saw the way that they were creating new and consolidating old elites in all sorts of corrupted and corruptive ways in order to build up a stronghold which supports the Oslo process.

At the same time, I saw the Israeli ongoing colonization very clearly. I saw it was done in order to sustain Israeli Jewish hegemony. But then, because I'm very aware of my theoretical in-built assumptions (I cannot even help it; it's not that I'm a scholar in Marxism—I'm not), I was very careful to collect a lot of information. I was very, very careful when people told me about Arafat's people starting to accumulate capital in the occupied territories while most of the people went through a process of impoverishment. I was very careful and didn't immediately write about it; because I'm inclined to believe that first I have to collect more information. So in a sense, I'm sometimes more careful about it because I'm aware of the impulse to theorize.

Tell me a little about your craft as a writer. Your pieces are beautifully written. They are comprehensive and they detail everyday life. There's an eye for things that people ignore. How do you do this?

Thank you. That's not the basic requirement of journalism.

Sometimes I see a kind of a film rolling in front of my eyes, and I feel a need to describe it in words. If I were a filmmaker, that's how I would have done it, but with pictures. Then, also, of course, I don't only write features; I write op-eds. I know that I have to expose the analysis, but I prefer to expose it through examples from daily life, and not to burden with slogans. I'm trying to avoid slogans as much as possible, because I live in a society, both Israeli and Palestinian, that is really overcrowded with slogans and one-sentence exclamations. And I'm appalled by it.

You're not driven by the headlines as many journalists are.

I don't need to be, because I don't cover daily news. I know some things are structural, and they might not get the headlines. They are structural, and they are developed within Israeli policy or within Palestinian tactics. So I pay attention to this much more than to what seems to catch the attention of everybody at certain moments, and then dies after two, three days.

Let's talk now about the Israeli occupation. You have delineated in an essay in Palestinian Studies *the structure of Israeli rule. Explain it to us. What are the by-products of the strategy that Israel is employing to control the territories?*

Let me first say this, that occupation is not necessarily a military occupation. It is enough when one people and one foreign government decide about the future and scope of development, and chances of development, of another people who has not elected this government. I came to understand what occupation is especially during the years of the Oslo process, which was presented as and believed by many to be a peace process. I observed the ongoing and ever-intensifying Israeli policy of control over Palestinian life, even though the army was not directly inside Palestinian-populated areas, and even though there were negotiations between Palestinian leaders and the Israeli government.

There were two main manifestations of this control, this Israeli persistent and successful attempt to dictate the Palestinian future. One is the policy of colonization or of settlement, whereby Israel got hold of much more land within Gaza and the West Bank during the Oslo process, and made sure that it created the infrastructure of one state in the one country between the land and the river. It was one infrastructure of very good highways, roads, and connecting remote settlements with the Israeli mainland, establishing the same sewage system, water system, electric grid, education system, of Israel in these remote places in the occupied territories; but it was an infrastructure for Jews alone.

Now in between this infrastructure, this grid of roads and settlements, you had Palestinian enclaves which were allotted self-rule, but the self-rule was in itself very limited. You could not expand in your natural territorial reserve because this had been taken by the Israelis in the time of the so-called peace process.

The second [way] to control Palestinian development was through a system introduced first in '91, which was practically a pass system, like the one in apartheid South Africa. Palestinians' right to freedom of movement was taken from them. What had happened between '67 and '91, in spite of the occupation and in spite of Palestinian armed attacks against Israelis in the years before Olso, was that the entire Palestinian community was allowed to exercise its freedom of movement in the whole country with certain and a few exceptions. After 1991 the policy was reversed: the entire Palestinian population was denied its right for freedom of movement, except for a few categories which were chosen by Israel.

Now, with the years, the system has perfected. It involves more and more people who need permits, and for smaller and smaller areas. At the beginning, you needed a travel permit from Gaza to Israel, or from Gaza to the West Bank, and vice versa; you now need a permit to go from one city in the West Bank to another city in the West Bank. In certain areas in the West Bank and Gaza, people who live near settlements need permits to go out of their own area in special hours through special gates. So what Israel has been doing during the last twelve years is fragmenting not only Palestinian territory but the Palestinian population into categories which are characterized by their access to the privilege of freedom of movement.

You write: "Time and space together make room in one's world, not only materially to accomplish one's tasks and activities, but at the level of the spirit, enabling both the individual and the community to breathe, to develop, to prosper, to create. Space in the occupied territories has been gradually but ruthlessly encroached upon for more than thirty years, as more and more land has been expropriated." This is kind of a theoretical statement. Give us an example in everyday life.

I'll share with you this story of a village, Jabara. It found itself locked between the recently built fence—Israel's security fence—and the former green line. This fence is allegedly built to prevent suicide bombers infiltrating into Israel. But the fence is not built along the green line, the border of '67, but it's built in many places deep into Palestinian territory in order to incorporate Israeli settlements. So it is upgrading the former border, and it is actually expropriating land from the Palestinian community, and it locks in people. People in these areas are not allowed to go freely to Israel and cannot go freely to Palestinian territory. In this village are only three hundred people, but you have one hundred children studying in a nearby village, which is actually the mother village of this little village. So the students have to cross through the fence to get to the other village for school. The fence has a gate. Sometimes it is opened; sometimes it is not opened. There are [also] teachers teaching in a nearby Palestinian city called Tulkarm. They have to cross from another place through an Israeli checkpoint with soldiers. Sometimes they are let through; sometimes they are not let through.

Now, the villagers need to have a special identity card, additional to what they [already] have, which is the Israeli authorization for them to live where they live. They live in an area that was declared a closed military zone, but only to Palestinians. Jews can go there and live there, but Palestinians cannot. Only those who live there already are allowed to stay, provided they get this authorization from the Israeli military. A few were already told that they are not allowed to stay there, because some of them were politically active years ago and were in Israeli jails, or so on and so forth. But this is their land, this is their home, this is their family, and now they're actually supposed to leave it.

This is something which happened on a different scale in the Gaza Strip. You have areas in the Gaza Strip where people need to go through fences and through gates twice a day, once a day, sometimes not, sometimes yes. They cannot go with their cars. They're not allowed to bring in things. They cannot market their agricultural products. So many people have been pushed to leave these areas, which are not, by surprise, the only vacant areas in the Gaza Strip, and where some of the big Israeli settlements are situated.[1]

So you see, it's slow. It's a policy in the name of security which forces many people to leave their own land and their own homes if they want to conduct a decent life. If they insist on staying there, they are doomed to impoverished life and pushed into becoming objects of charity, and they are not living off their own work.

This combination of the pass system and of the infrastructure to support the Israeli settlements leads to everyday problems, so that for an Israeli to travel on the highways that were built for the Israeli settlements, a trip could take, hypothetically, thirty minutes on a freeway. But for a Palestinian, who's not entitled to go on these roads, the same trip could take several hours.

[1] Israel withdrew from Gaza in August 2005.

Yes, or he could not leave at all. So it is not only the robbery of land, but you have a robbery of time. Palestinians' time has been robbed over the last thirteen years, because you have to wait for a permit and you don't get it, and then you have to wait again. Then you waste time waiting at the checkpoint, then you waste time in submitting another request for a permit, then you waste time trying to go through all kinds of small, dangerous bypass roads. And time is a means of production. Time is so precious for one's internal development and community development, and this has been grabbed by the pass system. This very important means of life has been robbed from the Palestinians. Sometimes I think it's more precious than land because land you can get back one way or the other. The lost time, you will never get back.

It must lead to a sense of helplessness, of frustration that eats away at the soul.

It's total strangulation. The thing is that people are not that aware of how huge this loss of time is. But I see how people—because of this loss of time and loss of space, because they don't have freedom of movement—they have lowered their span of expectations. They are not expecting much of their lives because they know that they will be disappointed. You cannot plan to go to see friends. I'm even talking about the years before these terrible times of armed clashes and constant military incursions. People have lowered, so much, their expectations of themselves. They restrict themselves to their narrow surroundings—family, work, home; family, work, home—nothing more than that. You don't even go in Gaza now. Even the sea, half of the shore, is blocked for Palestinians. You live four hundred meters away from the shore, and you can't reach the sea because there are settlements, and the security of the settlements comes first.

Help us understand how Israel came to adopt this strategy. In your readings I get the sense that initially these were ad hoc decisions with regard to control that have, in essence, turned into something else.

It's something that I'm always asking myself, to what extent it had been a master plan from the start. I'm still oscillating between the two possibilities. How much was it taken in '91 as an ad hoc policy, meant especially to contain the first Intifada? Because in '91, the first Intifada came to a standstill, in terms of Palestinian measures and an inability to continue a mass uprising, and the Israeli oppression came to a standstill, because at that time, Israel acknowledged its status in humanitarian terms as an occupying power. It had responsibility for the welfare of the civilian population. That's why it could not bomb Palestinians. It could not repress their uprising by dropping one-ton bombs on civilian areas, or by killing every day five, six, seven people and more, as it does today.

So it had to confine itself to bureaucratic logistic means, and the pass system was such a bureaucratic means. It tried to contain the Palestinian uprising from spilling over into Israel proper. And also, it allowed Israel much more control, because people were subject to all these extra documents, and then you can control people's movements, and then you contain their activities. But with time, and especially with the Oslo years, they understood how they could control economic life, how they could actually lead this economic war of attrition vis-à-vis the Palestinian authority, and thus force them to accept all kinds of concessions during the talks, during the negotiations, about the interim status and then the final status.

Then, I think, it evolved. I don't know at what stage. I think very early on it evolved as a means to achieve demographic separation. Not geographic separation, not political separation, but demographic separation, which means that Israel is still in control all over the territory where two peoples live, but it is separating the two peoples. It separates, but for the sake of one people, of one demographic group.

Let's talk a little now about the suicide bombers because in this recent phase, the series of bombings has in some ways shattered our ability to understand what is actually going on in the region. Help us understand how suicide bombers emerged in this conflict on the Palestinian side.

The first suicide bombings in this conflict occurred in Palestinian territory, not in Israel, in '93. This was ten years after the first suicide bombings in Lebanon, which means that for ten years, Palestinians, who are mostly Muslims, did not think of endorsing such a way of action. Their fight was always based on hope for life, not for death. Now, '93 is two years after the imposition of the pass system and of the closure policy. I think there was this terrible impotence that Palestinians felt in the times when their space was reduced. At this point in '93, it was only three or four suicide attempts inside the occupied territories—Gaza and the West Bank—against mostly military targets and settlers (who are seen by Palestinians as military, not as civilians).

The first suicide bombings inside Israel were in '94. These occurred one or two months after a Jewish American physician in Hebron killed twenty-nine Muslim worshippers in their holy place. So this was first an act of revenge. And then more revenge started. It started to be emulated by Hamas and by jihadis against Israel, always with the claim that it was retaliation against Israeli actions in killing those civilians.

But these bombings also had a clear political motive on the part of Hamas, and this was to foil the Oslo agreements, or to push to a corner the Palestinian Authority.

So the factions within the Palestinian leadership, in their competition with each other for popular support, see this as a tool?

In this Intifada, it became a tool in the competition between everybody. These factions are using people's fatigue with life, total loss of hope, the urge for revenge, because so many Palestinians civilians have been killed during the last three years, almost unnoticed by the entire world. They feel this need to take revenge, and they feel this need to get out, even for a moment, from their captivity and very limited space and to be omnipotent even for one moment. They're ready to die for this because they don't see any point in living. But then the factions are using this readiness, not because they strategize and they think this will bring them closer to independence, but because they compete with each other for popularity within the Palestinian population.

Let's broaden our understanding of this. What you have is a hypothetical person whose family's land is taken away, or who loses a relative, or . . .

Or who sees so much blood around them.

Who has been led to unbelievable depression and frustration and becomes a target of opportunity for factions among the Palestinian leadership, who want to use him in this way to strike back at Israel.

Very often they don't have to work hard to recruit him or her. Very often such people voluntarily look for someone and say, "We would like to make a suicide attempt." So they initiate the act themselves very often.

But from our side of the water, it's hard to understand what would lead a person to take this act. One is not sure whether they're motivated by religion, by going to heaven. Talk a little about that.

For me as a secular person, it's also very difficult to believe or to understand when people do talk about heaven. So I need the help of my Palestinian friends and acquaintances, who might not be very secular but are also not very religious. Most of them say that going to heaven, or the religious motivations of being *shahid*, being martyred and getting eternal life in heaven—these are not the main motivations; they only come last, or they are being adopted because it is accepted as the norm.

The real motivations are those drawn from the personal experience. I don't mean that a suicide bomber's individual life has to be a total wreck. No. We see that many of those who went to explode themselves had careers or had started to have careers; they were not coming from the poorest families; they were enrolled into universities. So it's not people who were a total loss in Western norms, or even Palestinian norms. But they felt they represented the society in its despair, and they wanted to do something, to make some use of this despair: revenge.

It is a very delicate interplay between the personal, though not immediate, despair and the political community's despair. Many of them got strength by becoming more observant, by going to the mosque, by praying five times a day, by reading the Koran over and over again. It's only then. Some of them started with the Koran at the beginning of the Intifada when they saw so much bloodshed. So many of their neighbors and friends and relatives getting killed, civilians getting killed by Israeli soldiers. They found compensation and solace with reading the Koran. So it strengthened them.

But this was not the motivation. It was, maybe, the support. At the same time, I did speak to one person from Hamas who eventually was killed, not in a suicide attempt but while confronting, with a gun, Israeli tanks and soldiers. We had talked a year before he was killed, and he told me he saw himself as a candidate for suicide. What he had chosen to do, to fight against the Israeli army, is almost suicide, because the proportions are such that you are always getting killed. He didn't mention religious motivations at all, only the national ones, only to think how many of his friends got killed. He was a very educated person, and also very religious, theoretically religious. He didn't use religion as the first motivation for joining the armed struggle. It gave him support, but not motivation.

On both the Israeli side and the Palestinian side, there seems to be a failure of leadership, a lack of a responsible leadership that sees both the implications of policies and the dynamic of the situation. Let's look at both sides. I want to ask you first about Israel, where it seems that even Labor governments who initiated and tried to implement the Oslo process continued to build settlements, and that that was a real failure of leadership. Do you agree?

Not at all.

You don't agree?

No—you say failure because you assume that Israel's main goal was just to have peace with the Palestinians.

Touché.

I think their main goal was to guarantee a stronger, bigger Israel, and an enfeebled Palestinian political entity. And they were very successful. So it's a very responsible leadership, if you think that this was their main goal.

So all of the sides of the Israeli debate are committed to enlarging the size of Israel through settlements?

I think so. This has been made clear during the Oslo process especially, and since. It's not a failure of leadership. It's a failure of Israeli constituencies that did not support these policies but let themselves believe that their leadership was going towards peace.

So why did these constituencies, then, fail to see what was going on, and try to build a political coalition to oppose that?

I guess that many people wanted to believe that it is possible to break the spell of conflict. People were very optimistic about the Oslo process. They thought their demands for a two-state solution and talk with the Palestinians in recognition of the Palestinian people were coming true under Labor. They just felt, "Oh, we were right all these years, and now there is a government which acknowledges we were right." So they paid very little attention to the reality on the ground. You can explain it psychologically without attributing bad motivations to these people.

But others thought that peace was possible with settlements, since in 1993 Arafat signed an accord which did not demand that Israel stop all settlement activity. So people thought that peace with settlements was possible and that maybe Palestinians were satisfied with it. After all, the settlement activity was beneficial for many segments of Israeli society. This is why these constituencies failed to understand the discrepancy between the promise of stability and normal life in a state, and the reality of permanent colonization.

Let's talk about the Palestinian leadership, then. How do we account for their failure? You suggest that important parts of that leadership sold out to the Israelis in the Oslo process—those are my words, not yours—but compromised themselves, creating almost a class system, among that leadership and the Palestinian people. And secondly, have they also failed by allowing the abuse of their own people, especially in the case of the suicide bombers, who are seen as tools for jockeying for position vis-à-vis the other factions in the cause?

I don't think that the Palestinian leadership sent suicide bombers. Maybe the leadership did not dare to stop it in time in this Intifada, but it did not use the suicide bombers itself. It's some of the factions in opposition to the leadership and some Fatah group-ings that used the suicide bombers. It is true, though, that the leadership failed to correctly analyze Israeli motivations and to conduct a better strategy of negotiation.

I think it's partly the naïveté of this Palestinian leadership; also, a human need to see a change. Let's not forget they were the weaker party. I think that they were very sincere in their readi-ness for a two-state solution as the final status solution. But they failed to see [or] to learn Israeli methods. And Arafat's people didn't consult with those inside the occupied territories who had known Israelis better. When they signed on the Declaration of Principles, they didn't even know what a settlement looked like. They thought it was a distant military position, so that's why they did not bother to insist on demanding a clear freeze of any Israeli construction in the occupied territories.

They let themselves be pampered by Israel's very colonialist tricks of giving an elite all sorts of privileges, especially of free-dom of movement, which allowed the Palestinian Authority to build up an entourage which benefited economically from the process and the presence of the Authority. That's why it gave its political support and participated in the negotiations.

So what you had were people who were economically depen-dent on the Israelis because of the privileges, and were also con-ducting the negotiations with the Israelis over how quickly the Israeli withdrawal/redeployment will be and how big the settle-ments will be or not be. So this was the by-product—what you feel as being sold out. I don't think it was intentional. Many of them did believe that if they served Israeli security demands for some time, they would guarantee the future and the stability of a Palestinian society.

Palestinians, as others, have always had their classes and elites. But the Palestinian Authority, internally, had a responsibil-ity for the welfare of the people. Instead of dedicating itself to the development of human beings inside, it invested a lot in all kinds of symbolic aspects of life which served the grandeur of the authority. It allocated much of its budget to security organs because Arafat needed this multiplicity in order to control. They did not develop enough the health system or the education system. I think this was their main failure. It stems from the fact that they were not really elected but came from outside; they were very indifferent to the people. They came from very undemocratic traditions, and this was a major failure. I think that if they cared more for their people and were more attentive to people's needs internally, they would have been stronger vis-à-vis Israel at the negotiation table.

What is the role that you as a writer can play in elevating consciousness of these dynamics? And in what way does that, in the long term, contribute to a change in the situation?

Sometimes I think that I'm only writing for the archives. But in five, ten years, people would say, "Oh, she wrote such-and-such."

Look, I didn't have influence. I've been writing about the discrepancy between the [rhetoric] and the facts on the ground during the Oslo period. I've been writing extensively in my paper and then my book. People read me. And certainly, there were other similar voices. But, somehow, it did not sink in. Most of the Israelis, I would say, did not get the message, because it's not for one writer to change things; you need a movement. You need a social movement, certain activity in the street of people who speak out clearly. And then this interplay between voices in the media and voices outside in the streets, in social activities, that can make some sort of a change or can be heard. When you're one voice . . . and I was considered a radical extremist, pessimist . . .

Cassandra?

Cassandra. Cassandra can be such a joy-killer. I'm always spoiling the party, so I was told. I was told by my editors, sometimes, "Everybody's talking about how Gazans are happy, but you only tell us about the pass system and travel permits and all this."

I was even told by somebody that I don't have perspective because I live in Gaza. So it's a new definition of journalism. So, no, I don't think I made a difference. On the contrary, I'm very frustrated because I documented and reported on so many clear and very logical voices among Palestinians which warned Israelis about the coming explosion if Israel continues this policy of pushing the Palestinians into a surrender arrangement.

What is your advice to people who are interested in this region, who may be driven in their understanding by what they read in the headlines in the English-speaking press?

One has to read other things than the headlines. There are all kinds of other messages, especially online. Not everything is always accurate, but people have to be very skeptical about what they read first, and then, always, to meet people within the region and maybe try to see Al Jazeera—news which is not only from a Western point of view.

Also one has to remember, no matter where one is, to be very skeptical about official versions. Power, any power, has to be suspected everywhere and has to be monitored. This is the main task of journalism. So they have to look for those kinds of writing which monitor power and which describe the situations not from the eyes of the ruler only.

I get the sense that you think and believe, both in word and in deed, that truth emerges from understanding, describing, and being immersed in the reality that you're writing about.

I believe that what I've been describing is the truth. I don't believe that it makes much change and much difference. It does not preach to the non-converted. It does not reach the non-converted. It reaches the converted. But, still, I know this is true, what I've been writing.

Jane Mayer
August 8, 2008

Where were you born and raised?

I was born and raised in New York City, into a family of historians, and I've dedicated my book *The Dark Side* to my grandfather, who is a historian.

What did your parents do, and how did it affect your thinking about the world?

Well, my dad is a composer and he writes modern music, and my mom is a painter. And how did it affect my view of the world? Well, my father's family were the Lehman family of bankers and philanthropists, and they were in public life, with Governor Lehman. And so there was kind of a liberal tradition in my family of politics. My dad was in intelligence in World War II, so I also had an interest in intelligence.

Was there a lot of discussion of politics around the dinner table?

There was some discussion of politics, and the arts, and it was a freewheeling, interesting family with a great sense of humor and a kind of interest in the underdog. I've always disliked bullies, maybe because my parents don't like bullies.

Talk about the influence of your grandfather, Allan Nevins, the historian. The bulk of his work was on what, on the American Revolution, or . . . ?

No, all the way through—a lot about the Civil War, and he wrote many biographies of famous figures in American history, and he won several Pulitzer Prizes, and he was the great man in our family. And so, I guess we revered history in my family and grew up reading a lot of it and talking about it a lot.

He also was a newspaperman, so I was brought up thinking it was a really fun life to be a writer, work on a newspaper, cover the living history, and maybe write books of history. It was something I just got interested in at an early age.

My grandfather's view of history was that individuals have tremendous impact. He didn't believe in the idea of Marxian forces that were creating history. He really believed that individuals could shape history, and in this book I think one of the things that really interested me was the personalities of the people that ran our government, and what an impact just a couple of people had.

And what led you to journalism? Why did you choose not to be a historian?

You know, I went to graduate school in history at Oxford and was on my way to doing a PhD and just completely flubbed out. I got lost in the library; I didn't know what to read. It was a lot easier just to do assignments for *Time* magazine in London where I was, some of the time—it just made more sense to me. So, I took a job with the *Washington Star* when they offered it to me and became a city reporter, and I think that's when I really started to understand what I wanted to do.

This particular topic seems to flow out of what you've just told us about your past, but was there one thing in particular that led you to focus on The Dark Side?

It's funny because I don't have a history of knowing much about torture, other than having had an older brother who beat me up!

But you know, I didn't bring any kind of expertise to this. This subject completely grabbed me. I didn't really choose it so much as it felt like it chose me. I had a long-standing interest that flows through the other books, in power and abuses of power. I've always been interested in questions of ethics, and people who are bullies, and in civil liberties, too. And so, this flowed directly out of that. The first book I did was about the Iran/Contra affair, which had a big impact on some of the characters in *The Dark Side*, and the second book I did was about Clarence Thomas, and his clerks are some of the key figures in this book. So, it's kind of the same cast of characters.

In a way, your work is about working through the conservative movement.

It is. And this was finally a moment when the people whose rise I had been covering got ultimate power, and the brakes came off, and this is what they did.

Cheney and Rumsfeld were characters from this previous era that you were just talking about.

Right. Their roots really go back almost to Watergate, and Rumsfeld and Cheney in particular are really savvy players of Washington. They understand the levers of power so much more than the president does. And so, they really get how to make things move in Washington and go their way.

You mentioned Watergate, which is important because when Ford comes in, he brings with him Cheney and Rumsfeld. And so, these are men whose formative experience in the executive branch comes at a time when the presidency really has imploded.

Exactly. And they really feel humiliated, and they feel that the curbs that are being put on the presidency are going to hurt the power of the presidency and hurt America. So, they've been chafing over these issues ever since Watergate, particularly Cheney, and itching to sort of get rid of the post-Watergate reforms. So, 9/11 happens, and they have that opportunity.

In the post-Watergate reforms congressional oversight was put on the intelligence community, and suddenly the CIA had to report to Congress. There was also the Freedom of Information Act that opened up the government, so people could see into it a little bit more. There was the FISA law, so you couldn't have warrantless wiretapping. All these things are sort of tying the president's hands, making the president more accountable to prevent abuses of power. Cheney was really unhappy with all of these.

You write about the Iran/Contra debacle and the report to which Cheney attached a minority report. What was his focus there?

It's so interesting because it was the most idiosyncratic lesson that Cheney took from Iran/Contra. Everybody else in the world, practically, thought that it was President Reagan who overstepped, but in Cheney's view, it was Congress's fault for impeding the President's right to make foreign policy. He draws this really eccentric conclusion, and later he talks about how he's very proud of that report. He basically sees Congress as kind of illegitimate. Cheney was a member of Congress, but he didn't really like Congress; particularly when he went over and became Secretary of Defense, people said he described congressmen as annoying little gnats. And so, he wanted to have free rein in the executive branch.

One of the things you say that Cheney really learned from his period in the Ford administration is the power of controlling what documents get to the president.

Well, you know, President Bush famously described himself as the decider, but the question is, what is he deciding between. Cheney had a cannier and more clever understanding of power, which is that if you can control what options are given to the president, you can control almost everything. Cheney's lawyer, David Addington, had the last inbox before documents went to the president, and he'd sometimes just slash things with a red pen and rewrite stuff before it got to the president. So, the president didn't get to see anything until it had been sort of filtered out by the vice president.

You've discussed how none of the key figures in the Bush administration were lawyers, and that was, in a way, unique in the history of national security because it has been lawyers and bankers who have made U.S. foreign policy.

It is interesting and different, certainly from recent administrations. The president's not a lawyer, the vice president's not a lawyer, Rumsfeld was not a lawyer, Condi Rice, national security advisor at the time, was not a lawyer, and Colin Powell is not a lawyer. So, when it came to 9/11 and the top people wanted to know what they could do legally, they really didn't know this firsthand, so they had to ask other people. There was kind of a vacuum of knowledge there.

It empowered Addington amazingly because he filled this vacuum. Basically the president and Cheney wanted to do everything possible under the law, and they had to ask lawyers what's possible. So, the lawyers became the people who made the policy. They defined the outer limits of what could be done.

Some of what happened post-9/11 was part of a conservative agenda that dates back to the early '80s. Can you talk a little about that?

It's not that there was a conspiracy to implement these programs, but there was an agenda that the conservative movement had prior to 9/11. So, when the Military Commission's order comes out, giving so much power to the executive to try people all on its own, that's when Michael Ratner, who's at the Center for Constitutional Rights, goes to his shelf and says, you know, "This rings a bell," and he pulls down *Mandate for Change*, which was this humongous, phonebook-sized book that was, in the Reagan administration, a kind of a wish list of Republican conservative ideas. Many of those ideas seem to be being implemented in America now. 9/11 empowered the people who were running the government to implement an agenda that probably never would have been able to be passed in a more democratic way before 9/11.

Now, what was the goal here? Someone commented that they wanted to put the terrorists they had captured in a no man's land where there was no law. Explain that to us.

There is a part of the conservative movement that has been suspicious of the rights of defendants and of international law. Some of them didn't even like the Miranda warning. They had many questions about the idea of international rights to begin with. And so, when they talked about what they wanted to do with suspects in the war on terror, they wanted to take them outside of domestic law, criminal law, and international law, too, so that these suspects wouldn't be called criminals nor prisoners of war covered by the Geneva Conventions. They're going to be a whole new class of people.

This is actually where I came into this story, to tell you the truth, because I heard Berkeley professor John Yoo, talking in a very tiny group at the American Enterprise Institute in Washington, about how there's a certain class of people, terror suspects, who really don't have rights. He was saying, what is it people don't understand about the fact that there're some people so bad they don't deserve any particular rights. And when I heard him say this, I just thought, as someone who's been interested in

American history and in civil liberties, it was a really frightening concept. That there would be people for whom there's no due process and that America would cast a whole category, a whole population of people, outside of any law.

And there was a name for them. They were the enemy combatants.

Illegal enemy combatants. Right.
     This was a really radical departure, which was to say that there's a certain class of suspect, a kind of human being, that's not covered by any law, not domestic, not international. They can make up their own rules in the executive branch about how to treat these people.

And there's another important choice that was made here that I think really affects everything, which is the idea that the primary concern after 9/11 is intelligence and preemption; it's not bringing to justice people who have committed crimes of terrorism against the United States.

It's understandable, in a way. They don't want to wait for terrorists to commit heinous acts and blow up innocent people in order to bring them to justice afterwards. They want to stop them before this happens. But they get you into the territory of thought crimes, and locking up people before they commit a crime is a complicated notion and a challenge to the justice system that we have, because basically you need to have proof of guilt, usually, in order to convict someone. So, they decide to kind of create these rules so that they can preempt crimes, and it creates all kinds of legal problems for them.

What sort of practices did they wind up getting involved in?

The lead role in the war on terror, in the very beginning, was given to the CIA, which, unlike the United States military and unlike the FBI, didn't have any history of interrogating people much. They didn't take prisoners before this, and suddenly they were given the role of jailers of the terror suspects, and they didn't really know how to interrogate people, and they had no rules at this point. So, they had to try to figure out how to make people talk, and they wanted to do it fast.They called Arab allies for advice and said, "What makes your people talk," and so they got advice from some of the more tyrannical governments around the world about using harsh methods. They also went to a military program, SERE, which teaches American soldiers how to withstand Communist torture methods if they're taken captive. They put advisors from that military program on their payroll and had them design what we started doing in our own interrogation program. So, basically we were copying the methods of the people that we had labeled the "evil empire" and of states that we considered torture states and enemy states. And so, it became this ironic thing where they turned everything upside down and we started copying what we had considered the worst examples of treatment in the world.

They also, believe it or not, went to the TV show *24* to get some ideas, which is just a fantasy show on Fox television. The swaggering hero, Jack Bauer, uses torture every week to make terror suspects on the show talk. And down in Guantánamo, when they ran out of ideas about how to interrogate people, according to Diane Beaver, the top lawyer down there, they would watch *24*, and they'd say, "Hey, let's try this. It worked for Jack Bauer. Let's see if it works for us." So, basically you've got this Hollywood fantasy dictating policy for the United States military there, too.

It's really not so surprising that they ran into some problems, because they weren't going to the wisest people. The people who really understand interrogation in this country are the FBI and the U.S. military, and they will tell you in a minute, you can't torture people. You're going to get unreliable information, and, as they'll say, the consequences for our own country are going to be just unimaginable.

There's another theme running throughout this, which is that this policy is not just immoral and illegal, but also didn't work. Torture doesn't work because either a person will not say anything or they'll make it up.

Exactly. It's been long known. So, why did they go this route? That is actually one of the questions I've had about this, and I have to say that I think it mattered that, at the top of our government, they, again, were not lawyers and did not know the Constitution. Also, Bush and Cheney famously were not military people, so they did not really know that much about the Geneva Conventions or the ethos that permeates the American military about the difference between how to fight an honorable war and a dishonorable one.

And I think there was a certain amount of vengeance that was in the air after 9/11. They were panicked, they felt they had dropped the ball, and they were angry. There's a statement from Colin Powell saying that when he looked at Bush in some of those early meetings, Bush looked like a man who wanted to kill someone. There was a certain amount of bloodlust, which you can understand, but it may have led us in the wrong direction.

There was also a period immediately after 9/11 with the anthrax scare, when Cheney and others thought that they might be facing a fatal attack. And so, for the people who were in charge of the government, this was really personal; it wasn't just political. They felt that their lives might be hanging in the balance, and they felt that the whole country's existence was in their hands. The feeling of panic was tremendous at that point.

Where is the loyal opposition to these policies? Where is the Congress, the Democratic Party?

If you can imagine that the ACLU is afraid to weigh in, you're really not going to see the Democratic Congress weigh in. You don't see any politicians for a long time, and when they test the waters—one senator, Richard Durbin, steps in in 2004, after those Abu Ghraib photos are published, and makes a statement critical of Guantánamo, and he is just absolutely clobbered for it, called un-American and anti-patriotic, and he winds up having to apologize in tears on the floor of the Senate. And there's another long pause before anybody steps up to this.

Following this in Washington, we realized there's pretty much only one person who has the right résumé and the moral stature to take on the subject of torture, and the community of opposition is begging him to get involved, and that's John McCain. And John McCain takes a while to step into this, actually. He's lobbied by a number of people who want him to get in, and he does, finally, and he changes the political equation. He's been tortured himself as a POW in Vietnam, he's a conservative Republican, a war hero, and he finally says that torture is anathema to America, and he says, in that wonderful, eloquent statement, it's not about them, it's about us. It's not that we love terrorists; it's that we're a country that's founded on inalienable human rights and on civilized practices, not barbarian practices.

Did the media fail on this, if not through individual reporters then through the collective wisdom?

I really feel that the media did a much better job than it's been given credit for. A lot of the stories were deep-sixed though. You could see that the editors were nervous, and at first they didn't really believe it. A lot of people did not believe what the detainees were saying about how they were being mistreated, including some of the liberal lawyers representing them. When those pictures of Abu Ghraib came out, Michael Ratner, who's one of the most left-wing, liberal lawyers in the country, said it was only then that he really believed what his clients were telling him, because it seemed so un-American to imagine that they were being tortured and tormented in this way, that they were sexually humiliated and stripped. It just didn't sound right to most people. I think there was just a kind of collective disbelief and maybe almost an unwillingness to think about this, too. We were told during the time by the government that we were being kept safe, and I think a lot of people just didn't want to know the details. So, I have to say, I think the American public is just as implicated in this as the press, and the Congress, and anybody else.

Let's go back to this discussion of your background and the way you personally were sensitized to American tradition, and history, and values. Was our fear so great that generally we all forgot what we stood for? Because the fact of the matter is, the separation of powers, the idea of our founding fathers, was to correct error.

I'm so glad you brought that up because people don't understand that the separation of powers is not just some kind of academic exercise, and Stephen Holmes writes beautifully about this in his book *The Matador's Cape*. It is to have a competition of ideas so that we don't make mistakes, so that if somebody does make a mistake somebody else can correct it fast and say, you know, that's not a good idea. When you take away all of those competing ideas and you give one branch of government all the power to run as far as they want to go—mistakes were made. And this whole experiment really proved, I think, the brilliance of the founding fathers in understanding that without some competition of ideas, the product could be really flawed.

You wind up, for instance, with innocent people being caught up in this and being renditioned, thrown in dungeons for months—and there's no process to take a second look at this Many of the people in the CIA thought they had an innocent person when they renditioned a German citizen named Khaled al-Masri to Afghanistan—they had a bad feeling about it from the start. They kept him for five months anyway because there was no mechanism, no check on their power.

And in that particular case, there was an intervention by an individual in the CIA to make sure he continued to be held, right?

That's right. There was a zealous person running the rendition unit, and she was just adamant that she didn't like the feel of this guy. We have a system of justice that's not supposed to be about hunches, but based on evidence. She didn't like the feel of him, so they kept him locked up. One of the top CIA officers told me he would come in every day and say, "Is that man still locked up in the salt pit?" And there was a growing worry. Finally a couple of the lawyers in the CIA went behind this woman's back to bring this problem to Tenet. And Tenet was like, "Are you telling me that we have renditioned an innocent person?" And he's saying, "Oh God, I hope we haven't used these so-called alternative methods on him."

But you know, the man lost seventy pounds, he was really sick, and I interviewed him later, after all this. They did release him and in a most extraordinary way. I mean, you cannot make up some of these stories.

I had a cup of coffee with him a couple years later, and he's one of the few detainees I got to meet with face-to-face, and you know, it's so different if you can see somebody. And he started to cry when I was having coffee with him, his eyes sort of welled up, and this was years later. He became very red-eyed, and he had to excuse himself and go out and smoke a cigarette. This thing was so painful, he couldn't talk about it, still. I was just trying to get some details about what he went through. It was just so horrific for him, still.

How did they release him?

They dumped him at a border with a picnic lunch and told him to start walking. And he thought he was going to be shot in the back, and he didn't dare turn around; he starts walking, and up ahead there's a border, and he can cross it and eventually gets to where he can take a flight home. By then his whole family had left, abandoned his house. The CIA gave him some money, too, and they kind of joked around about, "Well, you know, he never would've made this much money any other way," in the five months that he was being held, and so they're kind of cavalier about the whole thing. But people, some of the people in the CIA who were close to this, were really upset, too, and didn't want to have anything to do with it. A lot of good people left the CIA over these kinds of things.

What about holding people accountable now? Do we need a truth commission?

Well, I'm not a politician, so I'm not in an advocacy position. I'm a reporter covering all of these events, but as a reporter I really would like to know what the record is here. So many documents are still secret, and so many details of this program are still secret. I mean, people died in this program. Nobody's been prosecuted. There've been a number of homicides, but nobody in any senior level has taken any responsibility for it, and there've been recommendations that people be prosecuted that have been sent to the Justice Department. The Justice Department's not acted on any of them. I feel that the American public is owed some full account of what happened, because the government was acting in our name, and they've told us it was necessary and it had to be done, but I think it's worth knowing if that's really true.

What kept you going as you uncovered this? Because it must have been a very difficult task to confront.

You know, I think it probably sounds awful, but I really enjoyed reporting on this because it fulfilled what a reporter should do. I felt I had a really useful role to play, and I knew what it was, which was that I wanted the public to understand what the government was doing and to do everything I could to get the story. And I wasn't alone in that. What really was heartening was there were all these people who were trying to fix what they thought was wrong, and they were so passionate about it that it affected me. People in the FBI, like a former agent named Dan Coleman who said to me that we can't do this or we're going to lose our soul. It made me realize this is a really serious problem; it's not just some kind of game, it's not just "get the Bush administration." This is really, truly about what our country's about, and what our history means, and what our values are. So, I don't think there could be anything more interesting or important for a reporter like me, so I just feel I was lucky to be able to cover this.

And as you probed the story, you must have found out things that really amazed you.

Oh, my God! I couldn't believe some of the things that I was learning. I didn't think that this was possible, that we would have the extraordinary rendition program; I couldn't believe that we had a sleek, private Gulfstream jet that the CIA was flying around the world, snatching people off the streets, with agents wearing masks, no names—no one knows who they are, still—throwing people into dungeons forever. It seemed like a Robert Ludlum novel, not something real. And when I discovered the SERE program that we talked about earlier, I couldn't believe there's actually a curriculum for torture that the United States studied and then decided to apply as a policy ourselves. It seemed unthinkable. And then you've got these top lawyers in the Justice Department who are finally trying to push the government back into following the laws, and they felt so intimidated by Cheney's office that they were talking in codes to each other. They thought they were being wiretapped. It was an extraordinary time.

We should mention, also, the New Yorker, *because some of the best writing during this period came from you, Seymour Hersh, Lawrence Wright, and others. So what was it about the environment at the magazine that made this possible?*

We were up against really long odds in getting these stories. This was an incredibly secretive government, it was very hard to get your hands on documents, and it was a very intimidating environment in Washington, hard to get people to talk to you. So, it takes a lot of time. And the *New Yorker* gives its writers and reporters time to dig and dig and dig, and with that time you can get these stories. But increasingly—and it's something I think people should think about—newspapers have shorter and shorter stories; they have less and less money to report. You're not going to get this kind of information if people don't have the time and the luxury to really dig.

One final question, and let's go back to the beginning of the interview. Did you have a sense that you were carrying the torch of the values that you got from your parents and your grandparents?

I think so. I really do. And what I want to say is, you know, people sometimes say, "How could you be so anti-American?" To me, this is how you cherish America. It's dissenting in a way that's meant to try to correct what's wrong, and I really care about the country's history and values. And so, I hope I carry on my grandfather's legacy.

EMPIRE AND HEGEMONY

When powerful states attempt to control events in faraway lands, they set in motion political dynamics that can lead to war and conflict. In weak and fragile states, meanwhile, resistance to the erosion of national autonomy occurs when outsiders intervene. These struggles require the intervening power to maintain large military establishments with global reach. In democracies playing the game of empire, military expenditures increase at the expense of other priorities; in turn, opposition to the policies of intervention in faraway places emerges at home. The human cost of these misguided ventures sets the stage for political awakenings. Pakistani journalist Ahmed Rashid discusses how superpower intervention and then withdrawal from Afghanistan shaped the politics of the region and led to the rise of Al Qaeda and the Taliban. Social scientist Chalmers Johnson discusses the implications of a large military establishment for democracy at home and influence abroad. Finally, New Left writer and movement organizer Tariq Ali sees common elements in national liberation struggles, the continuing abuse of power by outside actors, and the importance of protest in response to wars such as those in Vietnam and Iraq.

Ahmed Rashid
Ahmed Rashid is an international journalist based in Lahore, Pakistan. For more than twenty years, his reporting on Afghani-

stan, Central Asia, and Pakistan has provided a rich understanding of the region's complex politics, religion, and terrorism. He is the author of *Taliban*, *Jihad: The Rise of Militant Islam in Central Asia*, and *Descent into Chaos*. He is the recipient of the 2001 Nisar Osmani Award for Courage in Journalism.

Chalmers Johnson

Chalmers Johnson is President of the Japan Policy Research Institute. A distinguished social scientist and public intellectual, he is the author of fifteen books, including *Peasant Nationalism and Communist Power*, a classic in Chinese studies, and *MITI and the Japanese Miracle*, a classic in Japanese studies. Professor Johnson is a former professor of political science at the University of California, Berkeley, where he also served as chairman of the department as well as chair of the Center for Chinese Studies. He is also an emeritus professor of political science at the University of California, San Diego. His most recent books focus on American power in the world and include *Okinawa: Cold War Island*; *Blowback: The Cost and Consequences of American Empire*; *The Sorrows of Empire: Militarism, Secrecy, and the End of the Republic*; and *Nemesis: The Last Days of the American Republic*.

Tariq Ali

Tariq Ali is a novelist, historian, campaigner, and one of the editors of the *New Left Review*. A Renaissance man, Ali practices a unique combination of activism and analysis that has inspired and enriched political dissent as well as our understanding of the politics of empire, the consequences of inequality and underdevelopment, the role of religion, the resiliency of national stuggles for liberation and autonomy, and the dynamics of regional politics and superpower intervention. He is the author of many books, including *The Clash of Fundamentalisms: Crusades, Jihads, and Modernity*; *The Duel: Pakistan on the Flight Plan of American Power*; and *The Protocols of the Elders of Sodom and Other Essays*.

Ahmed Rashid
March 26, 2002 and June 12, 2008

Where were you born and raised?

I was born in Ravapindi in Northern Pakistan. After the Second World War, my family was based some of the time in Pakistan and some of the time in London. So I grew up in both places. In the fifties, I had, if you like, quite a cosmopolitan life and education. And then, subsequently, I went to college in Pakistan, and then went to university at Cambridge.

How did your parents shape your character, do you think, in retrospect?

I dedicate the *Taliban* book to my mother because she was an incredibly inquisitive person who paid attention to absolutely everything. She was a very traditional Indian Muslim woman, grew up in British India. But she had incredible curiosity about everything, and while we were kids, she used to take us on these wild trips, even without very much money. We were sleeping in the car, I remember, as kids, traveling and camping in Europe. We drove once from London to Karachi in the '60s with her. She was just a very adventurous person. My father was the more stabilizing influence, if you like, in the family.

Was there a discussion of politics and current events and world affairs at the dinner table?

Yes, always. You know, I don't think any society was more politicized than Pakistan, because we had been through so many traumas and so much political upheaval and unrest. When Pakistanis get together, the first thing they talk about is politics at home and what's going on.

Where were you educated?

I went to college in India and in Pakistan and then got my degree from Cambridge. I was at Cambridge in 1968, during the anti–Vietnam War movement.

How did the '60s affect you, do you think, in retrospect?

Well, certainly, it radicalized me very much. The experience is there. I was [also] in Paris in '68. But, really, Pakistanis in particular were very radicalized from '68 to '70 because of the war in Bangladesh, which was then East Pakistan. This had a very traumatic effect on Pakistani leftists, on liberals, because the military conducted this war in a particularly brutal fashion, killing tens of thousands of Bengalis. When Bangladesh became independent and the army was defeated, there was a major political upheaval in Pakistan. So, you know, that was a period of enormous political ferment in Pakistan, where the left was very strong at that time.

I notice that history is a subject that you find very important as you unravel these current events. Tell us about navigating between research that you might do in a library versus on-the-spot reporting.

My first book came out in '94. It was called *A Resurgence of Central Asia*. It was the first book on Central Asia to come out after the breakup of the Soviet Union. I had been traveling to Central Asia; I had no clue of the history. There was very little at that time in English on Central Asia. You had this whole Soviet school in America and all over, but nobody covered Central Asia. I didn't speak Russian or any of the local languages. I was having to read books from the '20s and '30s and '40s that I got in secondhand bookshops. I started reading very extensively on history then.

But I'm fascinated with all academic disciplines. I read anthropology, I read history, I read economics. And I try to have a multidisciplinary approach in my books, where I'm looking at social and economic and cultural issues along with the politics and the investigative journalism side, so that it gives you more depth, a greater richness, and adds to the unfolding of these dramas, if you like.

Let's talk about Pakistan. Is Pakistan a rogue state?

No, I wouldn't describe it as that because I think the problem in Pakistan has been this perennial conflict between military power and civilian power. You had bouts of civilian rule, but essentially the military ruled the country, especially for the last thirty, forty years, and they have controlled foreign policy, particularly towards Afghanistan and India. And it's been very, very difficult for these intermittent civilian governments to encroach upon the military's control of foreign policy.

It's 160 million people with a very high population growth rate, dwindling resources, huge problems now of energy, of water, of land, and we're going to be over 200 million very soon, and certainly a major economic crisis is probably pending.

Is it a fair assessment that Pakistan never sort of carved a national identity that all groups and ethnic groups could agree to?

Well, exactly. Pakistan was born out of British India, a separate country in the name of Islam, but the founding fathers of Pakistan never imagined that it would be a theocratic state or a state run by religious leaders. Instead they wanted a British-style democracy. The constitution we have is a parliamentary democracy very much modeled on what Britain has. But the whole problem has been that after three wars with India, the national security issue with India, the dispute over Kashmir, the desire to have a pro-Pakistan government in Afghanistan—all these issues have really been driven by the military, and they have controlled these policy issues. As a result, at one point we were spending like 30 percent of the budget on the army. Education—literacy is about 50 percent, one of the lowest in South Asia. We're not spending enough money on developing human capital in the social sector. And this has been one of the very, very big problems.

The military defines the national interest in terms of the enemy, India, and bolstering military capability—this is the reason Pakistan went nuclear. The civilians, if you ask them, would define national interest completely differently, in terms of democracy, a vibrant economy, education, mass literacy. These kinds of categories don't come into the military's thinking processes, unfortunately. The other thing is that the military has not just grown politically powerful, but it has grown economically powerful, especially under General Musharraf. He has given incredible perks and privileges to the military. A lot of the land in the country is owned by the military, or if it's not owned it's seized upon by the military and developed according to what the military wants. The senior officers get far more perks and privileges than anybody in the civil sector. Almost all of their children are studying in America on scholarships. They are *the* most privileged group in the country.

At one point you quote the famous expression, "All countries have an army but in Pakistan the army has a country."

That's what many Pakistanis think because everything is dictated by the army, and no civilian leader can afford to rub the army the wrong way.

You've also discussed the relationship of the state to Islam, and you've made the point in Descent into Chaos *that the military has used Islam as an instrument. Talk about that.*

The political parties view the founding fathers as being modernist, democratic, and having intended to set up a democratic system where all the non-Muslim minorities have the same rights, and religion is part of the culture and tradition of the country, but it does not dictate the political process. Now, the problem with the military is that in order to further their foreign policy aims in Kashmir, towards India, and towards Afghanistan, they fueled Islamic extremist groups.

Since the 1980s, when the Americans came and trained the Afghan mujahideen to fight the Soviets in Afghanistan—since then the military has used these militants for their favorite proxy force to fight in Kashmir and in Afghanistan. And that, of course, has created a blowback in the country. I mean, you can't create militant groups and then expect them to just stay outside the country and fight foreigners. They will want to do the same thing internally, they will want to set up an Islamic state at home, and this blowback is what we have really suffered from very badly.

After 9/11, for the first time we have developed what we call now the Pakistani Taliban. And these are fighters who are militant groups; they are mostly from the Pashtun ethnic belt in the northwest part of the country, but they're linked to other groups, the Kashmiri groups, the Punjabi extremist groups, and they all want to carve out a sharia state, that is, a state for Islamic extremism in the northwest part of the country. The blowback from the post-9/11 period has been deeply affecting the whole fabric of society because we gave refuge to the Afghan Taliban; we allowed them sanctuary in Pakistan, and we allowed them to recruit and rearm in Pakistan. You know, I was warning, in 2002 and 2003, that if we continue this, we are going to Talibanize Pakistan.

There's no way you can keep these guys separate or put them out in the mountains and expect them to go and attack the Americans in Afghanistan without them influencing Pakistanis, and that's precisely what's happened.

The invasion by the Soviet Union of Afghanistan was a pivotal turning point in affecting the radicalization of some sectors of Islamic society. Tell us a little about the consequences of the Soviet invasion and the American response as a factor in creating this witches' brew that we now live with.

Essentially, what the U.S. launched in Afghanistan was a jihad. The Pakistani, the American, and the Saudi intelligence services were all joined together in bringing into Afghanistan thousands of militants from all over the Islamic world. At that time the American aim was simply to show that the whole Islamic world was resisting the Soviet invasion. But, essentially, they brought together these *jihadi* groups. And naturally, the militants who arrived to fight in Afghanistan from the Arab world, from all over, came from the most militant groups in this part of the world.

Now, many of these Muslim regimes also saw this as a good way to resolve their internal tensions by sending these militants out; you know, "Go and fight in Afghanistan, don't bother us here at home." That, of course, created the roots for Al Qaeda and bin Laden, and even the Taliban, and for the subsequent upheavals that have occurred in Central Asia. Because Central Asians came in the 1980s also, to fight in Afghanistan, and linked up with all sorts of Arab groups and Pakistani groups. So that legacy is what the world today is faced with.

The Pakistani military has seen Afghanistan as giving it strategic depth in the threat that it perceives from India. Talk a little about that.

Historically Afghanistan is a landlocked country. It has depended upon Pakistan for all its imports, its exports, its trade, and everything else. And in the '50s, to the '60s and '70s, in order to balance off this kind of overwhelming influence that Pakistan had, it always played the India card. It cozied up to India; it tried to play this balancing act between India and Pakistan so that it would not become wholly dependent on Pakistan and Pakistan would not attempt to swallow up Afghanistan. Now, it was a weak state, it was a state without an army, it was a state that depended on foreign aid, American aid, Soviet aid. And so, for its own national interest, it was a good way to go, but it never opposed Pakistan as such. Now unfortunately, what has happened after that is that Pakistan, once the mujahideen started their war in Afghanistan, saw that the Indians gave very strong backing to the Afghan Soviet regime in the 1980s, and they didn't want that to be repeated because at that time they accused the Indians of intervening in Pakistan's ethnic groups, arming and subverting them.

And this is a proxy war, of course, that has gone on between India and Pakistan for the last fifty years. Their intelligence agencies operate in our territory, our intelligence agencies operate in their territory, we've intervened in Kashmir, we've helped arm the Sikh rebellion in the '70s and '80s in India, they have done the same in Baluchistan. But the danger was that if the Indians were to consolidate in Afghanistan then we would be caught in this kind of pincer movement, the Indians coming from both sides as it were, and the army became very paranoid about this. You know, I've always written that this threat is far more to do with the army's paranoia and a perception of what could happen rather than what is actually happening. Now, after 9/11—of course, the Indians didn't have any presence in Afghanistan throughout the '90s—the Taliban were vehemently anti-Hindu, anti-Indian, and as a consequence we backed them because we wanted to strengthen their anti-India feelings. After 9/11, of course, the people who come into power are the Northern Alliance who had been fighting the Taliban, and the Northern Alliance had been armed and supported by India, by Iran, by Russia, by other regional powers. And consequently after 9/11 and the war ended, we took back the Afghan Taliban, even though we had pledged to the Americans that we would be supporting the war on terror. We took back the Afghan Taliban in the hope that even though we helped defeat them, we now needed them again because we feared that India would once again come to play a major role in Afghanistan. Now, if you ask the army today, if you ask any leading person in the foreign ministry, they will tell you India is playing a dominating role in Afghanistan. Well, I mean, I think that's nonsense. The Americans, and NATO, and about thirty other countries who have troops in Afghanistan, are playing a much more important role. They're giving more money; they're giving troops, et cetera. India is playing a role, but it doesn't have any troops there. It has an aid program for the Afghan reconstruction, but again, this tit-for-tat war has started. Pakistan is accusing the Indians of intervening in Pakistan. And this is why the army has used the India factor as an excuse for maintaining support for the Taliban.

One of the tensions that you talk about in Islam is the local versus international, provincial versus cosmopolitan. And you've suggested in your writings that what you get is a global jihad without a programmatic content, without a vision of what a future Islamic state would look like. Explore that a little with us.

The history of Islamic fundamentalism as an alternative to British imperialism and the whole colonial era was very rich in the 1920s and '30s, and especially in the Middle East, with the creation of an Islamic state. There was a very rich debate about this. These groups in the Middle East, and then in India (British India at that time), explored the idea of how an Islamic state would run—Islamic economics, the treatment of minority groups, the treatment of women, education—all these major issues.

Now, during the war in Afghanistan and events elsewhere in the Muslim world, you get a completely new generation coming up who are not rooted at all in the history of Islam and Islamic fundamentalism in the twentieth century. Who are not rooted at all in the wars of liberation against colonialism, which the earlier Islamic fundamentalists were rooted in. All you get is a kind of blind hatred against the West, against the Americans.

But primarily what drives them is a hatred for their own regimes. Because they don't have this intellectual background, they are not Islamic scholars, they are not historians, they have very little knowledge about what has gone on in the last one hundred years, they have a kind of blind faith that toppling "our" regime—the Saudi regime, the Pakistani regime, whatever—toppling "our" regime and bringing in sharia, Islamic law, will automatically resolve all the problems of the country.

[But] the evidence is there already: Iran failed. The Iranian Revolution wanted to do just that, and it failed. The Taliban wanted to do it in Afghanistan, and they failed, too. There's no intellectual interest in *What are they going to replace their regimes with? What are they going to offer the people?* I think that's why they remain on the extreme terrorist fringe of society. They never develop into mass parties, you know. Their action is militant, is to topple. It's not to build or create.

You write in your book Jihad: The Rise of Militant Islam in Central Asia, *"The genius of early Muslim Arab civilization was its multicultural, multi-religious, and multiethnic diversity. The stunning and numerous state failures that abound in the Muslim world today are because that original path, that intention and inspiration, has been abandoned either in favor of a brute or a narrow interpretation of the theology." Tell us about that.*

One of the cultural tragedies is that the fundamentalist parties today do not study history. It's not a subject in the madrasas, in the religious schools. They don't know about their own history. They don't know about the Islamic culture in Spain—the Muslims ruled Spain for nine hundred years, alongside Jews and Christians, and built the most magnificent monuments which are standing today. Or the history of multicultural, multiethnic Muslim empires that ruled in North Africa, and in the Middle East, and even in South Asia, of course. If you look at the Moguls, who ruled India for four hundred years, they came out of Central Asia. They brought with them a Central Asian culture, the culture of Afghanistan and Persia; lived with Hindus and mixed with Hindus and Farsis, Buddhists and other religious sects in India, ruled over them. This is the legacy specifically of South Asia. Unfortunately, the fundamentalist groups in the most recent twenty or thirty years have failed to grasp the diversity because they don't study this [history].

In the fundamentalist context, the word "jihad" takes on an entirely different meaning from its original meaning, is that correct?

Yes. Jihad is one tenet of Islam. It's a very important tenet, but it's one of the five major tenets of Islam. What the global jihadists do is to elevate jihad to be the only tenet of Islam, and the most important tenet of Islam. Well, you know, prayer, charity, performing the Hajj—there are all sorts of other things that Muslims have to do. So the first issue is that.

The second issue is that in the Koran, it says very clearly that there are two sides to jihad. There is certainly a side where Muslims have to defend themselves if they're attacked by unbelievers, which is, if you like, the militant side of Islam. But that is what the prophet Mohammed called the lesser jihad. The greater jihad is the improvement of self and the improvement of community. As in all great religions, Islam has an enormous legacy of questioning how do you become a better human being, how do you become an asset to society, how do you help other people. Religion is supposed to be about building community and civil society, and improving yourself in the process while you worship God. The greater jihad is all about that. But, of course, that has been totally ignored by such figures as Juma Namangani, Osama bin Laden, and mullah Muhammad Omar.

Let's talk about U.S. policy and the western response to events, especially in Afghanistan. We supported the Mujahideen through Pakistan which then unintentionally led to Al Qaeda; Clinton in the '90s let the Saudis and the Pakistanis take the lead with regard to the Afghan civil war; then, as we've just talked about, the Bush administration after 9/11 was narrowly focused on Al Qaeda and really sort of missed all the big picture.

You know, the Afghans in particular are very bitter about this because they consider that the real betrayal of the U.S. took place in 1989 when the Soviets withdrew from Afghanistan and the U.S. walked away as well, not helping rebuild the country or form a government. That, of course, led to the civil war that we had in the '90s in which ultimately the Taliban came up on top. After 9/11, the first problem was the sole focus on Al Qaeda at the expense of any kind of reconstruction, and the second was the very quick decision to go into Iraq. By March or April in 2002, twelve weeks after the war was won—I mean, people were still in a state of shock—the few resources that the U.S. had in Afghanistan, the special forces, the satellites, the imagery, the reconnaissance, et cetera, they were all taken out and they were sent stateside and sent in for retraining for Iraq, and you got the second string of perhaps not such highly trained U.S. forces coming into Afghanistan. And then as a result of this focus on Iraq the CIA basically had a policy of maintaining law and order in the country, or so they thought, through the warlords. So, there was this policy of arming and putting the warlords on the American payroll, and that was devastating because the warlords had been driven out by the Taliban precisely because the Afghan people were so fed up with them. The warlords, throughout the '90s, had devastated the country. They had pillaged and harassed and stolen people's property, and here were the Americans, the liberators of Afghanistan, the people who've overthrown the Taliban, who freed us from oppression, bringing back the warlords on their payroll. And that was something that the Afghans became very, very bitter about.

Of course, the problem with the warlords was that they began to defy Karzai. They said, "Well, look, I mean, who are you? I mean, you might be the president but we're on the CIA payroll. I've got three thousand militiamen." You had warlords who had two hundred tanks, three hundred tanks. I mean, you couldn't annoy them. So, Karzai's hands were tied in that sense.

And this only stopped around 2004, but by then these warlords had gone into drugs and business and trafficking, so they remained incredibly rich, politically powerful, ruthless, but now they were wearing suits. They weren't wearing militia uniforms; they would be wearing suits and ties; they found places in parliament; many of them stood in the presidential election.

This warlord policy was actually the creation of Paul Wolfowitz—whom I sometimes call "Warlord Wolfowitz." He was trying to sell the policy in Somalia, and in Sudan, and in other parts, saying that we should be arming and funding independent militia warlords who would go after Al Qaeda. So, the other problem, of course, was that these warlords were told to hunt Al Qaeda, but half of these warlords were taking money from Al Qaeda. No warlord has ever delivered a senior Al Qaeda figure to the Americans.

Let's talk a little about this drug business because I think it becomes very important, especially in a situation without nation building, or reconstruction, or the security required for development and reconstruction.

You know, right after the war myself and a bunch of scholars who were working on Afghanistan in America, we literally begged the State Department and the Agency for International Development, USAID, to invest in agriculture. Eighty percent of Afghans were living on agriculture. Within the next few months 2.5 million refugees came back home from Pakistan and Iran. What were these people supposed to do? There were no jobs, the land was devastated, and they all went back to their villages and their farms, and there was no investment in agriculture. And it would have been a minimal investment. You needed new crops, you needed fertilizer, you needed some farm-to-market roads, you needed better water distribution, et cetera, and agriculture was such a thing that we said, you can have a turnaround in one or two harvests, in one or two growing cycles. You can turn the whole economy around. Perhaps you can get them to grow crops which you would buy up yourself and pay more money than the crop was worth, simply to get the farmers on their feet again. But there was no investment in agriculture, and the result was that everybody went back to growing something that didn't need any infrastructure.

To grow poppies, you don't need fertilizer, you don't need water, you don't need infrastructure; it grows anywhere on almost anything, and that's what the poor farmers did, and eventually it became, of course, a major source of livelihood for millions of farmers across the country but particularly in the south of the country.

And very quickly the Taliban were back. In 2003, they first started taxing the farmers. After that they started taxing the local traffickers who were picking up the opium at the farm gate and then transporting it to a big trafficker; then they started taxing the big traffickers. So, there was this progression, and today, I have no doubt that Al Qaeda and the Taliban are heavily involved in not just making money at the bottom end of the ladder, which is where the farmers are, but also making money at the top end of the ladder. This is where the distribution is in Europe, where, of course, that opium doubles and triples and quadruples in price, and you rake in far bigger profit.

And if you look today at the Pakistani Taliban and the Afghan Taliban, they have enormous sums of money with which they're able to keep thousands of militiamen in the field—they're paying their soldiers now. You know, in the '90s the Taliban never paid their soldiers. It was a holy war. Now they're paying up to $100 to $150 a month to the soldiers, which is about twice as much as what an Afghan soldier in the regular army gets. They are paying the families of the suicide bombers, so if your son goes to commit suicide and kills a few Americans, depending on how successful he was, the father and the mother get a huge lump sum of money to compensate for the son's death. So, now we are seeing an insurgency and a movement that is flush with cash, and a lot of it is coming from the drug trade.

And now Afghanistan produces what percent of the world's drug supply?

Well, Afghanistan today produces 93 percent of the world's heroin, and unfortunately the international community has had no real strategy. We're not asking for American soldiers to go into the fields and hack down the poppy crop and antagonize the farmers, but at least what American forces could have done was interdiction, stopping the convoys, picking up the really big traffickers, who everybody knew who they were and everybody still knows who they are. The Americans had the helicopters, they had the special forces, they had the troops. The Afghan government didn't have any of these resources. You could have picked up a lot of people and brought them to justice either in Afghanistan or in America, or anywhere else, and this was just not done because Rumsfeld refused to involve the U.S. military in any form of counter-narcotics. And the State Department fought a running battle with Rumsfeld on that issue but got nowhere because Rumsfeld was controlling the military.

It's like all of the actors, for their own narrow vested interests, refused to see the big picture. But instead, they created a system that produced more and more terrorism by not dealing with the politics, and the economy, and the society in a comprehensive way.

I think you're absolutely right. I mean, if you look at all the major players, whether it's Musharraf or Bush or Karzai, or anyone, they were dealing with their own local problem rather than looking at the big picture. But I think most at fault were the Americans because the Americans had an obligation to look at the big picture. They were the leading player in Afghanistan. Now I think partly why they just utterly failed was the focus on Iraq.

But I think precisely this point is what the U.S. has to do in future. You have to look at the region in a strategic way. For example, if you want to deal with Afghanistan, you have to deal with the sanctuaries in Pakistan. If you want to deal with Pakistan, you have to get the Indians on board to give the Pakistan army some kind of feeling of security; you have to help resolve the Kashmir dispute. If you want to settle Afghanistan, you have to talk to the Iranians, and you have to give them some reassurances.

You need a dozen hands; you have to conduct multiple diplomacy at a dozen different levels with half a dozen countries, all at the same time, to resolve one problem.

You also suggest that the United States has failed beyond this in terms of implementation because you say we're not willing to devote the resources, and we don't have the institutions in our government to make a lot of this happen, even with a strategic vision.

During the Cold War the U.S. had the tools of nation building, if you like. You rebuilt Europe after the Second World War with the Marshall Plan, you had people who were knowledgeable about the world, about economics, et cetera, you had agencies like the USAID—when I was young and AID was working in Pakistan they had agronomists, and water engineers, and bridge builders, and road engineers. Today you wouldn't find any technical person in AID; you'd find a bunch of bureaucrats who sign checks to contractors. You used to have the U.S. Information Service, which was incredibly good at putting out the U.S. message in all these countries, and also influencing the local press—you did away with all that. And a lot of this was done away with at the end of the Cold War by the Clinton administration. It wasn't deliberately done; it was just run down. And Bush came in and merged AID and the Information Service with the State Department.

The wars of the future are not going to be fought just by special forces and high-tech gadgetry and satellites and drones, and all the rest of it. They're going to be fought by what comes after the war, what kind of political deal can you put together after the war to settle political differences and issues in countries. And of course, we've seen the tragedy of Afghanistan and Iraq.

If young people were to read this fascinating story, what advice would you give them in terms of preparing for the future?

One of my real complaints, especially for my colleagues in the media in America, is that there has been a horrible dumbing down of America in the last decade on foreign policy issues. The ignorance in the United States is huge. I think the media—and the government, perhaps, but certainly the media—is very much at fault here. There has to be a much greater awareness of foreign policy issues. U.S. governments have got away with either doing nothing, or doing the wrong thing, or getting involved under various pressures, because there has been no real domestic debate about foreign policy. Foreign policy issues are not on anybody's agenda. It's very important for young people to get involved with foreign policy issues and to understand the world around them.

In today's age—I mean, I'm an old man now—but I think in today's age, what I admire so much about so many students I talk to at universities is their multidisciplinary approach. Yes, you have to focus on your degree and your subject and your discipline, but you've got to be interested in other things also. I would love the students who come out of American universities to be interested in everything, curious about everything. It can mean travel, it can mean reading the newspapers, it can mean watching different TV programs, whatever. But I think there has to be a curiosity about what's going on in the outside world.

Going back to my mother, [like her] I'm still immensely curious. I never met Osama bin Laden, and I never met Juma Namangani either, but I'm very curious about what makes these guys tick. Why is it they do what they do? And to understand that, it's not just understanding the individual or the personality; it's understanding history and culture and tradition and geography and anthropology, and all sorts of things. I would love to see that kind of curiosity among young people.

Chalmers Johnson
January 29, 2004, and March 7, 2007

How can we explain your movement from being a social scientist to a public intellectual?

Well, don't ask for excessive consistency. John Maynard Keynes, when accused of being inconsistent, said, "When I get new information, I change my position. What, sir, do you do with new information?"

I've received quite a bit of new information, particularly since 1991 and the collapse of the Soviet Union. Until that time, it's quite true I was a cold warrior. I believed in the menace of the Soviet Union.

And you even called yourself a "spear-carrier—"

"Spear-carrier for the empire."

"—for the empire," yes, yes.

That's the prologue to *Blowback*; I was a consultant to the Office of National Estimates of the CIA during the time of the Vietnam War. But what caused me to change my mind and to rethink these issues? Two things: one analytical, one concrete. The first was the demise of the Soviet Union. I expected much more from the United States in the way of a peace dividend. I believe that Russia today is not the former Soviet Union by any means. It's a much smaller place. I would have expected that as a tradition in the United States, we would have demobilized much more radically. We would have rethought more seriously our role in the world, brought home troops in places like Okinawa. Instead, we did everything in our power to shore up the Cold War structures in East Asia, in Latin America. The search for new enemies began. That's the roots of the neoconservatives in the Bush administration. I was shocked, actually, by this. Did this mean that the Cold War was a cover for something deeper, for an American imperial project that had been in the works since World War II? I began to believe that this is the case.

The second thing that led me to write *Blowback* in the late 1990s [was something concrete]. Okinawa prefecture, which is Japan's southernmost prefecture, [is] the poorest place in the Japan, the equivalent of Puerto Rico; it's always been discriminated against by the Japanese since they seized it at the end of the nineteenth century. The governor at that time, Masahide Ota, is a former professor. He invited me to Okinawa in February of 1996 to give a speech to his associates in light of what had happened on September 4, 1995, when two marines and a sailor from Camp Hansen in central Okinawa abducted, beat, and raped a twelve-year-old girl. It led to the biggest single demonstration against the United States since the Security Treaty was signed. I had not been in Okinawa before. Back during the Korean War, when I was in the navy, I took the ship in to what was then called Buckner Bay, now Nakagusuku Bay, and dropped anchor. Other officers on board went ashore. I took a look at the place through the glasses, and I thought, "This is not for me." But we were anchored in the most beautiful lagoon, so I went swimming around the ship. So I had been in Okinawan waters, but I'd never touched ground before.

I have to say I was shocked to see the impact of thirty-eight American bases located on an island smaller than Kauai in the Hawaiian Islands, with 1.3 million people living cheek-by-jowl with warplanes . . . the Third Marine Division is based there; the only marine division we have outside the country. And I began to investigate the issues.

The reaction to the rape of 1995 from, for example, General Richard Meyers, who became chairman of the Joint Chiefs of Staff—he was then head of U.S. forces in Japan—and all he said was that these were just three bad apples, a tragic incident, unbelievably exceptional. After research, you discover that the rate of sexually violent crimes committed by our troops in Okinawa leading to court-martial is two per month! This was not an exceptional incident, expect for the fact that the child was so young and, differing from many Okinawan women who would not come forward after being raped, she was not fully socialized and she wanted to get even. This led to the creation of a quite powerful organization that I greatly admire called Okinawan Women Act Against Military Violence.

I began to research Okinawa, and my first impulse—again, as a defensive American imperialist—was that Okinawa was exceptional: it's off the beaten track, the press never goes there, the military is comfortable. I discovered over time, looking at these kinds of bases and other places around the world, that there's nothing exceptional about it. It's typical. Maybe the concentration is a little greater than it is elsewhere, but the record of environmental damage, sexual crimes, bar brawls, drunken driving, one thing after another, these all occur in the 725 bases (the Department of Defense–acknowledged number; the [real] number is actually considerably larger than that) that we have in other people's countries. That led me to write *Blowback*, first as a warning.

But it also led you to publish this book Okinawa: Cold War Island, *edited by you, which looks at the various aspects of this. And what you're saying is, it's not only the social cost; it has impinged on the people of Okinawa's right to have some kind of democratic existence.*

Oh, no question about it. One of the things that I thought was most outrageous in the discussion of the United States in Iraq is how Bush and others have spoken many times of our wonderful [act] of bringing democracy to Japan after the war, as if to say that our military missionaries were really good at doing this. And using Japan, you'd have to say they always must leave out Okinawa, because between the battle of Okinawa—the last great battle of World War II, and one of the bloodiest—down to 1972, it was run entirely as a Pentagon colony. It was not included in the peace treaty. The head of Okinawa was a lieutenant general in the army. It was a safe house, very rarely visited by anybody.

Then in 1972, after tremendous protests over the conditions in Okinawa, it reverted to Japan and came under the security treaty. But the understanding that Nixon and Kissinger had achieved at that time is that there would be no change in the bases, and they are still there. Essentially, Okinawa is used as a dumping ground by the Japanese. They want the security treaty, but they don't want American troops anywhere near mainland Japanese. So they put them down, as I say, in the equivalent of Puerto Rico, and the conditions fester. The governor of Okinawa today, a very considerably conservative man, Mr. Inamine, is still, nonetheless, always saying, "We're living on the side of a volcano. You can hear the magma down there. It may blow. And when it does, it'll have the same effect on your empire that the breaching of the Berlin Wall had on the Soviet empire."

If I could summarize what you're saying, there was a kind of a synergy between two things. One is your realization that the Cold War institutions weren't being dismantled.

Right.

And because your interests are so broad and your scholarship is so deep, you're also talking about economic policies toward that region. So there was no adjustment at the end of the Cold War with regard to our policies toward Korea, with regard to our policies toward Japan.

But the Okinawa experience allowed you to get inside this dimension, which was a key part of these Cold War institutions.

I think it's well said. To put it in a nutshell, Gorbachev really did attempt to dismantle the Soviet empire. He was one of the exceptional cases in history in which an empire sought to dismantle itself, because of the need for reform and things like that. The Russians, by 1989, wanted contact with France and Germany more than they did with these miserable little states in East Europe. He was stopped cold by vested interests in the Cold War system as structured in the Soviet Union. I began to discover the exact same kind of Cold War–vested interests existed in the Department of Defense, in the military industrial complex, in the intelligence agencies. And they were having their way.

In one of your books, I think it's in the introduction to The Sorrows of Empire, *you say that as a consultant or an adviser to the CIA, you were not impressed with the reports and analysis that you were viewing. So we were not in a position to understand what was going on, just as a matter of the information we were getting.*

This is what blowback means. "Blowback" is a CIA term that means retaliation, or payback. It was first used in the after-action report on our first clandestine overthrow of a foreign government, the overthrow of Mossadegh in Iran in 1953, when, for the sake of the British Petroleum Company, we claimed he was a communist when he just didn't want the British to keep stealing Iranian resources. In the report, which was finally declassified in 2000, the CIA says, "We should expect some blowback from what we have done here." This was the first model clandestine operation.

By blowback we do not mean just the unintended consequences of events. We mean unintended consequences of events that were kept secret from the American public, so that when the retaliation comes, they have no way to put it into context. Just as after 9/11, you have the president saying, "Why do they hate us?" The people on the receiving end know full well that they hate us because of what was done to them. It's the American public that is in the dark on that subject.

As you're coming to these realizations and moving in this new direction, you move from being a traditional social scientist to a public intellectual. Talk a little about that transition. Was it because of the nature of the problems you were seeing and new responsibilities you felt you had? As a public intellectual, you can't use as much jargon as one might as a social scientist, although I don't think you use a lot of jargon. Talk a little about that.

I try to avoid it. One of the things I dislike about academic social science is this tendency to mesh it all into a framework by people who don't really know what they're talking about. I retired from the University of California in 1992, and *Blowback* was not written because I needed tenure. It certainly grew out of my main specialty in East Asian politics, Japan, and the growing realization that Japan was a satellite of the United States—that its foreign policy was entirely in an orbit around Washington, D.C., and that this required explanation.

I conceived of *Blowback*—written in 1999, published in 2000—as a warning to the American public. It was: you should expect retaliation from the people on the receiving end of now innumerable clandestine activities, including the biggest one of all, the recruiting, arming, and putting into combat of mujahideen freedom fighters in Afghanistan in the 1980s who are the main recruiting group for Al Qaeda today.

The warning was not heeded. The book, when it was first published, was more or less ignored in this country. It was very nicely received in Germany, and in Japan, and in Italy, in places like that. But then after 9/11, when all of a sudden, inattentive

Americans were mobilized to seek, at least on an emergency basis, some understanding of what they were into, it became a bestseller. My publisher—she's a very lovely woman—said to me, "It's a hell of a way to sell books, but it's better to sell than to not sell them." Her offices are down on West 18th Street, not too far from ground zero, and she called me on the morning of September 11, 2001, to say, "Blowback big-time just hit, and I'm getting out of here, but I thought you on the West Coast ought to get out of bed and turn on the TV," which I did.

You're raising a very important point, which is that our policies often lack an understanding of our own actions. But also—

Not just lack of understanding. They've been kept secret. That's why the subtitle of *The Sorrows of Empire* is "Militarism, Secrecy"—I want to stress secrecy and say a word or two about that in a moment—"and the End of the Republic."

Two days after 9/11, when the president addressed Congress and asked rhetorically, "Why do they hate us?" my response was: "The people immediately around you are the ones who could tell you with precision why. That is, Cheney, Rumsfeld, Rice, Colin Powell, Richard Armitage"—these are the people who ran the largest clandestine operation we ever carried out, in Afghanistan in the 1980s. "They could explain to you, in detail, why." Once the Soviet Union had been expelled in 1989 from Afghanistan and we simply walked away from it, the people we had recruited, trained, and equipped with things like—

Stinger missiles.

Stinger missiles—the first time the Stinger was ever used against a Soviet gunship was in Afghanistan. Once we had achieved our purposes, we just walked away, and these highly armed young men felt, "We've been used. We were cannon fodder in a little exercise in the Cold War, in a bipolar competition between the Soviet Union and the United States." Then we compounded that with further mistakes like placing infidel troops (our troops) in Saudi Arabia after 1991, which was insulting to any number of Saudi Arabians, who believe that they are responsible for the most sacred sites in Islam: Mecca and Medina. Osama bin Laden is so typical of the kinds of figures in our history, like Manuel Noriega or Saddam Hussein, who were close allies of ours at one time. We know Saddam at one time had weapons of mass destruction because we have the receipts!

It strikes me that there are two things going on here. One is that these small powers or medium-sized powers—well, really, small powers— aren't doing what we're telling them, but they also bite the hand that fed them at one point.

They certainly do. These people remember with a vengeance. Osama bin Laden comes from a wealthy family of a construction empire in Saudi Arabia. He's the sort of person that you would more likely expect to see on the ski slopes of Gstaad with a Swiss girl on his arm, or as a houseguest in Kennebunkport with the first President Bush and the notorious "petroleum complex" of America. But he was insulted. He had been in Afghanistan. The base where he trained mujahideen, at Khost, the CIA built for him. It was one of the few times we knew where to hit. Because we built it, we did know where they were. He then was disgusted with us and certainly gave us fair warning in the attack in 1993 on the World Trade Center.

You bring to your books the erudition that was apparent in all of your early works. In talking about the events of 9/11, you make reference to the Sepoy incident. Tell us about that, because it's quite striking.

It's a little off the subject we're talking about, but it relates. One of the problems of the American empire right now is we're running out of cannon fodder. That is, here we are in January of 2004; within a few months, 40 percent of our troops in Iraq will be National Guard or reservist. There just aren't that many Americans [available to fight], unless you want to go to the draft, and that would probably be politically very difficult. Imperial powers have always faced this in the past; they go around looking for foreigners who can do their dirty work for them. We did it in Vietnam with the Montagnards, with any number of people we tried to sign up. I refer to one way to solve this problem as the Sepoy strategy.

The Sepoy strategy refers to the British armies in India that were 95 percent made up of Indian soldiers, who in 1857 revolted against them. This ended the activities of the British East India Company in India. India then became directly ruled by the Crown, and became a much more imperialist enclave than it had been prior to that.

You make the comparison with Osama bin Laden and his role in Afghanistan.

In a certain sense, one might argue that 9/11 was a new example of the Sepoy mutiny of 1857, in which the Indian troops believed that they were being misused by their British officers. The Enfield rifle, particularly an early version of it, had just been introduced. It had a bullet that came soaked in grease, and you had to bite off a piece of paper around it in order to use the cartridge. The Hindu troops believed that this was cow fat, the Muslim troops believed that it was pig fat, and [both believed] that the British were trying to force them to blaspheme against their religions. Also, the British were using Christian missionaries to try and convert them. It led to a massive revolt. The Indians do not call it the Sepoy Mutiny; they call it the first revolutionary activity leading ultimately to Indian independence. I think that something like that may be happening to us today, too.

So with this background, you've now just published your newest book, which is called The Sorrows of Empire: Militarism, Secrecy, and the End of the Republic. *You're trying to help us understand, to show us what the nature of the American empire is.*

Yes.

Central to that is understanding what the military is, what militarism is, and what imperialism is. Talk a little about that.

What I want to introduce here is what I call the "base world." According to the Base Structure Report, an annual report of the Department of Defense, in the year 2002 we had 725 bases in other people's countries. Actually, that number understates in that it does not include any of the espionage bases of the National Security Agency, such as RAF Menwith Hill in Yorkshire.

So these are bases where we have listening devices?

These are huge bases. Menwith Hill downloads every single e-mail, telephone call, and fax between Europe and the United States every day and puts them into massive computers where dictionaries then read them out. There are hundreds of these. The official Base Structure Report also doesn't include any of the main bases in England disguised as Royal Air Force bases even though there are no Britons on them. It doesn't include any of the bases in Uzbekistan or Kyrgyzstan, any of the bases in Afghanistan, the four bases that are, as we talk, being built in Iraq. They put down one major marine base for Okinawa—there are ten—and things like that. So there is a lot of misleading information in it, but it's enough to say 700 looks like a pretty good number, whereas it's probably around 1,000.

The base world is secret. Americans don't know anything about it. The Congress doesn't do oversight on it. You must remember, 40 percent of the defense budget is black. No congressman can see it. All of the intelligence budgets are black.

No public discussion.

In violation of the first article of the Constitution that says, "The American public shall be given, annually, a report on how their tax money was spent." That has not been true in the United States since the Manhattan Project of World War II, even though it is the clause that gives Congress the power of the purse, the power to supervise.

The base world is complex. It has its own airline. It has 234 golf courses around the world. It has something like seventy Lear Jet luxury airplanes to fly generals and admirals to the golf courses, to the armed forces ski resort at Garmisch in the Bavarian Alps. Inside the bases, the military does everything in its power to make them look like Little America. A Burger King has just opened at Baghdad International Airport.

There are large numbers of women in the armed forces today, [yet] you can't get an abortion at a military hospital abroad. Sexual assaults are not at all uncommon in the armed forces. If you were a young woman in the armed forces today and you were based in Iraq, and you woke up one morning and found yourself pregnant, you have no choice but to go on the open market in Baghdad looking for an abortion, which is not a very happy thought.

Militarism is not defense of the country. By militarism, I mean corporate interest in a military way of life. It derives above all from the fact that service in the armed forces is, today, not an obligation of citizenship. It is a career choice. It has been since 1973. I thought it was wonderful when PFC Jessica Lynch, who was wounded at Nasiriyah, was asked by the press, "Why did you join the Army?" She said, "I come from Palestine, West Virginia; I couldn't get a job at Wal-Mart." She said, "I joined the Army to get out of Palestine, West Virginia"—a perfectly logical answer on her part. And it's true of a great many people in the ranks today. They do not expect to be shot at. That's one of the points you should understand; it's a career choice, like a kid deciding to work his way up to Berkeley by going through a community college, and a state college, and then transferring in at the last minute or something like that.

Standing behind it is the military-industrial complex. We must, once again, bear in mind the powerful warnings of probably the two most prominent generals in our history. George Washington, in his farewell address, warns about the threat of standing armies to liberty, and particularly republican liberty. He was not an isolationist; he was talking about what moves power toward the imperial presidency, toward the state. It requires more taxes. Everything else which he said has come true. The other, perhaps more famous one was Dwight Eisenhower in his farewell address, where he invented the phrase "military-industrial complex." We now know that he intended to say "military-industrial-congressional complex," but he was advised not to go that far.

So as we try to understand how your thinking evolved over time, you're saying that suddenly you confronted what is essentially a system of Okinawas.

Yes. Well said: a base world.

A base world in which we put bases for purposes that then change.

And we never close them.

And we never close them. We create kind of—

We may close some now in Germany, because we're mad at Schröder. . . .

And we're probably going to close some in South Korea, because it's very possibly the most anti-American democracy on earth today. With 101 bases, the South Koreans are fed up and they don't think they need them any longer.

And in these bases, the American citizens who are serving as soldiers lead a good life. We're talking country clubs.

It's a volunteer army, so you've got to make life halfway decent. It's state socialism—that is, you're not paid a huge salary, but you have free housing, free healthcare, free education for your children—you're taken care of in many different ways. There's no question the troops of the Third Marine Division, located on Okinawa, are living better than they would in a stateside town like Oceanside, California, right next door to Camp Pendleton. They remind me very much of the Soviet troops that were based in East Germany when the Wall came down, and they didn't go home for four years. They knew that life was better where they were in Germany than it was going to be back in the old Soviet Union.

You write: "Empire is a physical reality with a distinct way of life, but also a network of economic and political interests tied in a thousand different ways to American corporations, universities, and communities, but kept separate from everyday life, that is, in the United States." And then you go on to say, "What is most fascinating and curious about the developing American form of empire, however, is that in its modern phase, it is solely an empire of bases, not of territories. And these bases now encircle the earth."

The bases are the equivalent of what used to be colonies. They exist from Greenland to Australia, from Japan to Latin America. For your viewers who are veterans (I'm a veteran of the Korean War), for veterans of World War II or Korea, or Vietnam, [military] life is not the same. You don't do KP anymore. You don't clean latrines. That's farmed out to private companies like Kellogg, Brown & Root, a subsidiary of Dick Cheney's Halliburton Company. At Camp Bondsteel in Kosovo, they do everything for you. They even do the laundry. The troops at Bondsteel say, "There ought to be a little patch that says, 'Service by Kellogg, Brown & Root' on your uniform."

Let's explain to our audience. This is a base in the Balkans which—

It's not in the Base Structure Report either, for reasons I don't know.

But apparently set up to facilitate the humanitarian intervention and—

Peacekeeping operations in Kosovo.

Right. But you point out to us that when you move to the systemic level, then it looks like a base that helps secure [access to] oil.

That's right, you've got it. The army likes to say facetiously that there are only two man-made sites you can observe from outer space: one is the Great Wall of China, and the other is Camp Bondsteel. It was built in 1999 by Kellogg, Brown & Root. It's the most expensive base we've built since the Vietnam War.

Bill Clinton said we would be out of Kosovo in six months. Bush II ran on a campaign that we shouldn't be there at all and should get out. This base is considerably more than you need to do peacekeeping in Kosovo. So what's it all about? Well, it's about our efforts to extract oil from the Caspian Basin, bring it across the Black Sea—not having to take it through the Dardanelles—transfer it across the Balkans to the Adriatic Sea and through Albania, and then on to the rest of the world. This base lies directly astride the Trans-Balkan pipeline that we are in the process of building. It is also an ancient Roman Empire military route.

What interests me here is that we're talking about something that looks very much like the end of the Roman Republic—which was, in many ways, a model for our own republic—and its conversion into a military dictatorship called the Roman Empire as the troops began to take over. The kind of figure that the Roman Republic began to look for was a military populist; of course, the most obvious example was Julius Caesar. But after Caesar's assassination in 44 B.C., the young Octavian becomes the "god" Augustus Caesar, behaving not unlike our own boy emperor, Bush II.

When a former "spear-carrier for the empire" turns that spear on the empire, the results are impressive. You may be one of the few people not affiliated with the government who has read these reports that tell us about the bases and the number of soldiers we have. You point out that when you add up all of what's there, you're talking about $118 billion of capital investment, which may be a low number.

This is the so-called plant replacement value, a typical piece of Department of Defense jargon. They calculate plant replacement values for all these things, and it's not that the numbers are any good, but they give you an idea of how the DOD evaluates them. You discover that Kadena Air Base, which was built for thermonuclear war in the middle of Okinawa, is the most valuable base we have in East Asia. Certainly, Ramstein Air Base in Germany is enormously valuable. Again, bear in mind here, we're talking about bases that have been there for sixty years. World War II is long over, and that's also when we got the bases in Korea.

In the same way, the new series of Persian Gulf Wars, Iraq I and Iraq II, are producing a plethora of bases around the Persian Gulf in deeply unstable, antidemocratic, Islamic autocracies. In Central Asia, where we're beginning to implement Dick Cheney's oil strategy, we are heavily invested in places like Uzbekistan and Kyrgyzstan. In Kyrgyzstan, we've named our air base "Captain Peter J. Ganci Air Base." Peter J. Ganci was the highest-ranking member of the New York Fire Department to be killed on September 11, 2001. But these countries are leftover autocracies from the former Soviet Union. They're among the least democratic places on earth. They compare in quality with North Korea.

You write in the new book: "After the attacks of 9/11, we waged two wars in Afghanistan and Iraq, and acquired fourteen new bases in Eastern Europe, Iraq, the Persian Gulf, Pakistan, Afghanistan, Uzbekistan, and Kyrgyzstan."

The only place left out in the old southern Eurasian countries, of course, is Iran. We've got it squeezed now between Afghanistan on one side and Iraq on the other.

So, two points I want to emphasize here. One you already touched on: when you put one of these bases down, you get a reaction like the reaction in Saudi Arabia when we put a new base in or refurbish the base that was there as a result of the first Iraq War.

It's a foreign antibody stuck into a functioning culture that we don't understand, and of which our troops are actually almost cultivated to be systematically contemptuous. There's no way to avoid the racism and arrogance that goes with the way our people are educated and what they do when they come to countries like this.

I'm not trying to be a sensationalist, but I actually do worry about the future of the United States; whether, in fact, we are tending in the same path as the former Soviet Union, with domestic, ideological rigidity in our economic institutions, imperial overstretch—that's what we're talking about here—the belief that we have to be everywhere at all times. We have always been a richer place than Russia was, so it will take longer. But we're overextended. We can't afford it.

One of my four "sorrows of empire" at the end of the book is bankruptcy. The military is not productive. They do provide certain kinds of jobs, as you discover in the United States whenever you try and close a military base—no matter how conservative or liberal your congressional representatives are, they will go mad to try and keep it open, keep it functioning. And the military-industrial complex is very clever in making sure that the building of a B-2 bomber is spread around the country; it is not all located at Northrop in El Segundo, California.

Even if the Republicans are defeated, no matter who replaces Bush, I have grave difficulty believing that he or she can bring under control the Pentagon, the secret intelligence agencies, the military-industrial complex. The Department of Defense is not, today, a department of defense. It's an alternative seat of government on the south bank of the Potomac River. And, typical of militarism, it's expanding into many, many other areas in our life that we have, in our traditional political philosophy, reserved for civilians. [For example,] domestic policing: they're slowly expanding into that.

Probably the most severe competition in our government today is between the Special Forces in the DOD and the CIA over who runs clandestine operations.

Let's break this down a little and put it in context. What you're really saying is that, lo and behold, we've created an empire of bases, a different kind of empire, and that it's basically changing who we are and the way our government operates.

The right phrase is exactly what you said: "lo and behold." It reminds you of the Roman Republic, which existed in its final form with very considerable rights for Roman citizens, much like ours, for about two centuries. James Madison and others, in writing the defense of the Constitution in the Federalist Papers, signed their name "Publius." Well, who is Publius? He was the first Roman consul. That is where the whole world of term limits, of separation of powers, things like that, [began].

Yet by the end of the first century B.C., Rome had seemingly "inadvertently" acquired an empire that surrounded the entire Mediterranean Sea. They then discovered that the inescapable accompaniment, the Siamese twin of imperialism, is militarism. You start needing standing armies. You start having men who are demobilized after having spent their entire lives in the military. It's expensive to pay them. You have to provide them, in the Roman Empire, with farms or things of this sort. They become irritated with the state. And then along comes a military populist, a figure who says, "I understand your problems. I will represent your interests against the Roman Senate. The only requirement is that I become dictator for life." Certainly, Julius Caesar is the model for this . . . Napoleon Bonaparte, Juan Perón, this is the type of figure.

Indeed, one wonders whether we have already crossed our Rubicon, whether we can go back. I don't know.

I remain enormously impressed by the brilliant speeches that Senator Robert Byrd, from West Virginia, gives week in, week out, to an empty Senate chamber. They sound like Cicero. They really do sound like a passionate lover of our constitution and what it stood for. Nobody is listening to him. The news media don't report it. And Cicero did end up with his head and both hands nailed to the Forum wall by the young Octavian.

In your indictment of what we are becoming, or maybe have become, you go through a list. We can't do all of it; we don't have enough time. But, essentially, civilians who think in military ways now making decisions, the Pentagon expropriating the functions of the State

Department, a policy being perceived as military policy as opposed to all of the dimensions of—

People around the world who meet Americans meet soldiers. That's how we represent ourselves abroad, just as the Roman Empire represented itself abroad as the Legionnaires. People have to conclude, even if they don't come into military or armed conflict with us, that this is the way the Americans think. This is the way they represent themselves today. It's not foreign aid any longer. It's not our diplomats. It's not the Fulbright program. It's the military. It's uniformed eighteen- to twenty-four-year-old young men and some young women.

Moving on beyond the government—and we're not even going through the list; people should read the book for that—the privatization of the military; the development of the CINCs, that is, the military commanders all over the world who are proconsuls—

These people like to call themselves "old Roman proconsuls." They're not proconsuls, but they go outside of the chain of command, directly to the president and secretary of defense. They have a huge entourage around them, their own aviation, and things of this sort. Ambassadors report to them.

And then coming home, after 9/11, to changing the laws about wiretaps, about the use of the military domestically. What you're pointing to is an erosion, as you just said, of the foundations of our republic. And then, also, the world of ideas. Because I believe that what you're saying is that, on the one hand, you have one group that basically wants to use the military for domination and another group that says, "Oh, no, we're good guys. We want to use it for humanitarian intervention." And you don't see much difference. The point being that the system of empire is there to be used.

There's no question that a group of intellectuals who have served in the government for many years—in the Reagan administration, in the first Bush administration, now prominently represented in the Department of Defense; people like Wolfowitz, Richard Perle, others—these people made, in my view, a very wrong conclusion after the demise of the Soviet Union, namely that we won the Cold War. I don't think we did; I think we just didn't lose it the way the Soviet Union did. But they concluded from that we were a new Rome; that we were beyond good and evil; that our policy should be the famous old Roman phrase, "We don't care whether they love us, so long as they fear us." Wolfowitz was writing back at the very end of [the] first Bush [administration] that our policy should be the military domination of the globe to ensure that no one, enemy or ally, offers competition to our military force.

On the other hand, just as you were saying, particularly in the Clinton administration, there were those imperialists who spoke of the duty to intervene in the case where human life was at risk and things of this sort. The issue here is not that such a duty or obligation doesn't exist; it is how it's legitimatized. It is not just up to us to decide that we are now going to do a humanitarian liberation of Kosovo from Yugoslavia, but not Chechens, or Palestinians, or East Timorese, or whoever else that we don't want to get involved with. Humanitarian intervention, if it is not legitimatized—and the only form of legitimacy we have is by sanction of the UN Security Council—is simply a euphemism for imperialism, in which we declare that we have good intentions, but nobody is going to stop us.

So, for you, Iraq isn't surprising at all—that there are no weapons of mass destruction; that the Senate essentially passed the resolution; that we ignored the UN; and that, now, we've changed our mission. In the end, we may not get democracy, but we will have four or five bases.

There's a lot of continuity here, too. What Americans don't realize is how remarkably hard the Clinton administration worked at
promoting the Taliban in Afghanistan—our purpose then was to
get a stable government in Afghanistan with which we could, for
the sake of the Union Oil Company of California, build gas and
oil pipelines from Tajikistan across Afghanistan, and emptying
through Pakistan into the Arabian Sea. Jim Baker is a very distinguished former secretary of state; his law firm, Baker Botts, has five
attorneys in Baku, Azerbaijan. Now, I want to tell you, there's not
a lot of legal work going on in Baku these days. This is the military-
petroleum complex at work. The involvement of very high-ranking
advisers in our government, of the Kissinger-Brzezinski-Scowcroft
class, as advisers to these oil companies is ubiquitous.

We now know from former secretary of the treasury Paul
O'Neill, as well as from Condoleezza Rice herself, that on the day
the Bush administration was finally sworn in, they had decided
to go to war to conquer Iraq in order to steal its resources. It's got
the second largest oil reserves on earth, and it was also part of a
plan that includes Camp Bondsteel in the Balkans, that includes
the bases surrounding the Caspian Sea, the ring of bases along
the Persian Gulf, reflecting our increasing anxiety that we were
going to lose Saudi Arabia exactly the same way we lost Iran in
1979, as a result of our own bungling interventionist policy.

The decision on the part of, certainly, Vice President Cheney,
was that we needed the oil. And yet we know that we have the
technology today to completely eliminate our requirements for
Persian Gulf oil if we would simply institute fuel conservation
procedures. Instead, the symbol of the United States after 9/11
became, at least domestically, somebody driving a Chevrolet Sub-
urban down the freeway at high speeds with an American flag
attached to its antenna. Sales of this huge SUV have doubled
since 9/11. The gas mileage is rotten on the thing.

It was a decision on our part to go in this direction, also to
attempt to control the world . . . places like China. China is the

world's fastest-growing economy. It grew at 9.1 percent last year. The decline of American economic influence is, today, irreversible. There's simply nothing that can be done about it. We don't manufacture much anymore. We just trade in securities. But we can control the Chinese if we control the oil. They are now major petroleum importers too. This is the kind of geopolitical, geostrategic thought that was going on among the neocon defense intellectuals during the period they were out of power, between the two Bushes.

As a student of revolution and social change, can you point to any areas of hopefulness within the American system that might turn these things around?

The greatest source of hope in the world today happened in February of 2003, February 15th and 16th, when some 10 million people around the world in every democracy on earth expressed their overwhelming opposition to the war in Iraq—400,000 in New York City, 2 million in London, a million in Rome, another 800,000 in Madrid, equally large numbers in Berlin. These people haven't melted away. They're very sensitive to the way the world is going.

So I put it to you this way: the United States is having very real problems very rapidly. We are failing in Iraq. We have not produced a friendly regime in Afghanistan, which is looking more like it was before 9/11, the world's largest producer of opium and a major source of terrorists.

As a student of Asian political economy, you wrote the classic on MITI. In the final analysis, your judgment is that we will not only suffer political but also economic bankruptcy.

So, what do I suggest probably will happen? I think we will stagger along under a façade of constitutional government, as we are now, until we're overcome by bankruptcy. We are not paying our way. We're financing it off of huge loans coming daily from our two leading creditors, Japan and China.

It's a rigged system that reminds you of Herb Stein, [who], when he was chairman of the Council of Economic Advisers in a Republican administration, rather famously said, "Things that can't go on forever don't." That's what we're talking about today. We're massively indebted, we're not manufacturing as much as we used to, we maintain our lifestyle off of huge capital imports from countries that don't mind taking a short, small beating on the exchange rates so long as they can continue to develop their own economies and supply Americans: above all, China within twenty to twenty-five years will be both the world's largest social system and the world's most productive social system, barring truly unforeseen developments.

Bankruptcy would not mean the literal end of the United States, any more than it did for Germany in 1923, or China in 1948, or Argentina just a few years ago, in 2001 and 2002. But it would certainly mean a catastrophic recession, the collapse of our stock exchange, the end of our level of living, and a vast series of new attitudes that would now be appropriate to a much poorer country. Marshall Auerbach is a financial analyst whom I admire who refers to the United States as a "Blanche Dubois economy." Blanche Dubois, of course, was the leading character in Tennessee Williams's play *A Streetcar Named Desire*, and she said, "I've always depended upon the kindness of strangers." We're also increasingly dependent on the kindness of strangers, and there are not many of them left who care, any more than there were for Blanche. I suspect if the United States did start to go down, it would not elicit any more tears than the collapse of the Soviet Union did.

Do you see a configuration of external power, Japan, China, the EU, that will be a balancer that might not just confront us but might help guide us to changes that would be good for us and them?

Once you go down the path of empire, you inevitably start a process of overstretch, of tendencies toward bankruptcy, and, in the rest of the world, a tendency toward the uniting of people who are opposed to your imperialism simply on grounds that it's yours, but maybe also on the grounds that you're incompetent at it. There was a time when the rest of the world did trust the United States a good deal as a result of the Marshall Plan, foreign aid, things of this sort. They probably trusted it more than they should have. Today that is almost entirely dissipated by the current government that's been in power since the Supreme Court appointed it in 2000. At some point, we must either reduce our empire of bases from 737 to maybe 37—although I'd just as soon get rid of all of them. If we don't start doing that, then we will go the way of the former Soviet Union.

Tariq Ali
May 8, 2003

Where were you born and raised?

I was born in Lahore, long years ago in 1943, when it was still part of British India. When I was four years old, it became part of a new country, Pakistan, which very few of us imagined at that point would ever come to existence.

In looking back, how do you think your parents shaped your thinking about the world?

My parents both came from a very old, crusty, feudal family. My father had broken with the dominant ideology in politics of that family when he was a student, and had become a nationalist, a communist, fighting against the British Empire in India. My mother, too, belonged to the same family, and they met up; my mother became radicalized. My mother's father, curiously enough, was Prime Minister of the Punjab. Even though my father was from the same family—even, if you like, from a superior branch—my grandfather said that his daughter would never be allowed to marry a communist. And so there were massive rows going on in the family. This young couple was in love. Finally, my grandfather thought he would impose a condition on the marriage which would be completely unacceptable to my father. He said, "In order to marry my daughter, you have to join the army" (this was the British-Indian Army), imagining that my father never could—and he never would have. But then something else happened, which is that the Soviet Union was invaded by Hitler.

Once the Soviet Union was invaded, all the communists all over the world decided to back the war effort. So the wedding photograph of my parents is my father looking very jaunty in a lieutenant's uniform.

So political opportunity made possible the marriage, in your father's willingness to join the army. Tell us a little about your education, first in Pakistan and then here.

The choices were limited in those days, when I was growing up. One choice was to go to a very elite school, where the children of the aristocracy and the rich went. All my uncles had been there, but my parents said, "It's a school which wrecks lives. You're not going there." So the other choice was a school run by Irish-Catholic missionaries. There was a whole network of these schools, which were far more democratic in the sense that lots of kids from different social classes went there. And that's where I was educated. So one got a flavor of Catholicism and a Catholic education, but living inside a Muslim country.

You wrote in The Clash of Fundamentalisms, *"How often in our house had I heard talk of superstitious idiots, often relatives, who hated a Satan they never knew and worshipped a God they didn't have the brains to doubt?" Tell us a little about that. I know that your father, as a matter of form, permitted you to have some religious instruction, but you saw through it—and he saw through it, I gather.*

Yes, well, one was growing up in a Muslim country. You lived in an Islamic culture. All the noises of the Muslim city were present. But there were many of us growing up—it wasn't just me—who were not believers. My father at one point got worried—aunts and uncles used to be heard whispering: "At least give these children a chance! Don't wreck their lives like you've wrecked your own!"

So my father, who was a very fair-minded man, said, "I think you should at least know the fundamentals of the religion so you know what you're arguing against when the time comes," and attempts were made to do this. But often I found that the people engaged to educate me were not that knowledgeable themselves. Even as a child, one could see through the hypocrisy, actually. Many of them were discussing the Koran when they didn't understand it themselves, or what it was trying to say. This was very common in non-Arabic parts of the Muslim world.

So the attempts failed, and there we are: I grew up an atheist. I make no secret of it. It was acceptable. In fact, when I think back, none of my friends were believers. None of them were religious; maybe a few were believers. But very few were religious in temperament.

How do you account for the cosmopolitanism that was so much a part of your life? I want to know how that interfaced with Pakistani nationalism and whether you felt a strong identification with Pakistan.

We grew up in a town in Lahore, which had been one of the most cosmopolitan towns in India. Then you had the partition of India, and you had massive killings. This is not much talked about these days, but nearly two million people died, as Hindus, Muslims, and Sikhs slaughtered each other to create this state. So I remember when I was growing up, I would be sitting in the back of the car, and my parents were driving, and there was a sadness in the early days, a sort of semi-permanent sadness as we passed certain streets. They'd say, "Oh, God, remember 'X' used to live here." And "X" was always a Sikh or a Hindu name. These were the ghosts who were in that city as I was growing up. So when you realized what had happened, how much killing had gone on, you did ask yourself, "Was it worth it?"

And then you had another problem, which was that the Pakistani ruling elite was an elite with so many chips on its shoulders that I call it one of the few elites with a permanent inferiority complex. It never succeeded in developing a Pakistani nationalism, so that when Britain, France, and Israel invaded Egypt in 1956, Pakistan, more or less, supported that. They were allied to the West and were seen as a bridgehead of, first, the British Empire and later the United States in that region. So Pakistan could never actually develop. And because it didn't develop, we had no respect for them at all.

So there was a sense of alienation towards this state and its functioning, which in me was very strong from a very early age. I remember we used to say we wished our prime minister had been Nehru of India, because he believed in neutrality, trying to carve out a new politics, much more interesting . . . or Nasser, in Egypt. We were constantly looking at other parts of the world for leadership, never in our own land.

Pakistan, very early on, three years into its creation, decided that it was going to join the U.S. and British-sponsored security pacts, the first of which was the Baghdad Pact, which later became the Southeast Asia Treaty Organization. It put itself in this part of this world strategically. Whereas India, a much larger country, had the self-confidence to talk to Russia and America as equals. Nehru was a very distinguished politician, respected by both the White House and the Kremlin. We said, "Why can't we have leaders like that? Why do they have to hang on to the coattails of the West?" But that is the path they chose, and they stuck by it. The Pakistani army, still in power today, was a central conduit for the exercise of this power.

You went to Oxford. You were a president of the Oxford Union. Tell us how your education at that time shaped your consciousness.

Before I went to Oxford, I went to a university in Pakistan. We were very lucky that our college, the government college in Lahore, had a principal who was incredibly enlightened. He would

say to us, "Within the four walls of this college, you can think
what you like, do what you like, read what you like, and I will
defend you against all authority." This, at a time when a military
dictatorship had come into being and stopped politics. So we
were very lucky. We couldn't go out into the streets, though we
sometimes did as a collective, but within the college the atmosphere was very enlightened, and there were study circles discussing Marxism, discussing Islam, discussing anything you care to
think of. So that, already, was a good training.

But then, because I was very active and politically engaged at
the time in Pakistan, the governor of the big province banned my
speaking, even in the college. The principal was very upset he
couldn't stop it, and then, finally, my parents were worried that
I'd be locked up forever if I stayed there, and they pushed me
out. I didn't want to leave the country. I'm glad I did, in retrospect.
I didn't want to. But they basically pushed me out.

So I arrived at Oxford. And here, books—which weren't available in Pakistan or had been removed from the libraries—were
suddenly available again. The atmosphere was very open, and
I got engaged with the left groups on the Oxford University
campus very, very early on, and became very active. The Vietnam
War was then beginning, and I was pretty obsessed by that war.
It was my continent which was under attack. I knew we had to
do something about it, and I got very engaged in helping to set
up the anti–Vietnam War movement in Oxford, first, and then
nationally.

When I did my finals at Oxford, I had a bet with a friend that
I would bring Vietnam into every single answer. He said, "You
can't do it," and I said, "I will do it." He said, "They won't give
you a degree," and I said, "I don't care." So I sat down and did
that in philosophy, politics, and economics. One which drove my
economics examiner nearly crazy was the question, "Discuss the
cheapest forms of subsidized transport in the world," and I recall
writing that the cheapest form of subsidized transport was the

helicopter journeys made from Saigon into the jungles. I said the big tragedy was that often the passengers didn't return!

What do you feel is the main lesson of the '60s for you?

I was affected, also, by my origins and which continent I was coming from.

Bertrand Russell and Jean-Paul Sartre decided to set up an international war crimes tribunal to charge the United States with war crimes, and I was one of the people selected to go to Vietnam and find the evidence, which I did in 1967, when I was about twenty-three years old. I was in North Vietnam while the United States was bombing that country. So you got a real feel of it. You saw casualties every day. We were almost bombed ourselves on two occasions. And that was very formative—very, very formative.

I came back to Europe and reported to the International War Crimes Tribunal, and a big movement emerged in solidarity with the Vietnamese, in France, in Britain, and in different parts of the world. The key lesson one learns from that period is nothing will change if you just keep sitting where you're sitting. You have to get up and move and do something, even if there are very few of you for a start. But the passivity which later overtook the '80s and '90s generation was very sad to see.

Now, of course, it's a different situation. For a long time, it was socially unacceptable for young kids to be engaged. Now, we have a young generation for whom being engaged is socially acceptable again.

For me, the big demonstration [recently] against the war in Iraq, where a million and a half people assembled in London, was a wonderful occasion to see so many young people from the schools coming out. Kids invented their own slogans, and I couldn't even get the references of these slogans! It was some pop song which goes, "Who let the dogs out?" and the kids were chanting, "Who let the bombs out? Bush, Bush, and Blair." I said, "What are the origins of this?" and they said, "It comes from this song." "What song?!"

So the cycle has come around again. I often wonder what many of my contemporaries who are now serving on half the cabinets in governments of Europe, who gave up on all that and thought, "Now the world has changed. It's the end of history. We've moved on. There's no alternative," [I wonder] how they felt when they saw these amazing demonstrations in the United States and in Australia, Europe. I'm sure some of them must have felt a pang of conscience as they're preparing to go to war. The '60s generation is now in power in most parts of the world; [I wonder] what they felt when they saw millions on the streets?

For me, the lesson of the '60s always was be active, be engaged, and try and understand the world. So it's something I've not forgotten.

In your book The Clash of Fundamentalisms, *you draw heavily on the poetry of the period. Is there in the poetry an insight that allows you to make a point in a more compelling way?*

Absolutely. And, more importantly than that, poets have played a very big role in the culture of the Islamic world and also the non-Islamic world. If you take the role poetry played in Russia, both prior to the Revolution, during it, and after it, when Stalin had poets executed, the poets who survived said, "The one thing we cannot say about this regime is that it underestimates our craft!" In the West, poetry had become quite anodyne. There were very brilliant poets, but they didn't have that central role in the culture. Well, in the Arab world, they did. In the world of India and Pakistan, poets had a very important role. I think it grows out of the fact that the oral cultural tradition was very strong in that world. The written word obviously predominated, but large numbers of people couldn't read or write. When they went to hear a great poet recite, even if they couldn't read or write themselves, that poem left a deep mark on them. Often these poems were sung by famous singers, so they had a very deep impact.

This tradition is very deep in me because when I was growing up our house was a venue for poets and writers. They came and went, and, often, as a very young child, I would be sitting on the floor listening to people, very great poets reciting their poetry, so I was privileged. And then you could go to a poetry reading in a big open-air theater. The poetry reading started after dinner, at nine o'clock at night, a *musha'ira*, and it could go on until the early hours of the morning. By the end of it, the poets were reciting their poetry extemporaneously, inventing verses on the spot, and the crowds then made known which was their favorite poet. Often, poets too close to the government of the day were booed and heckled. So it's a very different tradition than has developed in the West.

Share with us your insights about poetry as an expression of protest and your analysis of the denial of that expression in our modern capitalist society.

The '90s of the last century were a decade when dumbing down became the form in most of the advanced capitalist world, including Britain. The BBC is still marginally better than most of the American networks, but I use the word "marginally" because if you live in that country and you see it every day, you see the big decline that has afflicted the BBC. Channel 4, which was set up by Parliament in 1982 to be an innovative, critical television channel—by the middle to end of the '90s had collapsed. A lot of experimental, very good work was done, but then it came to an end. It's almost as if one can trace this end to the collapse of the communist enemy; it's almost as if the rulers of the dominant capitalist world decided, "We don't need to educate our citizens so much. We have nothing to be worried about. If you educate them too much, give them too many opportunities, make them too vigilant and alert, they might actually turn on us." I'm not saying this is how they thought it concretely, but certainly it was what it seemed that they were trying to do. The dumbing-down seemed sudden: one day the networks were actually quite intelligent, and then six months later everything had disappeared. There's a very good Hollywood movie about it called *Network*, with Peter Finch, which describes the dumbing down in American television. But what happened in Britain has been every bit as disastrous.

To be cynical, I really do not believe that they want citizens in this world to think. They want a population which is more or less servile, which listens to them, accepts all they say, a population which is obsessed with consumerism and fornication, and carries on doing that. That's fine. But anything beyond that which challenges them, they more or less stopped. This has affected the control exercised now within television—and, shockingly, even in theater. I remember in the '60s, '70s, '80s, if you were head of drama at the BBC or Channel 4, you could do what you wanted. You went with your instincts. In the '90s came focus groups and marketing. You have to do the thing which gets the highest ratings. They assumed that the lowest common denominator is what got the highest ratings, and so they all started doing very similar things. Diversity in television began to die.

How would you advise young people today to prepare for the future?

I would advise them not to trust their politicians. And to doubt everything they see on the mainstream media and read in the press; to use their own brains and not accept what they are given as home truths; to ask themselves, "Could this possibly be true?" Always to question and to doubt.

We have a very clear-cut case in front of us. This government went to war to occupy a sovereign independent state, telling its people there were weapons of mass destruction, and that Saddam Hussein might give these weapons of mass destruction to Al Qaeda. Sixty percent of the American population believed in the link between Al Qaeda and Saddam Hussein where none existed. Anyone with the slightest bit of real knowledge would know that Saddam Hussein was a complete sworn opponent of Islamic fundamentalists. They hated each other. No one in the rest of the world believed the story of weapons of mass destruction to the same extent as in the United States. It's now turned out to be a lie: "There ain't any." And the neo-cons around Bush are saying, "Well, so what if we haven't found any? We got rid of him and brought freedom to the people of Iraq." But that "so what" is a very demeaning and debasing aspect of contemporary American politics. Unless the citizenry is vigilant and alert, they will carry on doing this. If you're not engaged in challenging the lies of the system, what's the good of living in this society?

Looking at your intellectual journey, what one or two themes do you think emerge that pull the ideas together that you've grappled with and continue to grapple with?

What played a very big part in my own formation [was learning from] the ideas of Marx and Lenin and Trotsky and various others when I was very young. From them, one learned and understood that the capitalist system was inherently unjust. Even with the best will in the world, it couldn't become a just system because it was based on the exploitation of the many by the few. That was its basis. We see this now reaching astronomical proportions, both inside the United States and globally. From that we learned that we have to have another system.

I was very critical of the Soviet Union from '56 onwards. I said, "This system isn't working." I was quite young, but I could see that this wasn't going to work. So what I learned from the failures and collapse of that system is that imposing that form of economic model without levels of accountability at every level, political and economic, is not going to work. So I became a believer in what I call socialist democracy. In my view, far from being the case that democracy is only compatible with capitalism, in fact, we see now that democracy is becoming incompatible with capitalism. Democracy will be only compatible with a system which is not based on exploitation. And that is something that I have believed in for a long time.

RESISTANCE
THROUGH ART

A novel, a movie, or a memoir can distill the essence of war, revolution, or the human struggle. The work of art becomes a form of resistance by raising important questions about what human beings and nations do to one another and by mobilizing the audience to see, understand, and resist destruction, oppression, and war. A teenager during the Iranian Revolution, Roya Hakakian discusses her disillusionment with the Iranian Revolution and how she slowly grew to understand the real meaning of freedom. Oliver Stone's political awakening came out of his experiences as a marine in Vietnam. That historical moment shaped his quest to understand the roots of that conflict and to convey through movies his insights about leadership, policy, and the human toll of war. Nobel Laureate Kenzaburo Oe's political awakening came during his first visit to Hiroshima, where he encountered the victims of the atomic bomb. The wise counsel of one of the attending physicians changed his thinking about the birth of his son, enriched his understanding of the human condition, and influenced his writing.

Roya Hakakian
Roya Hakakian is an Iranian American writer and documentary filmmaker. Her memoir of growing up a Jewish teenager in post-revolutionary Iran is *Journey from the Land of No: A Girlhood*

Caught in Revolutionary Iran. Hakakian is the author of two col-
lections of poetry in Persian, the first of which, *For the Sake of
Water*, was nominated as a poetry book of the year by Iran News
in 1993. She was listed among the leading new voices in Persian
poetry in the *Oxford Encyclopedia of the Modern Islamic World.* Com-
missioned by UNICEF, Hakakian's most recent film, *Armed and
Innocent*, is on the subject of the involvement of underage children in wars around the world.

Oliver Stone

Oliver Stone makes movies as a producer, screenwriter, and director. His movies—*Platoon, Born on the Fourth of July, JFK, Nixon,
Between Heaven and Earth*, and *Salvador*, to name a few—are, in a
sense, conversations with history. Intense, provocative, thoughtful, they are cinema which jolts our senses and stretches our
imagination, forcing us to confront our delusions about who
we are. Stone has been nominated for ten Academy Awards and
has won Oscars for writing *Midnight Express* and directing *Born
on the Fourth of July* and *Platoon*. Stone served in Vietnam, was
wounded twice, and received the Purple Heart and the Bronze
Star.

Kenzaburo Oe

Kenzaburo Oe's prolific body of novels, short stories, and critical and political essays has won almost every major international
honor. Oe's achievements as a writer committed to both literary
and humanitarian causes were recognized in 1994 when he was
awarded the Nobel Prize for Literature. In works such as *A Personal Matter, The Silent Cry, A Quiet Life, Hiroshima Notes*, and *A
Healing Family*, Oe's art moves from the personal to the political,
exploring how the individual, in confronting life's tragedies, over-
comes humiliation and shame to "get on with life," and in so
doing, finds personal dignity and a renewed sense of his responsibility to his fellow man.

Roya Hakakian
March 4, 2009

Where were you born and raised?

I was born and raised in Tehran, in Iran, and I came to the United States in 1985 when I was nineteen.

And looking back, how do you think your parents shaped your thinking about the world?

My father, who was a poet, had a great influence on me and made me absolutely fall in love with the task of writing. For all the years that I was growing up it seemed that my dad always had something to run away to. He had a sanctuary regardless of where in the house he was or what was happening around him. He could always pick up a notebook and a pen and be in a world of his own, and I think that made me embrace writing as a sanctuary, also.

And your mother?

My mom is probably the most generous person I've ever known, and she actually made me think from very early on what sort of a woman I wanted to be. Looking at her, I decided that I didn't want to get married because I would have to give everything over to the task of creating a family, I didn't want to have children because I didn't see myself all that interested in doing the things that she was doing. And so, in a way, I shaped an opinion about how I wanted to be based on the things that I saw my mother do, which, in many ways were things that she found herself doing out of generosity, and in many ways were things that inhibited her from her own self-development, which is not something that I wanted.

How did being Jewish in Iran affect you? Your family clearly retained their identity, but at the same time, you definitely are an Iranian.

Absolutely. You see, the reason we're having this particular conversation is because I am now in the United States and it's thirty years later. So, this very much is a retrospective conversation. When I was twelve and the Iranian revolution was taking place, I distinctly remember no one was thinking about religion as an issue. Iran, at the time that I was growing up, and even slightly prior to that, in the '60s and '70s, was religiously a very egalitarian place, especially as far as huge cities like Tehran where I was growing up or other big cities were concerned. I didn't grow up having the sort of preoccupations as a Jewish person that my mother or my father had had. My father was very much a target of bigotry where he grew up, in a very small village in central Iran. My mother had experienced a great deal, too. But in my years, these things were quite passé. We were modern people with modern aspirations, and talking about each other's religions didn't seem like a chic thing to do. And revolution especially, unlike what it seemed to people outside of Iran—and particularly in the United States—to the rest of us in Iran, educated, urban folks in big cities, was not about a religious undertaking.

For us in Iran, it was about all the great things that have brought revolutions about in history. It was about freedom, it was about democracy, it was about women's rights, it was about all the things that we thought modern Iran should have. And so, in that space nobody talked about religion. The revolution made it even more passé to entertain or discuss those issues. So, I didn't grow up thinking or debating these things until well into my teenage years when the mullahs took over, and the rules kind of changed.

So as Jews you were secular in Iran, but you maintained a piece of your identity with a commitment to the Jewish tradition.

Absolutely. It was only in my encounter with American Jews, when people asked me, "So, what were you?—were you reform, were you conservative, were you orthodox?," I began to kind of think about, "So what were we really?" And then I realized that these divisions are in some ways divisions that belong to democratic societies in which Jews have lived free enough to think of their own differences from one another, and therefore they have created subdivisions in which each feels more comfortable than the other. As Jews, we were something that is hard to describe. We observed; some of my best memories about my childhood are my synagogue memories. And more than anything, I remember playing with the other children, eating afterwards with the rest of the community, but it wasn't about a broader religious agenda. We were together, and it was how we experienced each other as a community, and that was precisely what I loved about it and what I continue to love about it and wish to pass on to my own children.

You describe in your book a moment under the Shah's rule when you're watching a friend read a women's magazine, and there're pictures of women in different roles, and you as a very young person were taken by the image of the woman truck driver. I raise this because there were aspects of what the Shah was doing to bring modernity to Iran, but in the end you see that it came with the denial of freedom. Talk a little about that because in a way the Shah's regime was quite friendly to the Jews, wasn't it?

Right. And I think that the Shah, in general, was the force behind the religious egalitarianism that came to Iran. I think it was part of the Shah's bigger strategy of bringing modernity into Iran to take away and try to soften religious boundaries in Iran, and it absolutely worked. We didn't have Jewish ghettos in Iran. You couldn't point to a neighborhood and say, this is a Jewish neighborhood. We had Jewish neighborhoods, but they were upscale neighborhoods where people lived and Jews happened to populate them heavily. So, it was very, very interesting to live at a time that was such a good time, not only for Iran but also for the cause of equality among various minorities in Iran. Those were the greatest years in the modern history of Iran when issues of religious differences had become so pale culturally. I have often been stopped by other Iranians who have said to me, "You know, it's only after we've come to the United States where Iranian Jews now say, 'I'm an Iranian Jew.' When we were in Iran nobody said anything other than, 'I'm an Iranian.'" And it's true. However, I think it came at a cost, which was that whatever Jews practice, or however it was that they experienced their Jewish tradition, it was very much done within the boundaries of the Jewish community. It was not something that had come as a result of a mutual understanding between Muslims and Jews. It was not that the Muslim community really knew who we were, not just as Iranian citizens but also as Jewish citizens. It had come at the cost of the Jews exercising however it was that they were Jewish behind closed doors and not displaying their Jewish identities overtly outside of their homes and outside of that sort of boundary. And I wish that hadn't been the case. I wish we as Iranians in those years had been better known, and I wish perhaps in the future we get to enrich the Persian culture in more overt and bolder ways than we have thus far.

How did you interact with Muslims?

The ways that I knew there was something different were very subtle, and so when Muslims were around I always knew that these people were outsiders, which is to say that they were not bad outsiders or good outsiders but they were outsiders. And so, I was on my best behavior, which is kind of like wearing my Sunday best, whereas when we were among relatives or other Jewish acquaintances, it was very comfortable. You didn't have to watch what it was that you were saying; you didn't have to worry that whatever language you used might offend someone else. I knew the neighbors who were not Jewish were outsiders, but I hadn't categorized them in any other way than a group of outsiders.

You were nineteen when you emigrated from Iran, and you had really no English when you came over, but you write such beautiful English. How did growing up in Iran influence your writing?

I have a passion for storytelling. I became a writer as a result of the Iranian revolution, because the revolution was a literary revolution for me and my generation and for the generation prior to my own. I was called to the cause by the greatest poets living in Iran in the '70s and '80s. I fell in love with their work, and as a result, with what it was that they were selling, which was the revolution at the time. The greatest person, the greatest influence on my life, was a poet who died several years ago, named Ahmad Shamlu, whose poetry took me several years to get. And my life was perfectly, irreversibly transformed as a result of that one reading when I finally understood what he was saying. So, I became a writer during a time when poetry, literature, were entwined with the concept of change, and with the concept of having collective convictions and a sense of collective commitment to Iran.

What does the evolution in popularity from poetry to prose mean in the historical context of the revolution in Iran?

I think in many ways poetry in Iran—well, poetry globally—is having a hard time anyway. And I think in Iran it's compounded by the fact that poetry was the language of the revolution for the educated, modern, city-dwelling people in Iran, and once the revolution didn't fulfill its promise, the vessel of the revolution—

the language—was something that people turned their backs on, and I think that's somewhat to be blamed for the additional fall of poetry from its historical pedestal in Iran. And I think, additionally, we as Iranians have had such a strong tradition of poetry writing, and we've had Rumi, we've had Hafez, we've had so many great giants in poetry writing, that our prose had suffered for many, many years historically, until the last thirty years. I think, as a result of the disillusionment in the revolution, we have turned to other mediums such as filmmaking and painting but also prose writing, which I think isn't such a terrible thing to have happened.

At least for me, as a young budding poet in Iran during the time of the revolution, poetry was all about very feverish emotions—not just ordinary "I feel blue" sort of emotion but passionate "Let's go make a fire" kind of emotion. And so, that was necessary for the sort of lyrical works created for many years in modern poetry of Iran. But at the same time, you can't do everything that you must do in literature by having these very intense emotions. You must take them off, so to speak, put them in a pot, put them on the stove, let it simmer, and kind of stir it and look at it, examine it, taste it, add spices to it, in order for it to process itself and become something else, which I think is the sort of work that if you're constantly writing these passionate pieces you would never allow yourself to do. I think prose writing gave us the opportunity to kind of say, okay, intense emotions are good and fine, but let's set them aside for a while, and let's look at this in a way that we have not looked at it before.

Do you think in Farsi when you write in English, before you write it down? What's going on in your mind?

When I first wrote the first draft of my book, *Journey from the Land of No*, I turned it in to my editor, and I think I had written it primarily with my Iranian head. My editor read it and after about a week, she called me up and said, "You know, Roya, this is very beautiful, but what does it mean?" It didn't offend me but I knew, as soon as she said that, that I had written that in the same way that we write poetry. You can get away with a great deal of ambiguity if you're writing poetry. But you can't get away with that in prose. And you can get away with even more of that if you write in Persian than if you write in English because, according to Strunk & White, in English you must be as simple and clear and concise as you can possibly be, and these are probably the rules that Persian prose writing would never recommend to you. We try to be complex and unclear and as ambiguous as possible. And so, I realized that somehow I have to marry these two aspects of my identity, my Iranian self with my American self, my drive for creating beautiful metaphors with my drive for being simple and concise and clear.

You went to Jewish school, and you describe in your book an incident when, the day after the revolution, you suddenly have a new woman principal who is a fundamentalist and a totalitarian. And she announces to the class that your Passover holiday is canceled. So, the young revolutionary Roya takes upon the task of leading a revolution against the revolution. Talk a little about that.

It was the first moment in my entire life that I was experiencing this Muslim/Jewish tension, because this principal who took over our school had come to convert us. She had come with an agenda to try to get us, a group of Jewish girls, to convert into Islam. It was the first moment that I realized that I was a Jewish person, and here was a fundamentalist Iranian who had other plans for me and wanted me to do something that I was unwilling to do. And I suppose the comedy in all of this is that it was also my first chance to apply the lessons of the Iranian revolution, which was to organize a rebellion. I was one among a few others who did that, and we had a Passover uprising. We wanted our full eight days of holiday, and we organized, we broke a few windows, and we stormed out of school, didn't come back until the end of the holiday, at which point she started to investigate and create files on every single one of us, which really haunted me until twelfth grade, when I left Iran. We paid dearly for that, but it was a great thing to do.

What was it like being a burgeoning writer in the midst of a revolution?

When I was young, I came home from school to find that my father had destroyed all of my books and diaries. It didn't take me years to forgive him. I forgave him the next day because the most dangerous period in the recent history of Iran were the years between 1981 and 1985, and in reality, he was just trying to protect me. Those were the years that the revolution was very young and a lot more merciless and brutal than it is today. The regime was quite insecure about its own existence, and therefore exercised far more brutality than it has ever since. I lived through a time when people who had sneakers or glasses on looked too much like somebody who was well-read—you know, glasses signaled erudition—and they were hauled away to prison because they didn't want book readers loose on the streets.

I really did know how dangerous it was to be keeping the sort of diaries that I was keeping and reading the sorts of books that I was reading. So, I knew sooner or later someone was going to destroy those things, whether it was the revolutionary guards storming our house and finding my stash, or my father—one of them, I knew, was finally going to do it. And of course, I'm glad that it was my dad as opposed to the revolutionary guards.

But you know, I suppose when you are fourteen, fifteen, sixteen, and seventeen, and these monumental things happen to you, of course they're traumatic. But outside of the trauma, if you're lucky enough to still have your brain intact and have some capacity intact to process things, you might arrive at some sense of insight and meaning. And I think up here in my factory, this was something that was happening over and over, encountering life in Iran on a daily basis. As a teenager, I was constantly looking at these experiences that should have completely obliterated and destroyed me, but I would just distance myself from it and ask, what does this mean, and what am I going to take away from this? I think what I took away from all of those experiences, including this moment of watching all the books I loved, every piece of writing that I'd ever created, burn, I realized that I was also thinking that I will do this for the rest of my life. I will continue to tell whatever perception of the truth I have. And so, in a way, it enabled me to continue to report for the rest of my life.

What was the source of that ability to draw strength?

I have to ask my therapist!

My role models were the poets I had fallen in love with: Ahmad Shamlou, Forugh Farrokhzad. I thought, "What would they do?" and my answer always was that they would certainly find a very beautiful and memorable way of capturing those experiences. And that's what I went on to do.

I'm curious what you have to say about freedom and how you think it can be nurtured by people who are outside a place that they have left. What is your take on that now, after all of this experience you acquired then and in America?

Well, up until the age of eighteen, my only experience of what a society was was my experience with Iran, which was really strongly shaped by my teenage years, which had taken place under the brutal rule of the post-revolutionary regime. When I came to the States, the sense that I was now free wasn't something that dawned on me the next morning when I woke up. Freedom is not something that you feel, like a shot of morphine into your veins, or a sugary drink that you suddenly gulp. In its best sense, it is something that you get to after several years. It's an awareness that sets in. It took several years until I realized that if I were to go back to Iran, I could never reprogram myself to live the way I had lived.

A year after I was in the United States, I met a boy in college, and I liked him, and we were on the street, and he wanted to hold my hand. I told him, "You can't hold my hand. We're on the street." And he said, "But this is New York," and I was like, "You can't hold my hand! We'll get arrested." And I knew how silly that sounded, even as I said it. I was intelligent enough to know that there were no revolutionary guards on the streets of Manhattan, but my emotional sense of who I was didn't know that. And so, it took many years until I stopped believing that someone was following me all the time. The day that I thought I could never go back and live in Iran again was the day that I realized that there was no way in hell I was willing to let anybody, let alone a seventeen-year-old wielding an AK-47 on his shoulder, ever stop me on the street to look into my bag or search me. I think that was the day I had a glimpse of what it meant to be truly free. I think about the absurdity of the fact that if I hadn't gotten on a plane sometime in August of 1984, my life would've been vastly different than it is today. And there is great injustice in that, and, of course, I think we have a responsibility to help not just with Iran but with every other injustice that goes on in the world. It's part of what we must do as global citizens.

Oliver Stone
April 17 and June 27, 1997

What would you identify as key to making a movie great?

There is the magic that occurs, very Frankensteinian, actually. The director is Dr. Frankenstein, if he's a good director. He is the doctor, playing, experimenting with the chemicals, and trying to bring them into some kind of collusion where they match, where they complement one another. You can have everybody very talented in your chemistry set, you can have the best cinematographer, the best designer, the best actors, the best script, and miss. I do think the scientist can screw up the experiment by misapplying the chemicals in the right quantities.

So we have the chemicals and the body parts, but there is that indefinable electric spark that transfers the gluten into life. When, where, angle of attack, trajectory, and just plain luck control the spark and whether it does or does not come to full, blooming life.

There is this magic thing, but based, I believe, on fundamental basics of good writing, drama, and character.

Among the body parts and chemicals: social breadth; galvanic excitement; burning commitment; a well-written if not great script; tolerant yet urgent direction; lighting that is both body and shadow and brings forth a rounded humanity; a camera that sees with the eye of *someone*, the god in the tapestry; actors that add the je ne sais quoi to the script, that added dimension of popping it off the page, making the audience feel they care more about these particular faces than people in their own life; and finally, a presence in time, a rightness to your moment, which is part marketing but mostly an indefinable moment of the zeitgeist—which in other words is "destiny." Each filmmaker has a destiny, each filmmaker of merit, I believe, has in him a few films that will strike that chord with destiny.

Lastly and above all, it is like sperm getting up the uterine canal and making it—that is to say, the odds are long, but if the desire for life is powerful, it will somehow emerge.

What is distinctive about movies as an art form?

Film is distinctive because it can cut through time with editing. Montage can create a three-dimensional space, great sensuality. There's an electrical thing about movies. And I've noticed it because I've written a lot of things that I've been able to direct and see how it works, and I am amazed constantly. Often something that will work on paper does not work when you see it on film. It sounds like a contradiction, but sometimes stuff that isn't so great on paper will be dynamite; it'll be electric because something— the look of an actor, the sensuality of a touch, the caress, an angle, the camera catches the light in a certain moment of time and it's just what I call magic. So those are elements that are very electric, stormy.

I always consider that when you tell a story on paper, it takes a certain amount of time to read. It has a given length, sort of a real time. But there's something about movies that always amazes me, their transcendence of time. There's a tremendous compression. It takes pages to read and to understand, but when you see it, it takes less than thirty seconds or sixty seconds to really get it. Because all of a sudden you're in history. You're in *Michael Collins*, for example; you're in Ireland, in Dublin in the 1920s, and you get it. You understand that all mankind has struggled in this same way, that there are classical verities that are true.

Movies tend to make optimistic the realities of life. Things are harsher, whether it's war in *Platoon* or caveman existence in *Quest for Fire* or history. In *A Man for All Seasons*, it looks very fine, but the people probably stank to holy heaven. They had terrible breath and terrible dentistry and doctoring, and people died, and there were all kinds of things like that that are not in movies. You don't smell the stink of the medieval ages. Greece, for example, has never been rendered honestly in its sensuality or its homosexuality. You don't see these truths in movies, to a large degree; it's very hard to get behind the canvas and go in. But you can, and in those moments that you do, that is when it comes alive. I hope, I really believe, that people know in their primal unconsciousness, which Jung talked about, there might be those moments that we all recognize from history. We feel that is right. The collective unconscious memory of the human race. In fear itself, the concept of fear that we all experience when we run into objects that frighten us. Fear may very well be a caveman fear of the predator, of the giant lizard chasing them—maybe that's what Steven Spielberg connects with so well in *The Lost World*.

We all have nightmares; we all have really horrifying fears. Mine may be being eaten by a giant snake or something. Perhaps I was in some ancient time. I'm terrible at horror movies, by the way. I get scared so easily. My son sits there, and he's amazed that I just can't watch some of that stuff that he watches. It's partly, probably, the fear of being eaten by a giant lizard.

Is that why, sometimes, there are scenes in a particular movie that people remember and they want to see them again and again?

You can in one second, in one frame, see something that will spark you as divine or genius. That's what great art is to me, the remembrance of it. You see, it can be a very great experience, but unless it somehow registers in your consciousness in some form inside the witness, it does not succeed on my terms. What is it that happens in movies, when you work so hard and all of a sudden, it just makes perfect sense in a twenty-second scene or a three-minute scene? That's the scene that everyone will remember.

Do different people see different things in those great scenes?

Absolutely. I believe in the blind man and the elephant here. I do believe that movies are subject to a million interpretations. Everyone is a critic; everyone can do it better. My father used to kid me. Whenever we saw movies when I was a kid, he said, "We could do it better, kiddo." Everyone is a movie director in their own mind.

Everyone has different reactions. I've met people who will go to a movie that I can't stand, and they say that they saw that movie ten times. There's something they like and identified in that movie, and I don't see it. Whereas the reverse is also true. So the movie critic thing is a dangerous thing because whose opinion is it? Consider the source. And also, how do we criticize a movie in terms of its achievement or acknowledge its objective? Do we say, "This movie, I may not agree with the objective, but this is what the objective is, and the filmmakers are trying to do this." That would be an honest criticism, it seems to me. Not, "How disgusting, this is a terrible subject." Or, "No one should be allowed to see this." There's this censorship going on, and that's not genuine criticism.

What happens to us when we watch movies?

I think you get in touch with your dream life, definitely. Or the collective dream life. Sometimes you're watching the eyes or the chemistry, or some aura that's coming off of the actor. That's why we have movie stars, I presume. It doesn't matter what they're in, people want to watch them. There's something, perhaps, primal about that. I guess what I'm talking about is something in the pre-brain, the dream-life brain of human beings.

I'm curious, did your experience in Vietnam make it inevitable that you would work with historical materials in your movies?

I think that anyone that lives through his life is going to end up dealing with his history. And his history sometimes inter-reacts with public events. And I think often in my life, my private sector has kind of come into collision with the public sector. And I'm looking back on my life, and I realize that the toll that I had to pay, or that my generation had to pay, to get through that period was unnecessary. It was unnecessary because it was all a series of expedient political decisions by Johnson and Nixon. And it changed the course of our lives and time forever. And it's hard to get back, because once you've lost that spot of innocence, perhaps, that you had when Kennedy got killed, and then Nixon performed his acts, his sinister designs, all that shaped us to the way we are now. We're all shaped by it. Life became what it did in America as a result of that, and that's what's fascinating. How do you avoid it? You make movies about historical periods so that you can avoid it. You can make, I guess, comedies where there's no social inter-reaction—although even *Ace Ventura: Pet Detective* posits an economic strata: that Jim Carrey has to exist in an economic level. He's never running out of money, even if he's a cable guy. In any film there's always a historical implication.

What is quite amazing about Platoon *and about* Born on the Fourth of July, *it's really the experience of the people, the soldiers who felt these decisions from the bottom up. Would you comment on that?*

That's probably, perhaps, one of the most significant things I learned over there was that there's sort of a perceived life that you get when you're raised. College students get it, you read it in books; your thinking is perceptions that have been taught to you. Very Pavlovian in a way. And when I got to the infantry, I really saw life smack up in front of my face. It was a noncerebral exercise. Six inches in front of my face—survive! You have to rely on your sense, your smell, your sight—all your senses come into play. Tactile. As a result, you never can get quite back. It's a question of what is authentic in your life, finally. What are your real feelings? How do you really feel about the way you are? How you are alive, what you are here for—once you ask yourself these questions (they're all Socratic ones, I guess), once you get into that arena, how do you go back into believing what "they" tell you?

You believe in recording the pain and the suffering as an entry point for the audience to experience a catharsis, and for the American people, in the case of your movies, to experience the trauma that was Vietnam.

You know, you don't set out to do that. You set out to be authentic to yourself and to put down the way that you feel it and you know it and you interpret it. And then others sometimes can key into it and get it. But a lot of people can see my movies, and they tell me they enjoy them or they don't, but they don't get into deeper analysis. Some people will say, "I was very moved by the picture," but may not even understand what feelings were working on them. *Natural Born Killers*, for example, evoked a very strong negative feeling in people. And I thought that that was the same thing to me as positive, because it's just a working out of feeling that they were regurgitating at the picture. People who saw *Born on the Fourth of July* said that they were healed because they felt that they were restructured. I don't know how true that is. But the films work at you on an emotional level, and you make of it what you can. And these movies are like Greek dramas. These are shards of the Greek vases that will endure. I hope movies endure.

Does a filmmaker's ability to tap into our feelings enable them to address a national experience?

Oh, I think so. I think that it happened in the Depression with the films of Frank Capra. At that time, of course, there was no television, and people really looked to movies. Maybe with David Wark Griffith earlier on, Chaplin and the stars they found—a longing was answered. But perhaps a lot of people wanted to believe. It's interesting that when economic times were the hardest, that's when many people embraced liberalism. But then Capra dealt very strongly with the fear of the ruling classes of losing control to this liberalism. I think that he was probably always criticized for his point of view, but I think he was beloved, in a way, until after the war. I think he kind of lost touch with his America, or America may have lost touch with itself after World War II, with the rise of Nixon and McCarthy. So there was no place for Capras. And it's interesting that the picture he did make, which was almost the great film of the '40s, *It's a Wonderful Life*, is really almost like a '30s movie, when you look at it. It's a harkening back to an optimism at a time when people cared about each other, and so forth. They don't in *It's a Wonderful Life*. The banks get bigger and bigger and practically ruin the man's life.

In some ways you're both radical and conservative. Your movies shake people up, but their goal seems to be also to restore the community to itself and its true story.

Movies have to make money; you've got to make them so they're exciting, they're gripping, people want to go see them. That's a very hard thing to do because people are more and more jaded, it seems, from the hours of television and the speed of modern life. So how do you make it exciting to tell the story? Well, first of all, you have to make the character strong so that people can follow that. And then hopefully that character can integrate with the background of the social situation that people can recognize. I'd love to do historical pictures more, but I don't know if I can. One of my fantasies in my life has been that I was granted access with a camera to go back in time, and to film the actual campaign of Alexander crossing into India through Iran and Persia. And I swear if I came back with that film and put it out there, that I would be attacked on all sides by the historians for having distorted the truth. I guarantee you, if I had been there, that that's what would have happened.

Let's talk about that, because you work between personal narrative and historical narrative. One runs into the problem, let's look at Nixon for example, where you told Nixon's personal story and created a character who's a Nixon for all time. On the other hand, you have historical "facts" in there that may be proven wrong. How do you want people to look at your movies in the future, distinguishing between the personal narratives and the historical facts?

Let's say I'm dead wrong about the facts, and time goes on. Fine. But you know I never put out a history; I put out a dramatic history. And that was labeled as such. I have the right to interpretation as a dramatist. I research. It's my responsibility to find the research. It's my responsibility to digest it and do the best that I can with it. But at a certain point, that responsibility will become an interpretation. And I will move on into closed-doors meetings, I will invent dialogue, I will create the fabric of a historical drama. I will come out with my interpretation. If I'm wrong, fine. It will become part of the debris of history, part of the give and take. You know, the movie will either work on its own terms, as a drama, in 2100, or it will also be perceived as having been historically perceptive. Shakespeare's dramas, thank God for him, lasted better as dramas than they did as history plays, didn't they? But that's not to say that they're wrong today.

Some have raised a concern that young people may not know history or read history, but instead see your movies and come to believe that they're absolutely true.

I hear that all the time. It's an amazingly, to me, superficial statement because first of all it implies that the teaching community has failed utterly to share a sense of history with their students. But secondly, movies have always existed to me as illusions. I've always accepted them as such. When I was a child, I'd see a movie, I took it for what it was, I enjoyed it. And if I believed it I would tend to be more interested in knowing more about it. *Lawrence of Arabia*—I went out and I bought *Seven Pillars of Wisdom*. When I saw *A Man for All Seasons*, I read Robert Bolt's book.

The world of analysis, the world of second opinion, reasserts itself very quickly. It's a natural given that if you're interested in a subject as the result of a movie, you will move on and learn more about it. If anything, if you can get somebody interested in something and get them excited, that's great. You should be praised for having opened the debate and having asked the right questions.

Every historical film that has been made has been called into question in some way. But generally speaking, the nonliteral person, the person who would enjoy a movie, would tend to view a movie as a first draft, would deepen his perception with reading around it. I mean, books are another medium. Books can go into more depth. But don't tell me for one second that a person who writes a book is more objective than a person who makes a movie. I don't buy that, because so many historians have axes to grind and have subjected their own judgment to their own perception and their own subjectivity and partisanship in some cases. It goes on all the time. And every history, in fact, is an omission of facts because there are too many facts to put in any history. Most historians will tell you that they make very discreet judgment as to what facts to omit in order to make their book into some shape, some length that can be managed.

I study history in order to give an interpretation. There are just too many facts to include in any historical work, if you have it all before you. I am not trying to be a historian and a dramatist: I'm a dramatist, a dramatic historian, or one who does a dramatic interpretation of history.

Let's talk about politics. How would you characterize your political philosophy?

In political terms, what is important is that you lived a life. I would vote for the man who's lived life, who's done different occupations, who's been out in the real world and struggled to make a living, struggled to raise a family, struggled with life as it exists. So I'd vote for experience, honest experience. I always feel comfortable with those type of leaders and with the Roman political philosophy. I'm very worried about professional politicians such as Mr. Clinton or Richard Nixon, in a way. I think experience will teach you a combination of liberalism and conservatism. We have to be progressive, and at the same time we have to retain values. We have to hold on to the past as we explore the future. It's a very delicate balance. That's the nature of existence. I was very influenced by Edmund Burke. So I'm not the dyed-in-the-wool liberal leftist that is painted by people who want to simplify and categorize me. I don't believe in left or right. I don't believe in liberal or conservative. I believe in both.

The "great man in history": do you subscribe to that theory?

I'm of two minds. I do believe there are leaders who are like lightning and they come along and they lead. The Lincolns of the world, the Alexander the Greats, they do exist. They have existed. Julius Caesar. They are men made for the moment. De Gaulle comes to mind most recently. Perhaps of all the politicians I've lived through, I'd say Kennedy.

At the same time, I'm of the mind that, like John Steinbeck said in his screenplay of *Zapata*: there is no one strong leader who can be held hostage or killed; each person is a leader in himself. It's because the people have the strength. Steinbeck paid homage to that in *The Grapes of Wrath*, too, which I think was really brilliant, the Tom Joad idea of everyone being on the move, the whole country, you can't stop it. I love that idea.

In your movies the other presence is what, in Nixon, *the young lady at the Lincoln Memorial calls "the beast," which I take to be "the system," the way it all hangs together, and which can grind people down.*

I do see "the beast" in its essence as the System, with a capital "S," which grinds the individual down to meaninglessness, Camus's insignificance. It's a system of checks and balances that drives itself from

1. the power of money and markets;
2. state power, government power;
3. corporate power, which is probably greater even than state power;
4. the political process or election through money, which is therefore in tow to "the system"; and,
5. the media, which mostly protects the status quo and their ownerships and interests like Doberman pinschers.

That would cover, I believe, all the beasts.

In this brief discussion, you've talked about what you do and your role as that of an artist. You're a storyteller, you're a historian in a way. And you're involved in a kind of a healing process in society. These roles—artist, healer, historian—do they conflict as you make a movie?

I don't think so. Probably at the very beginning of time we were all in this tribe, right? And we all sat around the cave, and some guy would tell the stories, you know. Homer would get there, and he'd say, well there was this great battle, and he did that, that family did this. And probably half of it was bullshit. But it went down into the history books because that was the first dramatic historian. Sophocles, Aeschylus, Euripides, they were all interpreting the various kings and rulers of their time. Socrates was interpreted by Plato. So where do we cross the line? Where do we get our first histories? All our histories have been debated. The interpretive battle. Now, there are facts, yes; there are memos; but even on paper, people are very careful about what they write. I think that historians underestimate that. Because I think historians are themselves subject to vanity and affectation.

What should be the role of a filmmaker in society, given all we've said about film and so on, and its capacity for dealing with historical materials?

I don't see that there is a defined role because that suggests obligation, and I don't think that the type of people who take this up would be in service or be "class president." People who are dramatists, at least I can speak for myself, tend to be rebellious, tend to go against the grain. Sometimes it can be the role, like in Indian tribes, of the guy who walks backwards. There's a special name in shamanistic terminology, the *heyoka*, the man or woman who is certainly interested in liberation for himself or herself first, but then that person perhaps can help others to be liberated. The raising of consciousness. Attacking Authority with a big "A"; not just being an attacker and a contrarian, but creating a body of work unto itself which is positive in itself. It's creative.

My dad always used to say to me, "They don't need all these schools. They should just live their life, get there and open their school under a tree, and if anyone wants to go and listen to them, they go and they listen to them. They'll find their own way."

What is the role of the movies in preparing us for the future?

Movies can really be a creative machinery. They can evoke a spiritual life, a higher ideal, models that are both negative and positive, or a paradigm for society to function by. That is, not just a comic book, but a mirror. I always think that life is more complicated than any movie. Life is chaos.

I'm waiting for the dramatist who will really capture the complexity of life. As great as they are, movies are all limited. A work of drama is inherently confined. Our lives are long, long—years and years.

Kenzaburo Oe
April 16, 1999

Where were you born, and where did you grow up?

I was born in 1935 in a small island of the Japanese archipelago. I must emphasize that the war between the U.S. and Japan began when I was six years old. And then at ten years old, I saw the war finished. So my childhood was during the wartime. That is a very important thing.

Were you the first writer in your family?

This is a very delicate problem. My family lived [on that island] for two hundred years or more. There are plenty of journalists among my ancestors. So if they had wanted to publish, I think they could have been the first writers. But unfortunately, or fortunately, they didn't publish, so I am the first man who published what I wrote; but my mother was always saying, "You men of our family are always writing the same thing."

What books did you read as a young person?

I didn't read many books before nine years old. I was fascinated by my grandmother's telling of tales. She would talk about almost everything about my family and my district, so it was enough for me. I didn't need any books at that time. But one day, there was some discussion between my grandmother and my mother. And my mother got up very early in the morning, and she packed one kilogram of rice—we ate rice—and she went to the small city of our island through the forest. Very late at night she returned. She gave a small doll to my sister, and some cakes for my younger brother, and she took out two pocket books. Tome one, tome two. I found Mark Twain's *Huckleberry Finn*. I didn't know the name of Mark Twain, the name of Tom Sawyer or Huckleberry Finn, but my mother said—and this was the first talk between my mother and me about literature, and almost the last talk. She said, "This is the best novel for a child or for an adult. Thus your father said." (The year before my father had passed away.) "I brought this book for you, but the woman who made the barter with the rice between us said, 'Be careful. The author is American. Now the war between the U.S. and Japan is going on. The teacher will take the book from your son. [Tell him] that if your teacher asks you who is the author, you must answer that Mark Twain is the pseudonym of a German writer.'"

You also read, according to your Nobel Prize speech, a book called The Wonderful Adventures of Nils.

Yes, a very famous Swedish female author [Selma Lagerlöf], wrote that book, a book for the children of Sweden to study the atlas of their country. [In this book] a kind of trickster is going through all of the country on the back of a small goose.

And one line in particular stood out for you. When the wanderer in the book returns home, he says, "I am a human being again."

Yes, the hero has become a very small boy through fairy magic, and he couldn't believe in the possibility that he would become an ordinary sized human being [again]. When he returns to his house, he secretly comes in the kitchen. His father finds him. Then a very kind, humane passion occurs in the hero; then very naturally he grows to ordinary man's size. Then he shouts, "Oh Mother, again I am a human being."

That was also very important for me. So in my childhood only two books are dear, and I also continued to read them again and again. I remember almost all of the words of those two books.

You have called yourself a writer of the periphery. In part, you are referring to your origins, but you also mean more than that. Explain what you mean.

I was born on a small island, and Japan [itself] is on the periphery of Asia. That is very important. Our very eminent colleagues believe Japan is the center of Asia. They think secretly that Japan is the center of the world. I always say that I am a writer of the periphery—periphery district, periphery Japan of Asia, and periphery country of this planet. With pride I say this. Literature must be written from the periphery toward the center, and we can criticize the center. Our credo, our theme, or our imagination is that of the peripheral human being. The man who is in the center does not have anything to write. From the periphery, we can write the story of the human being, and this story can express the humanity of the center, so when I say the word periphery, this is a most important creed of mine.

In A Healing Family, *you quote Flannery O'Connor when she speaks of the novelist's* habit, *the accumulated practice. What is that?*

At first, the word *habit* is not a good word for an artist. So I must use the word *habit* precisely according to the meaning of Flannery O'Connor.

The *habit* is this: when as a writer I continue to write every day for ten or thirty years, then gradually the habit of a writer is molded in myself. I cannot be conscious about it. Or I cannot be unconscious. But anyway, I have a habit to be reborn as a writer. So if I find myself in a crisis that I have never experienced, I can be born, or I can write something, by the power of the habit.

Even a soldier or a farmer or a fisherman can be reborn by the power of the habit when he meets the greatest crisis of his life. We human beings are born and reborn, and [if] we create our habits as human beings, then I think we can face [a crisis] even though we have not experienced it before. That must be the notion of Flannery O'Connor, and I am a student of Flannery O'Connor.

The birth of your son was the turning point in finding your voice as a writer. You have written that "Twenty-five years ago, my first son was born with brain damage. This was a blow, to say the least. Yet as a writer, I must acknowledge the fact that the central theme of my work throughout much of my career has been the way my family has managed to live with this handicapped child."

When I was twenty-eight years old, my son was born. When I was twenty-eight years old, I was a writer, a rather famous writer on the Japanese scene, and I was a student of French literature. And I was talking in the voice of Jean-Paul Sartre or [Maurice] Merleau-Ponty. I was always speaking about everything of this work. But when I found out one night that my son was born with very big damage in his brain, I wanted to find encouragement, so I wanted to read my book—that was the first time I read my book, [the only] book that [I'd] written up to that date—and I found out a few days later that I cannot encourage myself through my book; [therefore] no one can be [encouraged] by my work. So I thought, "I am nothing and my book is nothing." So I was depressed very strongly; then I was asked by a journalist who was editing a political magazine in Japan to go to Hiroshima, the place the atomic bomb [had been] dropped. There in Hiroshima, in that year the peace movement—the anti–atomic bomb movement—was meeting, and in those assemblies there was a big fight between the Chinese group and the Russian group. And I was the only independent journalist there. So I criticized both of them.

I found the hospital of the Hiroshima survivors, and there I found the very great Dr. [Fumio] Shigeto. In conversation with Shigeto and the patients in the hospital, I gradually found that there is something that encouraged me, so I wanted to follow this sense that there is something. So I returned to Tokyo and went to the hospital where my [newborn] son was, and talked to the doctors about rescuing my son. Then I began to write about Hiroshima, and this was the turning point of my life. A kind of rebirth of myself.

What you observed somehow moved you to another plane in dealing with your own personal tragedy?

Yes. Shigeto said to me, "We cannot do anything for the survivors. Even today we don't know anything about the nature of the illness of the survivors. Even today, so shortly after the bombing, we don't know anything, but we did what we could do. Every day a thousand people dead. But amidst the dead bodies, I continued. So, Kenzaburo, what can I do except *that*, when they need our aid? Now your son needs you. You must find out that no one on this planet needs you except your son." Then I understood. I returned to Tokyo and began to do something for my son, for myself, and for my wife.

Your novel about the birth of your handicapped son is called A Personal Matter, *and your writings on Hiroshima are collected in* Hiroshima Notes. *You write in the latter: "When the Hiroshima doctors pursue the A-bomb calamity in their imaginations, they are trying to see more deeply and more clearly the depth of the hell into which they too are caught. There is a pathos in this dual concern for self and others; yet it only adds to the sincerity and the authenticity that we sense." You are saying that in seeing this duality in the doctor, you were helped to see the complexity of the dilemma of Bird, the protagonist in your novel.*

Yes. Until then, my little theme was a duality or ambiguity of human beings. [This concept] came from existentialism in France. I think I found out the true duality and how I can be so-called authentic. But the word "authenticity" must not be so frozen in my case. I used the word from Jean-Paul Sartre. Today I would use another word. It is very simple. I wanted to be strictly an upright man. The Irish poet Yeats said in his poem, "The young man who stands straight." Straightforwardness. Erect. This kind of young man that I wanted to be, but then I used the word "authentic."

Lionel Trilling wrote that confessing to your feelings is one of the most courageous and valuable things a writer could do. That's what you did in A Personal Matter.

I wanted to do so. At the time I didn't think of the value of being an upright man. I [felt I] must write about myself. Why not? I cannot be reborn, and my son cannot be reborn, I felt, [if I don't]. So when I was by the sea, [I decided that] I must rescue myself and I must rescue my son. So I wrote that book, I think.

Your son became a composer. Your family—your wife, your children, and yourself—in caring for him over time identified his ability to communicate. Tell us how that came out.

Until my son was four or five years old, he didn't do anything to communicate with us. We thought that he cannot have any sense of the family. So he looked very, very isolated—a pebble in the grass. But one day, he was interested in the voice of a bird from the radio. So I bought discs of the wild birds of Japan. I made a tape of fifty specimens of birds—birdcalls. There are the birdcalls and a very flat voice, a woman announcer, says the names of the birds. "Tada-dada," then: "*Nightingale.*" "Tada-da." "*Sparrow.*" "This is nightingale; this is sparrow." We continued to listen to that tape for three years. During those three years, when we played the birds' songs, my son became very quiet. So it was needed to make him quiet. My wife must do her work, and I must do my work. So with the bird voices, we three lived on.

In the summer when he was six years old, I went to our mountain house, and while my wife was cleaning our small house, I was in the small forest with my son on my shoulders. Nearby there is a small lake. A bird sang, [one of a pair]. Suddenly a clear, flat voice said, "It is a water rail." Then I shook. Utter silence in the forest. We were silent for five minutes, and I prayed for something, there on my head. I prayed, "Please, the next voice of that bird and please next the remarks of my son, if that was not my phantom or dream." Then after five minutes, the wife of that bird sang. Then my son said "It's a water rail." Then I returned to my house with my son and talked to my wife.

For a long time, we waited for another voice, but there was not any voice during the night. We didn't sleep. But in the early morning, a small sparrow came to a small tree in front of our window. He made a small sound, and my son said, "It's a sparrow." Then everything began, and we played the sound of a bird, and my son would answer. We made many recordings of birds, even the birds of the U.S. and Europe. My son answered very quietly and very correctly if he listened to the name of a bird two or three times. We began to communicate by the word.

"Pooh-chan"—my son was called Pooh-chan, from *Winnie-the-Pooh*—"what is the bird?" [He would answer after I played the tape.] "Sparrow." "Pooh-chan, what do you want to listen to?" He thinks, [and says,] "Water rail." "Nightingale." Then I would play it.

Then, we began to communicate, and my son was accepted for a school for the mentally retarded. They are always playing FM broadcasts of Handel, Bach. Then my son began to listen to the music. After he is concerned with the music, he suddenly forgot almost all the names of the voices of the birds. When my son was sixteen, he had a very strong fit, and he lost the sight of both eyes. Through each eye he can see, but not through both. So he cannot look at the piano and the musical score. So he makes a missed note, and that is very uncomfortable for him. So he gave up the piano, and his mother taught him how to write music. In five weeks, he began to write the music of Bach with a pencil. At first, very simple music. In a year he began to compose his music by himself.

Now he has two compact discs which you were able to buy in Berkeley on Telegraph Avenue.

Yes, I went to Tower Records, and I bought some compact discs by Piazzolla. I checked [at the record store] and found two of my son's compact discs and played them this morning.

Your son has fulfilled the dreams of Nils—riding on the wings of birds or, in his case, the sounds of birds.

Yes, so besides [learning from] the birds [like Nils], my son can say, "Yes, I am a human being, I am a man." Beside the discs of my son, I thought, "I am a man."

In A Healing Family *you write that your son's music has shown you that in the very act of expressing himself, there is "a healing power, a power to mend the heart," and you go on to say, "For in the music or literature we create, though we come to know despair—that dark night of the soul through which we have to pass—we find that by actually giving it expression we can be healed and know the joy of recovering; and as these linked experiences of pain and recovery are added one to another, layer upon layer, not only is the artist's work enriched but its benefits are shared by others."*

I add something to my comment there. After writing that essay, I received many questions. And critics said, "Oe has become very conservative now. He is a very quiet man; he says, his [son's] music healed him, and he can be healed by the compact disc, himself. That is very negative and very conservative," they said. I must answer that. I don't say "to be healed" in Japanese. The verb "heal" must be used actively. I heal myself. A human being is healed by something. That is a very positive deed of human beings. When I listen to the music of my son, I don't experience any passive deed. I feel I am doing something positive with my son. We are looking out at the same direction. So if someone feels he is healed by the music of my son, even then I believe someone is looking in the same direction as my son. So he is positively healing himself with my son.

My son's music is a model of my literature. I want to do the same thing.

Do you believe that a writer chooses his themes or do they come upon him?

Nadine Gordimer has written that we don't choose a theme or a situation or story. The theme chooses us; that is the goal of the writer. The time, the days choose us as a writer. We must respond to our time. From my experience, I can say the same thing as Nadine Gordimer: I didn't choose the story of a handicapped son, or we didn't choose the theme of a handicapped boy's family. I wanted to escape from that if it were possible, but something chose me to write about it. My son chose me. That is one definite reason I continue to write.

You write in another essay, "The fundamental style of my writing has been to start from my personal matters and then link it up with society and the state and the world."

I think I am doing my works to link myself, my family, with society—with the cosmos. To link me with my family to the cosmos, that is easy, because all literature has some mystic tendency. So when we write about our family, we can link ourselves to the cosmos. But I wanted to link myself and my family with society. When we link ourselves to society, then we don't write very personal matters, but we are writing an independent novel.

You say in A Healing Family *that the lessons you learned in making a handicapped child an active part of your family were an example of how a society at large should treat the handicapped and how society should learn from them. In essence, one can create a healing society by creating a healing family.*

Yes, I hope so, but I don't want to emphasize the role of the family of the handicapped boy, I don't want to emphasize individuality. Always, when we linked our individual family to society, [it] has social value; if not, I think, we can only write very personal matters through our experience. When I named my first novel about my son *A Personal Matter*, I believe I knew the most important thing: there is not any personal matter; we must find the link between ourselves, our "personal matter," and society.

What does a Japanese writer need to add to the discourse in Japan?

In Japan, we wanted to create a truly new national attitude after our defeat in the war. For years, we wanted to create democracy, democratic man, a democratic country. I think we gave up. Fifty years have passed. Now there is an atmosphere of anti-democracy in Japan. So today, I feel very ambiguous. A dangerous atmosphere of nationalism is coming in our society. So now I want to criticize this tendency, and I want to do everything to prevent the development of fascism in Japanese society.

Do your novels and humane themes that you focus on contribute to the climate of ideas so that fascism becomes less of a possibility?

When I was in Hiroshima, Dr. Shigeto said, "When you can't think of anything to do, you must do something." So I think if I can have some power to influence young intellectuals, we can organize a different power. Because today's crisis is one of unconscious feeling of ultranationalism in Japan. A very big feeling, atmosphere. If we write about it precisely, if we attack it, then young intellectuals can become conscious of this feeling. It is very important in the beginning. I want to ask young men of Japan, the young intellectuals, to confront their reality.

Several of your works focus on youth; for example, Nip the Buds, Shoot the Kids, *on youth gangs where there are no values and the town has evacuated. What special role do young people have to play in shaping our ideas about the world?*

In the end of my new novel, my hero is creating a new charity, not Christian, not Buddhist, but doing something for the souls of the assembled young men. One day the leader reads a Bible in front of the people, the letter of Ephesians. In Ephesians there are two words: "New Man." Jesus Christ has become a New Man on the cross. We must take off the old coat of the old man. We must become the New Man. Only the New Man can do something, so you must become a New Man. My hero has no program about the future, but he believes that we must create New Man. Young men must become New Man. Old man must mediate to create New Man. That is my creed. I am always thinking about youth's role in Japan.

How should young people prepare to define a New Man?

First, I hope young men are upright, independent. Second, I hope they have imagination. The imagination is not to accept the other's image but to create our own image and more precisely to reform the imagination which was given to us. To be upright and to have an imagination: that is enough to be a very good young man.

You say of Dr. Shigeto, "Without too much hope or too much despair, he had simply dealt with the suffering as best he could," and you go on to say, "He was truly an authentic man."

My professor was a specialist of French humanism, and he always said to me "What is humanism? It is to be without too much hope and also too much despair today." Not too much hope, not too much despair. That is the model type of a humanist today. That was my teacher's comment, and I said that to Mr. Shigeto, and he said, "Yes, I know that through my life."

HUMAN RIGHTS
AND THE LAW

The law can be a powerful instrument for achieving justice, defining moral behavior, and responding to governments that violate the law. Tools of law—from precedent and tradition to international treaties and the marshaling of evidence—can ensure the dignity and the rights of the individual or expose the abuse of power disguised as lawful government action. Justice Albie Sachs used the law to fight apartheid in South Africa and through that struggle witnessed firsthand the triumph of humanity. Nobel Laureate Shirin Ebadi discovered in the law a vehicle for the struggle against the excesses of the Islamic Revolution in Iran, especially in its violations of the rights of women and children. With the law as his weapon, international lawyer Philippe Sands awakened the international community and the U.S. Congress to the costs of the Bush administration's torture regime.

Albie Sachs

Justice Albie Sachs is a leader in the struggle for human rights in South Africa and a freedom fighter in the African National Congress. Twice he was detained without trial by the security police under the Apartheid regime. He describes his detention in *The Jail Diary of Albie Sachs*, which was made into a play in London. He is also the author of numerous books on issues of gender, the law, and human rights, and most recently he wrote *The*

Soft Vengeance of a Freedom Fighter, which is an account of his recovery from an attempt by the South African security forces to kill him. He now serves on the South African Constitutional Court.

Shirin Ebadi

Shirin Ebadi is the 2003 Nobel Peace Prize winner. An Iranian human rights lawyer, she teaches at Tehran University and is the author of *Iran Awakening* with Azadeh Moaveni. Her Iranian legal publications include works on the rights of women, the rights of children, and the rights of refugees.

Philippe Sands

Philippe Sands, QC, is a barrister at Matrix Chambers and Professor of Law and Director of the Centre of International Courts and Tribunals at University College London. He has appeared before many international courts, including the European Court of Justice, the International Court of Justice, and the Special Court for Sierra Leone. He is the author of *Lawless World* and *Torture Team: Rumsfeld's Memo and the Betrayal of American Values*.

Albie Sachs
February 2, 1998

Tell us a little about your background, your parents and your family.

Well, I grew up in South Africa, and my first memories are of running on the beach in a very beautiful part of Cape Town called Clifton, and being told "your father's coming," and seeing big white tennis shoes. That was my father. He and my mother were separated at the time. I looked up, up, up. Way up there was a head, a body talking to me. He was a big figure. He was a trade union leader, Solly Sachs, very controversial. Always involved in scraps. He fought the bosses, he fought the government, he fought my mother, he fought his second wife. And when he ran out of everyone else, he fought his children. At his funeral in the 1970s, in London, one of the speakers there said, "And I'm quite sure if God exists, Solly's up there arguing with him right now."

So I grew up with that kind of a background. A very strong dad, remote; and my mother would be the one to type up the minutes of the meeting while the men were playing cards. She was very much also in the struggle. Very modest about her own abilities and capacities, but always doing a lot of hard work, getting things done, looking after two little kids. And surrounded by people who were strong personalities, vivacious, interesting, laughing. Many of them women on their own, sometimes with children, sometimes without. Ideas counted for everything.

I didn't know when my birthday was (to this day I don't care for birthdays), but my dad sent me a little card: "Dearest Albert, on your sixth birthday, many happy returns and may you grow up to be a soldier in the fight for liberation." That was during the Second World War.

So politics and the struggle were in your blood from the earliest ages.

Yes. I wouldn't even call it politics: it was living. There'd be strikes on, people were painting posters, and things were animated. There was lots of expectation and hope about the future. People mattered. There would be indignation about, "the bosses did this" or "the government did that" or "isn't it terrible." And of course we followed the Second World War with very great interest. There would be maps up on the wall with little flags to show where the Nazi troops were advancing, where they were defeated in Eastern Europe and North Africa. So it was a world of public events, a world where the public and the private interacted a lot. My dad might get into the newspaper for something that happened that involved him. A very lively, vivacious, active world—that's my basic memory. And me being a dreamy child— in the school reports it would say, "Albert is a dreamy child," and I'm a dreamy adult now. I think these things last with you right through life.

What books influenced you in those days?

The books I remember are of two kinds, the fairy stories and the legends, particularly those involving trials. The trial by ice, people climbing over mountains. The endurance and love. And later on in my life when I was in solitary confinement, I would think back much more on those books, the books of fairy stories from childhood, than I would on the great literary classics.

I just remember that sensation of pushing and pushing, and withstanding the pressures on you to succumb in some of these stories. And winning through. That would be one set of stories. The others were stories about the war, and about pilots who went up into the skies and shot down Messerschmitts. There was one chap called Rockfist Rogan who would go up in a plane, shoot down a few Nazi planes. And he was a boxer as well as a pilot. He would knock out the German heavyweight champion, steal a plane, and fly back to Britain. It was that kind of male heroics that played quite a big role as well in my imagination.

How did your parents address the problems of Apartheid when you were a child?

I wouldn't say they addressed it. We were different. We lived differently. My mother worked as a secretary for Moses Kotane. He was a very prominent African leader in the African National Congress and South African Communist Party, and she had taught him at night school. He used to say, "Well, Rae taught me to read and write and now I'm her boss," and he found it very amusing. But what was interesting for me was that she would say, "Shhh, keep quiet! Uncle Moses is coming." She had to get something ready for "Uncle Moses," and then he would come in. So I grew up in an atmosphere where it was absolutely normal for a white woman to be working for an African man, to have great respect for him. And he was a very admired figure. It was important when this leading political figure was coming to the house—she would be excited that he was actually coming to pick up some typing from our house.

What about ideology and your parents' political values, beyond just being involved in the struggle?

Well, the ideology, I would say, was much more what life was about, and you lived for making the world a decent place and for liberating humanity or being part of the process of humanity being liberated. It wasn't a concrete, very specific kind of a thing and I certainly didn't get any didactic lessons from them. But it was the example and the things that they thought were important that really mattered.

My subsequent approach to human rights and human dignity, and what matters, must have been colored by my experience of growing up in a home where these values were not simply abstract ideals. It was about people and about the things that diminished people and the things that ennobled people.

As a young person, you and your friends were imbued with the notion that conflict was something that would be out there and you would have to endure.

It was a world in which ideas mattered, in which you put yourself on the line, in which you believed questions of destiny and existence were fundamentally important. It was belonging to a community of people giving each other a lot of support and always anticipating the net result would be that one day the State is going to crack down, one day there's danger, and would we be able to withstand the trials?

Conflict was there. Life involved conflict, and then how did you relate to that? It could be international or local. The Rosenberg executions were something that excited the community that I was in a lot and we protested. We felt it was awful. The American connection was quite strong; Paul Robeson was a big hero. We loved his voice, and his picture would be up on our walls. But it was mainly focusing on Apartheid, South Africa, oppression, the pass laws, the victimization of people because of their skin color, their lack of opportunities. That was our main focus, but we liked to feel we were part of a worldwide struggle for freedom everywhere.

At the time you were pursuing a degree in the law and then went into civil rights work?

At university itself I was very torn. It was a five-year course; we had some outstanding constitutional lawyers. It was a time of constitutional crisis in South Africa, cases being litigated. This was the early 1950s.

I felt intrigued but alienated—all this is book stuff; it's ideas, very, very abstract. And by then I was involved in study classes in the townships, and we would meet. I'd have to speak quietly, at night. They asked me to be there. Frequently, it would be just by candle. And it's something very extraordinary, that when you only see people's eyes and cheekbones lit up by candlelight and you speak to them, it's like the face is so strong and the human experience is so strong. To me this was the real world, and this was real knowledge. This was what really mattered. And I turned my back on all that stuff on the campus, at the university—it was literally high up on the hill, and the townships were down on the plains. Years later, when we had to draft up a new constitution, it was actually by linking up the vitality of the lived experiences of the people (who are now educating me) with the grand concepts and ideas that my law professors had been teaching me. When they came together, we got our new constitution. It was important for me to see that the one set of knowledge is not opposed to the other set; they're not inherently antagonistic. That, in fact, the name of the game, if you like, for the lawyer, the constitutionalist, the scientist, is to link up the two.

And navigate that apparent chasm, that, in fact, the two enrich each other.

That's the point. It's not even navigating through the shoals; it's finding the streams flowing together and creating a new kind of a turbulence.

So you did become a lawyer, a civil rights lawyer. Tell us about that.

I was extremely ambivalent about it. I loved striding into court wearing my gown—"Advocate Sachs." I loved the cut and thrust, the parry, the tension. The judges asking you questions, cross-examining the witnesses, strategizing. It was engrossing. It was interesting. And I hated it! We were mercenaries. You could be employed by anybody just to argue for them. It didn't have that core sense of justice and right. So that was all kind of mixed in. The worst part wasn't even that; that's intrinsic to the legal profession anywhere in the world. The law was being used, the courts were being used, to oppress people, not to protect people. The judges were white, the police who commanded things were white, the prosecution was white, the laws were made by whites. And the majority of people whom I defended in criminal matters or who appeared in civil matters were black, and they had no say in the law. So it was injustice through law. And we had to follow the protocol and say, "Yes, my lord," "No, my lord."—the gymnastics we had to do even in terms of address. When an African woman, elderly, grizzled hair, who had seen a lot in life would be called "Rosie," and a young white woman would be called "Mrs. Stander" or "Mrs. Smith." If you called the African woman "Mrs. Shelbelila" when the judge just called her "Rosie," it would be like a slap in his face and your client might suffer. You're provoking, you're creating atmosphere. So you had to do an enormous amount of jumping around, acrobatics, not to buy into this whole Apartheid linguistics that could be so demeaning, but not to be too confrontational on the other hand.

When did you first affiliate with the African National Congress?

Basically it was while I was a law student. I sat on a seat marked "Non-Whites Only" during the Defiance of Unjust Laws campaign. We had sit-ins. We had civil disobedience in the early 1950s, before the wonderful movement here in the United States. And I led a small batch of whites, mainly students, into the post office, supporting the struggle of blacks who were denied equal facilities or integrated facilities throughout the country. They wouldn't arrest us. It was kind of embarrassing. We sat there trying to be heroic and militant, and the cops wouldn't arrest us. They whipped off any blacks who sat on seats marked for whites only. Eventually we were arrested. I was taken to court. The magistrate saw I was seventeen and said, "Oh, a juvenile." From then on my name wasn't mentioned. He asked if my mother was in court. She nervously stood up, and he said, "I'm sending you home to the care of your mother." And that was a terrible slap in the face for this young militant revolutionary, being sent into the care of his mother. So that was my first act, my first confrontation if you like, with the state, while I was still a law student.

Let's review this experience of detention and the subsequent book that emerged, The Prison Diary of Albie Sachs. *What were you arrested for, and how long were you in solitary confinement?*

I was detained under what was called the Ninety-Day law. You didn't have to be given a reason. It was enough for the security police to have a suspicion that you had information which could help them in their security inquiries. Then they could lock you up for ninety days, in solitary confinement, without access to lawyers, family, anybody else. At the end of the ninety days, I was about to be released. I packed everything. I was going out. I was extremely suspicious; it was the hardest period of my life by far. And before I could reach the front door of the discharge office, a cop was there. He put out his hand, shook my hand, and said, "I'm placing you under arrest again." And I went back inside. I had to unpack the few things that I had, sign the property receipt again for my watch, and back into my cell. So I spent another seventy-eight days. It was 168 days in solitary.

And the name of the game here by the authorities was to break your will and, as you say, to destroy your personality.

To destroy you, to get information from you, to get you to become a witness against others, and to terrorize other people knowing that this might happen to them.

And you survived this. In The Prison Diary of Albie Sachs, you seem to be saying that you had to come to terms with who you are. You say, "I am conciliatory rather than defiant. My manner is gentle, my demeanor quiet." On the other hand, you weren't going to cooperate with the authorities.

I was very worried. I felt a good revolutionary is angry, wants to storm the Bastille, wants to kill the oppressors. And I found I didn't have that sort of emotion. I thought there was something wrong with me, that I needed psychoanalysis or something to "let real anger come out." But that's just the way it was. I didn't hate the guards. I didn't want to pick up a dagger and plunge it into their back. Even with the people questioning me, interrogating me, I never had that immediate, feral, personal kind of anger. And in the end I decided, well, that's just the way I am. I might mention that amongst my greatest heroes, and I did reading afterwards (not heroes, I don't even like the term "heroes" and I hate being called a hero), the people I identified with very much were Gandhi—his description of his trials, what he did in jail— and the suffragettes. I love the suffragettes. And I think I loved them very much because they made a struggle with just themselves. They went to jail, and they resisted force feeding, and they didn't go out to kill the enemy and to storm and to break down. It wasn't physical in that sense. All they had was themselves and their will and their determination and their courage, and a sense of personal dignity and beauty. I identify very strongly with them.

You had very human conversations with your guards, with the commanders of the facilities, and in the end, without accepting their values, you accepted their humanity.

Yes. And not only at the end; it was right from the beginning. For me it was very important to have human contact with somebody. I needed it. The one station commander used to shout and swear and was extremely unpopular with all the persons underneath him. The only person he could speak to and get a hearing from was me. But it suited me down to the ground; it was breaking the silence. And some of the things he said were quite extraordinary and astonishing, but again maybe it was the writer in me. I would see someone sitting there—that's his worldview, that's how he sees things, that's what makes him tick. He had as much integrity, if you like, within his frame as I had within mine.

But in the end, human action did matter in this situation.

Yes, I nearly gave in on several occasions. If they had got their timing right, maybe I wouldn't be sitting here now, maybe I would have collapsed, maybe I would have cooperated with them. Maybe I would have been so demoralized I would have been just another victim, sad, trying to rebuild my life somewhere else. But they never got the timing right.

Subsequently, almost twenty years later, you were the victim of a bomb attack by the South African security forces. You almost lost your life, and you describe your recovery in The Soft Vengeance of a Freedom Fighter. *One thing you say in that extraordinary work is "I have to use my imagination," talking now about the process of your recovery; "this is where a certain measure of courage comes in perhaps. Not physical bravery but the courage of conception."*

This whole theme of courage has been with me since I was a kid, and courage for children, young boys, growing up in South Africa was military courage. We had the prototype of this brave man who would kill, risk being killed, and expressed courage in a physical sense. Afterwards that was a thing that we all had to do battle with in all sorts of ways, a very damaging, narrowing, inhibiting concept of courage.

Here now I'm getting an enormous amount of love and support, and so on, from all over the world, from people close to me and from people I've never heard of, because I'm the guy who survived a bomb. I'm so courageous, look at what I'm doing, sitting up in bed, writing, all the rest. And I didn't feel that was courage. To me, whatever courage meant, it didn't mean that. Courage was something where you pit yourself against something else, where you have to make decisions, where you are aware of the challenge. And you hang in there, and you see your way through. I think a lot of these great heroes of my childhood were psychopaths. I don't know if that's courage. It's problematic. Sometimes courage is perverse; you do things because you're driven. And it's not real, clean, open courage. But the courage I was speaking about in that excerpt would have been not dramatic, not visually available and there to be seen, not fitting into the prototype of this person who's strong and who stands up to something even stronger. It would be in the head. It would be the courage of thinking something through, of developing an idea, of following it through, and not being lazy.

You were ambivalent about the extent to which you were being made a hero. You were willing to do that for the movement, for the anti-apartheid struggle, but really that was not helpful to you.

I didn't like it then, I don't like it now. It's a label; it's an imposition. I sometimes joke that if you're a hero, you're expected to conduct yourself well. You're not allowed to do things that ordinary people do and commit all the little peccadilloes that ordinary people go in for. I do find it very intrusive. It's intrusive on me, my space, and my relationship to the world. And yet I used to love heroes. I used to read about the resistance heroes, heroes of struggle, and it energized me. But then I also became a little distrustful of that afterwards because you know how weak you are in those situations, how easy it is to break. And some people break. We all broke up to a certain point. And so that concept of a hero was actually destructive of the things we wanted to achieve.

People would be detained in solitary confinement, and people outside would say, "Oh, Sam says she'll never break, she's a hero." And after three days of sleep deprivation and standing with her ankles swelling up like balloons, she would break. Because the people outside felt no one breaks. So it actually became, even from a purely instrumental point of view, very damaging to the struggle. And I don't like role models and the whole idea of role models, and of people trying to be like someone else. We've all got to be more like ourselves and have the confidence to be like ourselves, to discover who we are. And to share with others and get things from others, but not be like wonderful people, not to be like them, to be wonderful in ourselves.

I did feel that in a way I was like an ambassador for our struggle. And it was easier for me to depersonalize myself in that way, and to see myself as an exhibit. My arm, the trauma, could be seen. And that was the physical sign of what millions of people were suffering, and I was willing, in that sense, to allow my body to be used as an exhibit, if you like. Not as a crude exhibit, but as a living, active, participatory exhibit in the anti-apartheid struggle. Now I don't like it anymore. Now we're getting on with our lives. And my body is my body, and it belongs to me. It doesn't belong to the struggle. I wrote it there, it's in the books, people can remind me of it. It's for the public record. But I'm back into myself again.

You call your book, which is an account of this recovery, The Soft Vengeance of a Freedom Fighter. *What did you mean by "soft vengeance"?*

I heard they'd caught the guy who'd put the bomb in my car. To this day, I don't know if it was true or not, but I said, "Fantastic, I'd love to meet him. I'd love to have a human, face-to-face contact with him." To humanize the relationship. The idea of being almost blotted out by someone who doesn't know me, who's only seen me in a photograph as an object to be eliminated, was unbearable. And I just wanted to speak to him. And then I felt, let them put him on trial, and if the evidence is sufficient to convict him beyond reasonable doubt, then let him pay. If the evidence is insufficient, he must be acquitted. And that will be my soft vengeance; his acquittal will be my soft vengeance. Because it means we're living in a country where the rule of law functions, due process functions, these values have triumphed. That will be my soft vengeance. Now I said that in the narrative, and I remembered that twenty pages earlier I also used that phrase, "that will be my soft vengeance, democracy will be my soft vengeance." And I realized that that was what the book was about.

What are your feelings about participating in this transformation of South Africa?

It's very satisfying to know, not so much to say I told you so, but to know that the things that you put yourself on the line for, the beliefs that you had, the marginalization that you were subjected to, that in fact that call was right. There's a vindication, a validation of your whole life and of the things that you suffered, and so on, the discomforts and the terror. Everything makes sense; it was justified. And that's very, very thrilling. And it's thrilling in a personal sense, but it gives one courage about the world, that it is possible to have simple, naïve beliefs in human goodness and the capacity of people to change and to transform their lives; it's a living experience of it. And at the same time the skepticism. It wasn't as easy as we had thought; there were betrayals along the way. Everything is precarious; we don't quite know how it's all going to work out. It's not given, it's not certain, the insecurities continue. That's also something that's very valuable along the way. But basically it's an intense optimism that results from all this struggle.

Talk a little about your story in relation to the larger struggle and the importance of the group in sustaining you.

Particularly when we were tested, these experiences were intensely subjective. You were on your own, literally on your own, when you're in solitary confinement. When you're blown up and almost dead, you're on your own. But you still have those moments of unconsciousness fading in and out. Communicating with others, hearing a voice. And that slow, long recovery was very personal. But then there was also the knowledge that I'm part of a community, a group, that what got me there wasn't just a purely personal idiosyncratic thing. That I'm in history. There are thousands of others out there crying for me, laughing for me, cheering me on. I'm doing it for them. It's about something. It's about the world out there. It's not about becoming famous or becoming rich or being powerful or enjoying sex. It's about who you are in the world. And that was very, very sustaining.

In solitary confinement, it was more difficult because you forget the world out there, and you really are driven in unto yourself. And you don't quite know what it's all about or why. And what kept me going at certain moments had nothing to do with the struggle. These questions of ideology, of knowledge, became more and more remote, and I relied more and more on a kind of concept of honor that was very intense—I'm not going to let these so-and-sos tell me what to do. I don't know why I'm holding out; all I know is that I'm holding out. And I sometimes suspect boxers get like that. They don't know why they're carrying on; they're just going to carry on. There's something inside that keeps them going. It has a lot to do with training, I'm sure, and preparation.

But in the end, I became a member of this wonderful, huge, South African family that had all sorts of different appearances and backgrounds and spoke different languages. But because we had to overcome barriers to be associated with each other, we just shared so much it was very, very intense. I learned to sing through the ANC. I would be stiff and white and tight inside myself and think I had to go to singing lessons, and I'd be up on a platform and everybody's singing, or marching through the streets and everybody's singing, and I just learned to loosen up, to let go, to go with the flow. Often I wouldn't know the words, but it didn't matter. I would sing with my body. I would sing with the fun and the musicality and join in. That was very, very sustaining as well for me.

We weren't interested in politics and office and power, becoming prime minister or president. We would have scorned that. The prospects we had were of jail and torture and exile and underground. The only thing we could see in front and the only liberation would be for humanity, for the world, for the people. And it was intensely life-enhancing and giving to feel that you're part and parcel of that. Very, very vivid and real on a day-to-day basis. The kingdom of heaven is within you; you are part of the struggle. You are joining with others. You have these intense beliefs. And then you see people whom you believe in behaving abominably, and it's under a lot of pressure, and people crack up and people get old and people give up. All that happens, but there's that stream, that core, that's running on and on all the time. And often I would say to myself that the whole is bigger than the parts. Individuals can be very fragile and very awful, but somehow interacting with each other, there was something decent that was maintained all the way through.

We never let go of the basic ideals. And they were simple ideals. Apartheid was awful. We could all live together as equals in this country. We could work out solutions the minute we accepted that kind of shared patriotism or a shared citizenship. We never let go of that. And what gave us the courage and the strength was when, in our daily activities, we achieved that. You called it a civil society within our own ranks. That sense of community, the enjoyment, the fun of doing things together. That was something that was very sustaining and interesting all along the way. Maybe I would say that looking back, we were a little bit arrogant and harsh. We felt that we had the truth. And in a way we did, and it sustained us. But, I would also say to others today, to just be a little bit accepting of others and try and find the good in others, try and listen to others and understand their positions without capitulating to them. You don't have to come out slugging all the time. There's a lot of power in forgiveness, in reconciliation, in listening, in putting yourself in the shoes of the other person. This isn't weakness, it isn't diminishing, it can actually be very, very enhancing.

Shirin Ebadi
May 10, 2006

Looking back, how do you think your parents shaped your thinking about the world?

I was born to parents who came from educated backgrounds. My father deeply believed in the equality of rights between men and women, and he practiced that in his day-to-day life. My father had a very large library, and I don't recall seeing him without a book because either he was busy with some work or when it was his free time, he was reading a book.

Your family was very much affected by the fall of Mossadeq through the CIA intervention. Tell us a little about that.

I was young when the CIA started a coup in Iran that overthrew the national hero Dr. Mohammad Mossadeq. He was consequently arrested. A number of his followers, too, were arrested. Some were forced to give up their jobs and stayed at home. My father also was forced to give up his job for a few years, and naturally that affected our lives.

How did your mother affect you and shape what you became?

My mother was extremely kind, and she devoted all her attention to raising her children. She believed that that was the most important task for a mother. When I had my own children, too, I took that lesson to my house and believed that good motherhood is the most important role for every woman.

SHIRIN EBADI245

What led you to decide to become a lawyer?

Immediately after finishing law school, I became a judge. I was part of the first series of women who entered the system to become judges, and I was the first woman who started presiding over a court.

Following the revolution, I was told that I could no longer serve as a judge because I was a woman, so I decided to join the Iranian Bar Association and practice law.

I had lost my job, and I had realized that it was not just my job lost but that the system was hurting, in fact, women and society. And that was indeed what had happened. That was the beginning of the attack on women, and a series of laws were passed consequently that were very discriminatory. So, I decided to focus all my attention on promoting women's rights and issues. For me, the practice of law is a tool to serve justice.

One of the turning points in your life after the revolution was the killing of your brother-in-law. That sensitized you to a need for a new sense of justice in the system.

The execution of my brother-in-law made me very sad, but what was even sadder was that in a period of probably just a week, about three thousand young people were executed only for being active in political life.

As a lawyer, I realized that justice was at stake, greatly, and that my political defendants were at the core of my attention, that they were the most oppressed people in our society, because they were not only arrested innocently, they were also treated worse than any common criminal in prison.

I am reminded of the story you tell in your book about you and your husband signing a postnuptial agreement after the revolution. Tell us about that, because it gives us a good sense of what the law means to you and what a society without law cannot give.

I always believed that law must serve justice, and when it fails to do so, I try to find ways to make sure that the law brings us closer to justice. Before the revolution, my husband and I married under very fair and equal conditions according to the law. However, after the revolution, I lost all my rights. I was turned practically into a slave, whereas I was an equal partner before the revolution. The injustice that I felt was affecting my behavior at home. One day I spoke with my husband and told him that I suffered from this legal injustice, and I proposed that we sign a new agreement by which he would restore my equal rights. He agreed. It's interesting that when we actually went to sign the contract, the clerk there who was sitting in the office turned to my husband and said, "Are you crazy to do this?" And he said, "Well, in order to save my family life, I need to do this." I felt that justice was created afterwards. And fortunately to this day, our marriage life has stayed together.

Help us understand how justice moves forward in Iran. On the one hand, you have to navigate between Islamic law, the traditional text, the interpretation; on the other hand, you have a sense of international law, for example, in the case of women's rights.

The government justifies the unsatisfactory laws that prevail in the country by claiming that they are Islamic laws. But I have studied Islamic text and law very carefully, and my efforts are geared towards proving to the government that they are, in fact, basing the law on a wrongful interpretation of Islamic law and that there are other interpretations. The cases that I generally work on are those that can demonstrate to the people the practical results of law. Oftentimes when I take a case to trial, I invite reporters to come and write about the case beforehand and to raise public awareness of the results. Once that awareness is created, people put pressure on the government and demand the change in laws. By carrying out this technique, I've, in fact, succeeded in changing a number of laws.

In your book you talk about the time you advised the women's caucus in the parliament on some new legislation. Tell us about that, because your arguments were showing that Islamic law had many interpretations, and that was what the debate was about.

On the suggestion of some reformist members of parliament, I drafted a family law that was compatible with Islamic law and at the same time served justice. In a meeting that I had with members of parliament, there was a group of members of the clergy present, most of whom were fundamentalist. They strongly opposed the draft law. I walked into that meeting with a number of religious texts, and whenever I made an argument I would show the people the text that I was referring to, to prove to them that, in fact, these are religious texts that defend my case. But eventually, one of the clergy who was sitting there, who was very fundamentalist, decided that he no longer wanted to hear the case, and I noticed that he whispered something in the ears of the tea server, [who] left the room and then came back to me and said, "There is a phone call waiting for you." When I left the room, I realized that, in fact, there was no one calling for me, and when I tried to reenter, he informed me that I was no longer welcome in that room. So, because what I was saying was based on the truth and justice, they couldn't accept it any longer, and they couldn't justify another argument, so they chose not to have me in the room. In fact, our problem with Islamic fundamentalists is this very issue. They simply don't want to hear what others have to say.

I have always tried to prevent abuse of power, whether that abuse is to get political gains, or to play with religion or the religious feelings of the populace, or to use power to add to wealth.

In looking back at this evolution of the law, and the really hard work that you had to do, how did you do all that you had to do? Because you were still a mother, raising a family, but you were also confronting these very difficult cases that put you in the public eye.

Since a young age, I got used to working twelve to thirteen hours a day, and in fact, when you get used to working that kind of schedule, you realize that twenty-four hours is, in fact, a lot of time. I compare my situation to a person on board a ship. When there is a shipwreck, the passenger then falls in the ocean and has no choice but to keep swimming. What happened in our society was that the laws overturned every right that women had. I had no choice. I could not get tired, I could not lose hope. I cannot afford to do that.

We say that the strength of the chain lies in the smallest and weakest part of the chain, so you must always protect that so that the chain does not fall apart. Women and children and political prisoners are the weakest members of our society and need our protection.

Tell us about your discovery that you were on an assassination list that had been prepared by agents of the intelligence service.

I was, more than anything, surprised. I was surprised because I was a person who was not involved in any political agenda that sought to undermine the government, and I had served the people on a pro bono basis, and yet I was so hated that the ministry of intelligence would order my murder. And then I became very sorrowful when realizing that our government isn't capable of making the distinction between friends and foes.

What are the roots of your courage?

When you believe in the rightfulness of your path, you take stronger steps. At the same time, I'm a Muslim and I believe in God, and that gives me additional strength. When I choose the path that I'm sure is the right path to take, I make my best effort to succeed, and when I carry out my best effort, then I leave it to God and let Him turn the rest of the events forward for me. Courage comes from confidence. When you are confident that your decision is correct, then you will make all your efforts to make it happen. Those who lack courage are often those who are not confident enough on whether their decisions are right or not.

Translated from the Farsi by Banafsheh Keynoush

Philippe Sands
November 18, 2008

Where were you born and raised?

I was born in London, in 1960.

Looking back, how do you think your parents shaped your thinking about the world?

Hugely. My mother was a refugee. She was born in Vienna, in 1938, and left Vienna, being Jewish, in circumstances of obvious difficulty. And she ended up in Paris, where she was brought up in a Catholic orphanage, and survived the war and then met, as a very young lady, my father and moved to London, England. So, the international dimension, and the context of conflict and suffering, and the idea that people keep with them damage that has been done decades ago, was present in my life, I would say.

Was there a lot of talk about these experiences in your family?

In my experience, people are divided into two categories. There are those who want to talk about it and those who don't want to talk about it, and I grew up in a household in which one didn't really talk about these things. I was very close to my grandfather who survived the whole war experience and who was a remarkable individual, a sort of young socialist in Vienna in the 1930s, and I talked politics a lot with him. He was a pretty formative influence in my upbringing, but there were things he wouldn't talk about.

What do you see as defining the path that you took?

I'm the first lawyer in my family. My mother didn't go to university. My dad's a dentist, no interest really in the political world, but I grew up in a household which was touched by foreignness, and so I was always interested in things that were international. If you asked me what was the single moment I remember in my childhood at school, it would be an economics teacher who took us down a coal mine when we were fourteen-year-olds, and, being a sort of north London middle-class boy, that was a pretty powerful experience. And then when I went up to university, at Cambridge, I was exposed for the first time to international law and I sort of fell in love with the subject. We had a wonderful teacher, a Yorkshireman named Robbie Jennings. I remember him standing up in October 1980 to the whole classroom, three hundred of us, and saying, "I'm going to teach you for the next year about international law, and probably out of the three hundred of you, if one of you ever has an issue of international law in your working life, that will be a decent result."

Tell us about practicing international law.

When I studied international law, there was basically one court, the International Court of Justice. As I mentioned, we had a teacher who basically said, "You may find it interesting, but it's going to be of limited practical relevance." I sort of fell into it by accident. I did a master's in international law at Cambridge so I could specialize in it for a year. At the time I had an American girlfriend who was doing an MD/PhD program, a Marshall scholar in Cambridge. Then she went back to Harvard, and I followed her. I had no job, no position, no nothing. I needed some money, I needed to live. And so, I got a job as a research assistant to a young academic in international law at Harvard Law School, a guy called David Kennedy, and was his research assistant for a year, and was a visiting scholar at Harvard Law School for a year. That was a big experience. It introduced me to the American way of lawyering, and after the dullness of Cambridge, where we were taught that law and politics are two separate things, here all of a sudden I was exposed to the world of critical legal studies, and all the battles that were going on at Harvard Law School then.

We studied international law in Cambridge, England, in a context in which we were not encouraged to find the links between politics and law. And then I went to spend a year in America and it was the very opposite. You could not divorce law and politics. Law was so deeply connected to political process that one had to look at them as flip sides of the same coin. That encouraged me to look at law in a much more policy-oriented way, and I think that was an important development. If I hadn't spent that year in America I would've followed a very different path. Later I took a reseach fellowship and became an international lawyer and qualified also as a barrister. I've always taught and practiced.

What would you say are the skills that are required to do international law well?

I think the most important ability is the ability to disconnect yourself from your own milieu and understand how other cultures, and other societies, and other political persuasions think of the issues you are interested [in]. Try to put yourself in the position of the other to see how they will react to the same facts or circumstances, which they may do in different ways. When I appear before the International Court of Justice and I'm making an argument to a bench of fifteen international judges, I'm scanning the bench looking at the fifteen different nationalities, appreciating that they all come with their own emotional, intellectual, political baggage, and trying to understand how they come to the same set of problems we're all looking at.

And international law is about taking the law to a higher level than one might find in one particular national setting?

International law is defined as the law that governs relations between states. It's evolved since then. It also governs relations between states and individuals, between states and corporations, involving international organizations, the OECD, the UN, and other bodies, but essentially it's the law that binds the globe. And it has a role at the international level, but it also, in many countries, has a role at the domestic level. So, now I would argue international law before the English domestic courts, and the English courts now are taking international law arguments pretty seriously.

How do you account for this neoconservative agenda having such animus against the whole body of international law, and an insistence on going it alone?

I think it's a complex question, and the answer to that question is built on deep theory and individual fear. I think it's entirely legitimate for the neocons to have put on the table a question as to how international law is effective at the domestic level. But at the other end of the spectrum, there's also a concern about personal well-being. So, we know, for example, from various accounts that have been written, that when Donald Rumsfeld came back to the Department of Defense, he initiated a review of various international norms, which for example, made it difficult for people like Henry Kissinger to travel abroad because of fears of investigations or the tap on the shoulder which might lead to arrest. And Donald Rumsfeld saw norms of international law as undermining the ability of the United States to exercise choices in particular directions, and he wished to remove from the equation such norms of international law which would impose constraints:

constraints on the use of force, foreign travel, the promotion of particular values. It was a sort of à la carte multilateralism.

If people say the United States is against international rules, that's not right. It turns out that the economic prosperity of the United States, which has been built on free trade rules, foreign investment protection rules, intellectual property rules, many other rules with an economic objective, lies at the heart of the United States' remarkable ability to export economic intellectual ideas and develop its own economic well-being. What President Bush did in the past was essentially say there is good international law—the economic stuff—and then there's the bad international law—the noneconomic stuff. You pick and choose the bits of international law you like, and you get rid of the other ones.

But I don't think there's a simple answer to your question. I think different people were motivated by very different considerations. What they were joined with was somehow a belief that the very nature of international law was inconsistent with core American values of democracy and individual freedom. I think that's wrong, and I think, in fact, that international law such as it is encapsulates core American values, and I think the pendulum will now swing back the other way.

Let's talk about your book Torture Team. *Tell us about that creative moment when you decided to pursue this topic.*

I had published *Lawless World* in 2005, and I'd written it as sort of a macro-picture of the world and its international rules, and I was being asked, what was I going to write next. And a number of people who had read *Lawless World* said that the one chapter in there that they thought contained the nuggets of an interesting story was the chapter on Guantánamo. I'd dealt with it in *Lawless World* but very generally and just on the basis of the documents. That conversation which took place with a number of people in the summer of 2006 coincided with my coming across an old movie that I'd not seen for many years, *Judgment at Nuremberg*. I think I had the flu or something; I was ill, lying in bed, channel surfing, and I came across the opening shots of this remarkable film that tells the story of the prosecution by the U.S. military of some of the worst lawyers in the German Nazi regime. And it chimed with a concern that I had, looking at some of the documents, including the press conference with Alberto Gonzales and Jim Haynes after Abu Ghraib, how on earth did the U.S. lawyers authorize techniques of interrogation which on their face were inconsistent with the very international laws the United States, more than any other country, had put in place—the Geneva Conventions, the Torture Convention. And so, what I decided to do was abandon my normal processes, which is to do things on the basis of documents, and I thought, "Let's go and meet these people. I want to talk to them, I want to hear their stories, I'll try to do it with an open mind. I'd like to see what motivated them, I'd like to see what the true story is," and I decided to adopt a different methodology. I'd write to them, I'd track them down, I'd see if they'd speak to me, and basically, most everybody did agree to speak to me.

Now explain what the Rumsfeld memo was. What was in that memo?

It was written by Mr. Haynes, who was Mr. Rumsfeld's lawyer, General Counsel of the Department of Defense, on the 27th of November, 2002. It was signed by Mr. Rumsfeld a few days later, and in the document Mr. Rumsfeld gave blanket approval for fifteen techniques of interrogation at Guantánamo, including water-boarding. And below his signature he writes, "I stand for eight to ten hours a day. Why is standing limited to four hours?" This appears to be the very first time that the line has been crossed of formalizing the use of cruelty in order to protect the interests of the United States since 1863. Now there's not to say there hasn't been cruelty before—in Vietnam and Korea, in

Central America in the 1980s—but what you won't find is a document that is equivalent to this one. It's a very significant change
when you institutionalize cruelty, when you legitimize it in a
piece of paper which someone as significant as the Secretary of
Defense then signs. And so, this was an act which took the United
States into a different place.

*There were a number of attorneys from the Justice Department and
throughout other government agencies who helped to legalize these
interrogation policies. Help us understand these lawyers, the role they
played and what was wrong with what they did.*

These lawyers, who were joined by a distinct ideology and brought
in to do a particular job—the legal advices and the processes that
they followed are not characterized by independence of thought.
So, unhelpful authorities are ignored, contrary decisions are bypassed and simply not addressed, and what you have is a situation in which the lawyers appear to be simply rubber-stamping
predetermined executive policies. When you go to your lawyer,
you don't expect your lawyer to say to you, "Well, you tell me what
you want to do, and I'll find you a legal argument that justifies it."
That's what happened in this case. They abdicated a legal role
and, in so doing, crossed a line that separates good advice from
bad advice, and possibly also the line that separates unprofes-
sional advice into advice that gives rise to criminal liability. Let's
not forget, Article 4 of the Torture Convention criminalizes com-
plicity and participation in torture.

To what extent was this about power, or was it really self-delusion?

Ideology is the first source that led to these actions. The individuals who were driven in this direction had a particular vision of
America's unfettered and unconstrained ability to act and a particular ideological approach to the interpretation of the Constitu-

tion. The second thing was about incompetence. The people who were advising on these areas of the law actually have no background in this area of the law and gave incompetent advice. And thirdly, it's about hubris. It's not listening to others who may have a better understanding. And the consequence of all this is that it's taken us to a seriously bad place. It undermines our ability to work with our allies. Allies are not going to hand over detainees to countries that engage in abusive techniques of interrogation. And, I think equally significantly, it creates a recruitment tool. I've been told time and time again that the effect of the Abu Ghraib pictures and the Guantánamo stories has been to enrage people. Abu Ghraib and Guantánamo will have made it more difficult for us to contain and respond to a real and present threat that we face.

One final question: What do you think that President Obama needs to do to walk us back from these mistakes to atone in a way that would help restore America's legitimacy?

I think he's got a very difficult task ahead of him. He has to repeal the entirety of the Military Commissions Act and do away with these military commissions and restore some semblance of due process to the system of justice that is to be meted out to various people. He needs to send out clearer signals that the United States will not torture anymore. He needs to extend the prohibition on the use of these techniques from the Department of Defense to the CIA, which of course, President Bush vetoed. If he doesn't do those things, I think people will begin to get concerned. I think he'll go pretty far, pretty quickly. More complicated for him is looking back. What does he do in relation to the crimes that have been committed? I think the first step is to sort out the facts, and the process of an administration that is not fearful of sorting out the facts will go very far in allowing the United States to move to the next stage and help us all move on.

RADICAL INSIGHTS
THROUGH HISTORY

History can contribute to the political awakening of the young, opening their eyes to the powerful lessons of the past. Unfortunately, traditional history has too often failed to offer a comprehensive narrative that includes injustice and oppression, resistance and dissent, and the experiences of minorities, women, and the poor. This failure necessitates a fresh approach to the subject, which the distinguished historians included in this final chapter have so masterfully provided. Joan Wallach Scott and Howard Zinn have undertaken the formidable task of examining the history of *all* people and correcting the biases of the establishment's narrative. The civil rights, antiwar, and women's movements impelled them to create new categories of historical analysis that reveal important truths about our past in order to inform our future.

Joan Wallach Scott

Joan Wallach Scott is Harold F. Linder Professor in the School of Social Science at the Institute for Advanced Study. Her work has challenged the foundations of conventional historical practice and has contributed to the formulation of a field of critical history. Written more than twenty years ago, her now classic article, "Gender: A Useful Category of Historical Analysis," continues to inspire innovative research on women and gender. In her latest work, she has been concerned with the ways in which difference poses problems for democratic practice. She has taken up this question in her most recent books: *Only Paradoxes to Offer: French Feminists and the Rights of Man*; *Parité: Sexual Equality and the Crisis of French Universalism*; and *The Politics of the Veil*.

Howard Zinn

Howard Zinn is an activist, a historian, a writer, and a playwright. He is the author of many books, including *A People's History of the United States*, *The Zinn Reader*, and an autobiography, *You Can't Be Neutral on a Moving Train*. His three plays are *Emma*, *Daughter of Venus*, and *Marx in Soho*. He is a professor emeritus of history at Boston University. He has received the Thomas Merton Award, the Eugene V. Debs Award, the Upton Sinclair Award, and the Lannan Literary Award.

Joan Wallach Scott
February 26, 2009

Where were you born and raised?

I was born in Brooklyn, raised in Brooklyn.

And looking back, how do you think your parents shaped your thinking about the world?

My parents were both high school history teachers, although I like to think that's not the reason I became an historian. It was definitely a family in which ideas and politics mattered. They were both on the left. In fact, my father was fired in 1953 from his New York City schoolteacher position for refusing to cooperate with a McCarthy-like investigating committee in New York City.

What was the conversation like around the dinner table, a lot of talking about political issues?

Analyses of politics and issues, and also discussions about history. My mother continued to teach all of those years, so stories about students, about how my parents taught the Civil War or various things in American history. My mother would puzzle over why kids could understand some things and not others. The idea of teaching, and the importance of teaching, was very much present in the dinner-table conversations.

It sounds like there was a lot of talk about methodology, even before you went on to university. Any high school teachers that particularly influenced you, or any setting, before you went to college?

Yes. There was one particular high school Advanced Placement English teacher, whom I always credit with teaching me how to read. We used those old Brooks and Warren *Understanding Poetry* and *Understanding Literature* books, and he taught us how to read poems and how to read between the lines in literature. I didn't know it then, but I think that was when I fell in love with language and ideas of literary representation.

Where did you do your undergraduate work?

At Brandeis University.

And what did Brandeis contribute to the shaping of your intellectual mind?

The first year I was at Brandeis as a freshman, Herbert Marcuse gave a lecture to the incoming freshman class that was called "The Nuisance Value of an Education." The idea was that you were supposed to do something with what you learned, be critical, be politically engaged, and I've never forgotten that. And then the next influence was being taught by Frank Manuel, in the second half of "Introduction to Western Civilization." That is why, I think, I became a historian, and I know from my own friends that Frank Manuel's course was one of these places where converts to history were made. He mostly was interested in the history of ideas and intellectual history, and we read original texts and talked about them.

Did you get a greater sense of activism at Brandeis?

Yes. I started Brandeis in the fall of 1958, graduated in 1962. Nineteen-sixty was the sit-ins in Greensboro, North Carolina, and Michael Walzer, who had graduated several years before, did a tour to Greensboro, North Carolina, and around the South, and came back and reported to us about what he'd seen and urged us all to picket Woolworth's. And so, that was another of those influences. But those were the years of real engagement. It was hard not to be engaged in student politics at Brandeis in those years.

Were there inklings of the Women's Movement during your years at Brandeis, or did that come later?

I always say that there was an influence in my family, because my father, who was very secular as well as politically engaged, would always tell us when we were young that the Bible was a book not to be trusted because it said that God had created woman out of man's rib and that there was an inherent inferiority assumed in that, that you had to be suspicious of. My mother worked the whole time that I was growing up, and we were raised to believe that there was no difference between what men and women could do. And many of my parents' friends were also teachers— women and men—so there were examples set for us as kids. But when I was at Brandeis, it was other kinds of politics, antinuclear politics, civil rights stuff. At Wisconsin it was civil rights first— '64 was the Freedom Summer—and then Vietnam. Feminism came later. It wasn't until I was teaching at the University of Illinois at Chicago in 1970 and there were friends who were organizing courses in women's history. That was the beginning, and I was part of a group of female faculty members. We founded a daycare center, a women's studies course—which then became a program—and it was there that I began to be interested in the feminist movement and in women's history. It was actually when

I went to teach at Northwestern two years later that I agreed to teach a course in women's history. And the students were the ones who would come into the classes demanding inspiration, demanding stories about women in the past. That was how I became a women's historian: I had to teach myself something of the history in order to be able to teach the course, and then I began to be really interested in some of the problems that were raised about women's history, particularly because I was a labor historian to begin with.

What was graduate school like?

Well, I came into Wisconsin in the fall of 1962, when it was teeming with graduate students. The chairman of the department, Merrill Jensen, was known for preferring not to have women in graduate seminars, thinking that it would destroy the camaraderie of the men in the seminar.

When you came to graduate school at Wisconsin, you met with the chair, and you were then assigned a seminar for life. I came in, and he said to me, "What language do you have? What history do you want to do?" and I said French because I'd had that from junior high, actually. And he said, "Okay, French history seminar." And that's how I became a French historian.

Later, a couple of professors formed a social history seminar. It was the beginning of the movement for social history, and we read E.P. Thompson's *Making of the English Working Class*, and a number of other books which inspired not only me but a whole generation of people to become social historians. I was particularly interested in labor history. And so, I did my dissertation on glassworkers in a town in the south of France.

And this was at a time when authority across the board was being questioned, the war in Vietnam, and all the way around.

That's right. I think that it provided the opportunity to further question authority. When I was an undergraduate, I did my politics and I did my history, but I never thought of them as being part of the same project. But it wasn't until I began doing women's history that I began to realize that there could be a relationship between the academic work I did and the work of challenging prevailing ways of thinking. That my scholarship could have some inherent political effect, as well.

Give us a bit of insight into your education as a scholar. What social theorists influenced you the most?

For me, it was particularly post-structuralists like Michel Foucault, who allowed me to think differently about doing history, and particularly about doing women's history at a point where I just couldn't figure my way out of "women" as a kind of supplement to the main story. One of the things that Foucault writes about is the fact that the questions you have about the past in the present are not innocent or objective questions. They're questions that are related to the time you live in, to the political justifications or challenges to the politics of the time you live in. For example: to do women's history would mean not just to ask what women did in the past but to say, what is it now that lets us think about gender relations between men and women in the ways we do? Did people always think that the differences were entirely natural? What's the difference if you say there've always been changes in the categories— the very meanings of the terms—even of men and women, over time? And we need to know what those differences are because not only will it help us understand the past, but it'll make us realize that things can be changed in the present, that things don't always have to be the way they always seem to have been.

How did reading Foucault shape your perception of education and learning in general?

There was some dimension of me that was always a little bit rebellious. But at Brandeis, you learned that the best essay exams
you could write were ones that challenged the premises of the
question. If you got an essay exam and said the Civil War was
caused by slavery—if you just said yes and wrote the answer,
that was not good enough. If you said the premise that the Civil
War was caused by slavery ignores questions of economics, politics, the economic interests of the states, et cetera, you could get
an A. I think we were taught to think critically and always to call
into question the presuppositions of anything that you were being offered.

So when I read Foucault, it was like another version of the
critical challenge. He's saying that you don't have to think of
history as a continuous linear development. You can ask where
the breaks are and why they happen. And even if the words used
are the same: "woman," "man," "reason," "passion"—they mean
different things at different times. What is it that brings those
different meanings into effect? And what effects do those new
meanings have? Then you get a whole different take—a much
more exciting take—on history and on what you can do with
knowledge of the past.

Let's talk about your book The Politics of the Veil. *You start with the
premise that history has an important role to play in contemporary
political discourse.*

I think I would call it critical history. Foucault actually calls it the
history of the present, which means that you take up contemporary issues. Not small political issues—not the stimulus package,
but the language used to think through the problems of the moment. The market might be one of them, right now, and whether
or not there's such a thing as a free market, and what's the history of the idea of the market. Are we in a period in which Adam
Smith's ideas are simply being reapplied, or is something en-

tirely different going on, which is using those ideas but for a very different set of issues?

So, it's a history that's sensitive to the conceptual categories with which people think, and which then critically looks at them and tries to disturb the power that they have. Actually in this book, if we want to take an example from the *Veil* book, it's the French idea of universalism that first got me interested in the question of the veil. In France the notion that everybody is an individual, all individuals are equal, that to recognize difference is to acknowledge cracks in the building of a unified nation, of a universal set of principles that are equally applied to everybody— I thought there was something wrong with that notion when you looked at any number of issues in French society. The one of the moment is the treatment of Muslim immigrants— some of whom are not immigrants at all, who've been there for generations—and the treatment of girls in head scarves in public schools. So, instead of writing a book in which I just told the story, I asked what is it that allows the French to think about Muslims and the wearing of a head scarf as an unacceptable form of behavior, and why head scarves, and why women? Why not go after imams? What is it that allowed this to become the symbol of what was wrong with Muslims in French society?

Do you think that we have to examine other issues throughout history—secularism, individualism—before we can really understand the course of events through time?

I wouldn't say that they continue through time in the same way, but that there are a set of concepts in this controversy about head scarves in France. It wasn't that these girls caused problems in school with their head scarves. There were probably, at most, a couple of thousand girls out of a population of Muslims of maybe six million, so we're not talking about a huge threat suddenly inundating the classrooms. We're talking about a heightened consciousness of the presence of Muslims, particularly after September 11th. The first explosion was in 1989, at the time of the bicentennial of the French Revolution. A junior high principal decided that he wasn't going to tolerate girls in head scarves anymore, even though they had been coming to school with head scarves. Jewish boys were coming in with yarmulkes; Sikhs were coming with their turbans; and none of this was an issue. It quiets down, there are negotiations, and in 1994 it erupts again, 2003 again. It seemed to be out of proportion—the hysteria about these head scarves, the speeches people were making, the articles in the newspapers, the ultimate destruction of everything that was predicted if girls were allowed to keep coming to school in head scarves, was so out of proportion to the phenomenon itself. It raised its own question: why is this happening? Each time, politically, it's the far right in France who's raising the immigration issue and trying to pull the center to their side.

And why do you think that people in France were so focused on this particular issue?

France has long been a country of immigration, but the requirement was that you assimilated to the culture, so if you came from Portugal, or Italy, or Spain, you learned the language, you behaved like everybody else, you looked like everybody else. There are three problems with Muslims. One is that they're darker. Two is that they're coming from former colonies so that their social relationship to the dominant population in France is as people who have been defined as inferior for years and years, since the French conquered Algeria for the first time in 1830. So, you have a long history which associates these people with inferiority. And the third thing is that they are insisting on practicing their religion in a public way whereas part of the assimilation process in France is that religion is a private matter. If you do it privately at home there's no problem, but if you demonstrate your religiosity by wearing a head scarf, by praying five times a day, by refusing to eat certain foods that are offered in the school cafeteria, then you're breaking the rules and trying to introduce what ought to be private into the sphere of the public.

This expression of religion is also a youthful response to the issues raised by globalization and a statement of an identity that makes the young person part of a larger community.

Absolutely, and of an international one, not just a national one, even if the kids themselves are not political in the scary ways that those who want to outlaw the head scarf or ban immigration from these countries altogether say they are. If this had been the 1970s, some of these girls might have been Maoists, and now we're in the twenty-first century and what is available as a kind of radical departure from materialism, western imperialism, global economic transformations, is for some of them Islam, and for good reasons, not frivolous ones. It is a language of protest in the same way that it is also a language of religion. I don't want to say that it's not about religion, but it is the available language of a kind of radical stand that you can take.

I think it's also about a kind of identification that is a way of thinking yourself out of a situation of great discrimination in which a lot of these kids live, in France. You're talking about minority, often very poor, populations—unlike in the United States, where so much of the Muslim immigration is middle class and professional. In these countries you're talking about people who are, on top of being economically disadvantaged, discriminated against on the basis of what I would call race.

Talk a little about Western perceptions of Islam.

Well, you can't think of "the West" and Islam. Those categories hide the enormous social and religious diversities on both sides.

One of the ways in which I think that the issue of Islam and "the West" has been used politically recently is to cover over, in the West, all of the problems of gender inequality that are now being attributed to Islam. So, if we can say one of our objections to "them" is that women are unequal and wearing a head scarf is a sign of their inequality, even if the women will say to you, "No, I'm wearing this head scarf because it's my way of deferring to God. Just like a Jewish man will wear a yarmulke and say he's deferring to God, I'm wearing this to defer. It has nothing to do with my father, my brothers, or anybody else." I'm not saying that all of them do it for these reasons but that we can't assume a single reason. We can't assume that they are automatically unequal while we enjoy equality. The attention to the head scarf in terms of a sharp opposition between "them" and "us" makes it possible to overlook all of the inequalities that persist in Western societies. If you look at the numbers of women in the elected parliaments of France or the U.S., it's only about 16 percent. If women are totally equal, how do you explain unequal access to elected office, or unequal wages, or all the sorts of things that feminists have been politically active about? Once you introduce this "us versus them," then all of those issues of inequality pale, and as feminists we become interested in liberating "them" from their head scarves, and we forget about the kinds of problems that we face here.

So, this is about power and the way words and symbols become an instrument of power to essentially deal with a situation by, in a way, not dealing with it.

Yes, that's right. It's the way in which language structures relations of power so you don't even get to see how they're actually operating. In the beginning of the war in Afghanistan, Laura Bush was talking about how we were freeing these women from the oppression that they had suffered, even as her husband's administration was trying to take away the right to abortion and was being supported by Christian fundamentalists who believed that women's role was to stay at home to take care of their children. People who believed her rhetoric seemed not to realize that there were people at home in the U.S. who were interested in oppressing women in certain ways while "liberating" them in Afghanistan.

How do the French approach the problem with confronting differences on the basis of gender equality?

French political theory always has a difficult time with equality on the one hand and sexual difference on the other hand. There's one set of characteristics that cannot be abstracted—which is sex—and those characteristics are thought to be naturally different and therefore inescapable. This contradicts the idea that everyone gets to be the same as individuals by being abstracted from their social characteristics. We're all individuals; we're all equal. But sexual difference is the one thing that creates problems for this abstract individualism. During the French Revolution, liberty, equality, and fraternity were declared to be the principles of the nation, but it took until 1944 for women to get the vote, and until 2000 to pass a law that grants women equal access to elected office. My question is, what kind of equality was there for women during this period? What were the terms by which equality was defined? How do you explain this seeming contradiction between a nation committed to individual equality and the denial of full rights of citizenship to women?

What I argue in my book is that there is a tension between so-called natural difference on the one hand and abstract individualism which is the basis for equality on the other. French ideology addresses the tension by talking about sexiness and sexual seduction and flirtatiousness between men and women as a national character trait, what the historian Mona Ozouf referred to as *"la singularité française."* Muslims have a different system of representing and managing gender relations. Muslims argue that relations between the sexes are the source of difficulty and must be managed by keeping the sexes apart. So women (and men) should wear modest clothes that don't emphasize sexuality and sexual attractiveness. And there's a clash there between two styles of thinking about how to represent the relations between the sexes—the French which says gender is not a problem (though of course it is) and the Muslim which says gender is a problem that must be addressed. I think this fed into the French anxiety about Islam, and it was one of the reasons that the head scarf and women's dress became a hot political issue.

How can we all work together to find solutions to these problems that arise from all of us living in an increasingly globalized world? How can we compromise as parts of groups, within countries as well as globally?

Working together without difference being thought of as invidious, without difference being turned into a hierarchy, without difference being constructed as a difference of power. There ought to be a way of acknowledging that difference is, in fact, the human condition. A French philosopher named Jean-Luc Nancy says that instead of thinking about having a common being—that is all of us being somehow the same—we need to think of having "being in common," which understands "being" as a state of difference: individuals are different from one another, groups are different from one another. Difference is the human condition, and if you could think in those terms—it's utopian, I know— then you would be in a situation in which difference couldn't be used to structure relations of power.

Do you see this kind of historical work applied to policy debates affecting the discourse in real time?

Well, yes and no. I mean, we could think of books that blew up a way of thinking about things, but I think you only actually do that in retrospect. For example, you could say Simone de Beauvoir's *The Second Sex* became a crucial text, looking back on it twenty or thirty years later, when a women's movement came into existence and cited it. So I don't think theoretical thinking and critical thinking necessarily have an immediate policy impact, but what I hope to do with this kind of critical work is to get enough people thinking differently about the questions so that we shake the firmness of the ground on which some of these opinions stand. I want to introduce doubt about the certainty of certain predominant ideas, and if we can do that, we can begin to make a difference in the general way people think and then maybe ultimately in the policy arena.

There are social movements, there are individual experiences, there are books and movies—there's a whole set of voices that have come into a conversation of which historians, philosophers, theorists are one small part. I think that's the way social change happens, and it's as a participant in an ongoing critical conversation that some people will latch on to and disseminate that I imagine the work that my own writing does.

Howard Zinn
April 20, 2001

How did the circumstances of your youth affect the way you came to see the world?

This should be asked of all historians. Growing up in a working-class family, going to work in a shipyard at the age of eighteen, working for three years in a shipyard, getting into the sweat of industrial life and being aware of the difference between the way we lived our lives and the lives of the people we saw on the movie screen or in the magazines, developing a kind of class consciousness: I think that had an effect later on my teaching and writing of history. Then joining the Air Force, becoming a bombardier in the Air Force, going through a war, coming out of the war with very, very strong antiwar ideas, even though I was in "the best of wars," as they say—the "good war." And then, teaching in Spelman College, my first teaching job. Teaching at a black women's college in the South—Atlanta, Georgia. Seven years there. Going through and becoming involved in the civil rights movement—I think all of that shaped my thinking about history.

How, specifically, do you think your parents shaped your character?

My parents were not political people at all. My parents were just ordinary. They were Jewish immigrants who worked in garment factories when they came here, and then my father became a waiter. You might say he moved up in the world. He went from being a factory worker to being a waiter, and then he became a headwaiter. As far as political influence, no. The only influence they had on my life was my observation of their lives. My observation that my father was working very hard, an honest hard-working man. My mother was working very hard, raising four sons. And yet, of course, they had nothing to show for it. That is, they were perfect counterpoints to the Horatio Alger myth that if you work hard in this country, you will get somewhere. I think that intensified my feeling about the injustice of an economic system in which there are people all over the country like my parents who work very, very hard and have nothing to show for it.

One of the things that your parents did was obtain for you a subscription to a collection of Dickens books, and so reading became very important to you and also offered you insights, right?

Reading, reading, reading at an early age. My parents knew I was a reader even though they were not readers. My father was barely literate; my mother was somewhat literate. But they knew that I was interested in books and reading. They had no idea who Charles Dickens was, but they saw this ad; they could send away coupons and a dime for each book. So they got me this whole set, and I made my way through Dickens.

From Dickens what I got was this ferocious acknowledgment of the modern industrial system and what it does to people, and how poor people live and the way they are victimized, and the way the courts function. The way justice works against the poor. Yes, it was Dickens's class consciousness that reinforced my own. It was a kind of justification for the beliefs I was already developing. It did what reading very often does for you—tells you you are not alone in these secret thoughts you have. Not long ago I read that someone asked Kurt Vonnegut, "Why do you write?" and he said, "The reason I write is to tell people: You are not alone."

I have a sense that life and learning for you are never separated; that life informs your scholarship and your scholarship informs the way you live your life.

I think that's true. There is a strong connection between the two. I think that's probably because I had so many vivid life experiences before I entered the academic world, before I entered the world of scholarship. By the time I went to college under the GI Bill at the age of twenty-seven, I'd already worked in the shipyard, I'd been in a war, I'd worked at various jobs, and so I brought to my reading of history those experiences. And then I learned from my experience something broader, that is, a historical perspective which reinforced the ideas that I'd gained from my own life.

Before you were in college, you were working on the docks and you were involved in a demonstration at Times Square, and the police attacked. In your autobiography you wrote, "Henceforth I was a radical, believing that something fundamental was wrong in this country, not just the existence of poverty amidst great wealth, not just the horrible treatment of black people, but something rotten at the root requiring an uprooting of the old order: the introduction of a new kind of society—cooperative, peaceful, egalitarian." That is an example of a kind of event that changed your thinking, and that's an argument that you make in a lot of your history, that people can be changed by things that happen to them and act accordingly.

That's right. Sometimes it's one very vivid experience. Of course, it's never just one vivid experience, but it's that one experience coming on top of a kind of only semiconscious understanding that's been developed, and then it becomes crystallized by an event. I think that's what happened to me at the age of seventeen, when I was hit by a policeman and knocked unconscious. I woke up and said, my God, this is America, where, yes, there are bad guys and there are good guys, but the government is neutral.

And when I saw that, no, the police are not neutral, the government is not neutral, that was a radical insight.

Your first teaching assignment was at Spelman College, a black college for women in Atlanta. Tell us about that experience and the amazing events that occurred during your stay, that is, the large historical events.

Those seven years at Spelman College are probably the most interesting, exciting, most educational years for me. I learned more from my students than my students learned from me. Living in the South at a very interesting time, the late '50s, early '60s, just before the onset of the big civil rights movement, and then during those years.

For one thing, I began to look at history in a different way. I began to look at history from a black point of view. It looks very different from a black point of view. The heroes are different, and the eras get different names. The Progressive Era is no longer the Progressive Era, because it's the era in which more black people are lynched than in any other period in American history. I began reading black historians. Reading Rayford Logan, reading Du Bois, reading John Hope Franklin, reading E. Franklin Frazier, and things that weren't on my reading list right up in graduate school at Columbia University.

So that was one thing, learning about history, but the other thing—more important, I think—was learning by being in the movement. By moving out from Atlanta to Albany, Georgia, and demonstrations in Selma, Hattiesburg, Greenwood, Greenville, Jackson. By becoming a kind of participant writer in the movement, it taught me something very important about democracy, about the democracy that I had been taught in junior high school, and which people learn even in higher education: institutions, constitution, checks and balances, voting, all those things that political scientists concentrate on. Obviously, that was not democracy.

Those things had failed to produce equality for black people, had failed, in fact, to enforce the Fourteenth and Fifteenth Amendments. Every president in the United States for a hundred years had violated his oath of office by not enforcing the Fourteenth and Fifteenth Amendments.

Democracy came alive finally, when black people took to the streets and demonstrated and sat in and got arrested by the tens of thousands and created a commotion that was heard around the world. So it was an insight, suddenly. It shouldn't have been; I should have known that from before, that democracy comes alive not when government does anything, because government cannot be depended on to rectify serious injustices. It comes alive when people organize and do something about it. The Southern black movement taught me that.

You write in your autobiography, "I began to realize no pitifully small picket line, no poorly attended meeting, no tossing out of an idea to an audience or even to an individual should be scorned as insignificant."

I suppose that's something that people learn when they participate in social movements, especially if they participate in the movement long enough to see it develop into something that at first seems impotent and impossible and then becomes a force and brings about change. I saw that in the civil rights movement, and I saw that in the antiwar movement. Because in both cases, you could see little things happen which seemed as if they would go nowhere. It seems as if you are up against forces that cannot be dislodged.

In the civil rights movement, change took place in the most dangerous parts of the country, in the deep South, where everything was controlled by the white power structure and blacks didn't have the wherewithal. The only thing they had was their bodies, their determination, their unity, their willingness to take risks. And, yes, it starts with small things. You don't think they are going to get anywhere. Nobody really knew in the late '50s or even in the first years of the '60s that anything big would happen, and yet it did.

The antiwar movement started off with small antiwar gestures in little gatherings around the country, and it seemed impossible. How are you going to stop the greatest military power on earth from continuing a vicious war? And yet, those small meetings, demonstrations, turned gradually, over several years, into a movement which became powerful enough to cause the government to think twice about continuing a war.

You state a part of your philosophy of history: "I'm convinced of the uncertainty of history, of the possibility of surprise, of the importance of human action in changing what looks unchangeable." You participated in one of the first (if not the first) teach-ins on the Vietnam War on the Boston Commons very early in the game. It was years later that you were drawing massive crowds to a similar event on the Commons.

That's right. That very first antiwar meeting on the Boston Commons in the spring of '65, when Johnson had begun the real escalation of the war, begun the bombing, begun the dispatch of large numbers of troops. We had our first antiwar meeting on the Boston Commons, and perhaps a hundred people showed up. Herbert Marcuse spoke, I spoke; a few other people spoke. It looked pitiful. This was '65. In '69, another meeting on the Boston Commons, a hundred thousand people are there. In those few years, something very important had taken place. I think that showed the possibility of change if you persist.

Your involvement in the antiwar movement was informed, in part, by your experience as a soldier. In one of the last bombing missions of the war, you were a bombardier on a plane that was responsible for one of the first uses of napalm, on an innocent French village called Royan. Tell us about that experience and what you learned from it, and how it affected your activism in the antiwar movement and your view of war in general.

I enlisted in the Air Force. I volunteered. I was an enthusiastic bombardier. To me it was very simple: it was a war against fascism. They were the bad guys; we were the good guys. One of the things I learned from that experience was that when you start off with them being the bad guys and you being the good guys, once you've made that one decision, you don't have to think anymore, if you're in the military. From that point on, anything goes. From that point on, you're capable of anything, even atrocities. Because you've made a decision a long time ago that you're on the right side. You don't keep questioning, questioning, questioning. You're not Yossarian, who questions.

And so, I was an enthusiastic bombardier, as I say. The war was over, presumably—a few weeks from the end. Everybody knew the war was about to end in Europe. We didn't think we were flying missions anymore. No reason to fly. We were all through France, into Germany. The Russians and Americans had met on the Elbe. It was just a matter of a few weeks. And then we were awakened in the wee hours of the morning and told we were going on a mission. The so-called intelligence people, who brief us before we go into a plane, tell us we are going to bomb this tiny town on the Atlantic coast of France called Royan, near Bordeaux, and we are doing it because there are several thousand German soldiers there. They are not doing anything. They are not bothering anyone. They are waiting for the war to end. They've just been bypassed. And we are going to bomb them.

What's interesting to me later, in thinking about it, is that it didn't occur to me to stand up in the briefing room and say, "What are we doing? Why are we doing this? The war is almost over, there is no need." It didn't occur to me. To this day, I understand how atrocities are committed. How the military mind

works. You are taught to just mechanically go through the procedures that you have been taught, you see.

So, we went over Royan, and they told us in the briefing that
we were going to drop a different kind of bomb this time. Instead
of the usual demolition bombs, we are going to drop thirty
hundred-pound canisters of what they called jellied gasoline,
which was napalm. It was the first use of napalm in the European war. We went over. We destroyed the German troops and
also destroyed the French town of Royan. "Friendly fire." That's
what bombing does.

To this day, when I hear the leaders of the country say, "Well,
this is precision bombing and we are being very careful, and we
are only bombing military"—that's nonsense. No matter how
sophisticated the bombing technology, there is no way you can
avoid killing nonmilitary people when you drop bombs. It wasn't
until after the war that I looked back on that. In fact, it wasn't
until after Hiroshima and Nagasaki that I looked back on that.
Because after Hiroshima and Nagasaki, which at first I had wel-
comed like everybody at that time did—"Oh yes, the war is going
to be over"—then I read John Hershey's book *Hiroshima*, and for
the first time the human consequences of dropping the bomb
were brought home to me in a way I hadn't thought of. When you
are dropping bombs from 30,000 feet you don't hear screams.
You don't see blood.

I suddenly saw what the bomb in Hiroshima did. I began to
rethink the whole question of a "good war." I came to the conclusion that there is no such thing as a good war. They may start off
with good intentions, at least on the part of the people who fight
in them. Generally not on the part of the people who make the
decision; I doubt they have good intentions. But there may be
good intentions on the part of the GIs who believe, yes, we are
doing this for a good cause. But those good intentions are quickly
corrupted. The good guys become the bad guys. So I became convinced that war is not a solution, fundamentally, for any serious

problem. It may seem like a solution, like a quick fix, a drug. You get rid of this dictator, that dictator, as we did Hitler, Mussolini. But you don't solve fundamental problems. In the meantime, you've killed tens of millions of people.

You've argued that what is selected and who selects the facts for history is very important. In fact, you quote Orwell, who wrote, "Who controls the past controls the future. And who controls the present controls the past." How did these life experiences, your insight, lead you to focus on this alternative history, for example, of the United States?

My growing up and going to work and becoming, as I say, class conscious; and then going to school and reading in my history books, looking for things that I had begun to learn on my own. Working in a shipyard and actually organizing young shipyard workers and getting interested in labor history, reading on my own the history of labor struggles in this country, and then looking in the history books that were given me in school, looking for the large textile strike of 1912, the Colorado coal strike of 1913, looking for Mother Jones, looking for Emma Goldman, Bill Haywood. They weren't there.

So it became clear to me that the really critical way in which people are deceived by history is not that lies are told, but that things are omitted. If a lie is told, you can check up on it. If something is omitted, you have no way of knowing it has been omitted. Looking through history, looking at the treatment of race, looking at the treatment of women; it made me always ask the question: what has been left out of this story? So when I started out my book, I knew I had to start out with Columbus, because that's what all histories of the United States start off with, and I said, "What is left out?" The Indian point of view. And then Las Casas comes into the picture, telling the other side of the story.

Arthur Schlesinger writes this glowing book about Andrew Jackson and Jacksonian democracy. What else was going on? And then I find out that Jackson is responsible for the brutal treatment of the Indians in the Southeast, driving them across the Mississippi, thousands of them dying. Jackson is a racist. Jackson is a slave owner. Under Jackson, the industrial system begins with the mill girls going to work at the age of twelve and dying at the age of twenty-five. I became conscious of omissions in history, and that's what I was determined to try to remedy.

You're a person who is up front about his values and up front about the emotion that he feels about injustice. I want you to talk about how your writing is affected by these honesties about both your values and your emotions. Is that a plus in making it easier to tell these stories?

I know that there is a kind of conventional wisdom, or, as I put it, conventional foolishness, that if you're passionate about something you can't really write well about it. In the arts, we accept that passion makes the arts come alive. But we don't accept it in scholarship, and therefore we draw a false line between the arts and scholarship. But I believe that being passionate about your scholarly work, being passionate about history is something that needs to be expressed in order to be honest. I think there's nothing more important than being honest about your feelings. Otherwise you are presenting something that is not yourself.

There is another element to it, and that is, in being passionate about something, you are giving that intensity to what you write, which magnifies its power. In a way, you're trying to make up for the fact that people who have written other things dominate the ideological landscape. Because you're a minority voice, you have to speak louder, more eloquently, more vividly, more passionately.

You have written, talking now about history and the importance of education, "It confirmed what I learned from my Spelman years, that education becomes most rich and alive when it confronts the reality of moral conflict in the world."

My experience at Spelman College is an example of the interaction between education and activism. When my students went into town for the first time to sit in, to demonstrate, to be arrested in spring of 1960, I had colleagues at Spelman, Morehouse, Atlanta University—the complex of black colleges—who said, "This is bad, they are hurting their education." One of them wrote a letter to the *Atlanta Constitution* saying "I deplore what my students are doing; they are cutting class; they are missing out on their education." And I thought, what a pitiful, narrow, cramped view of education this is. To think that what these students are going to learn in books can compare to what they will learn about the world, about reality. They will come from town, they will come back from prison, and then when they will go into the library, they will go into it with an enthusiasm and a curiosity that didn't exist before.

You also wrote, and I think you are talking about your years at Boston University, "I wanted students to leave my classes not just better informed, but more prepared to relinquish the safety of silence, more prepared to speak up, to act against injustice wherever they saw it." What then is the link in the importance of history to activism?

I think the learning of history is a way of declaring, "I wasn't born yesterday; you can't deceive me." If I don't have any history, then whatever the person in authority—the president at the microphone announcing we must bomb here, we must go there— the president has the field all to himself. I cannot counteract, because I don't know any history. I can only believe him. I was born yesterday. What history does is give you enough data so that you can question anything that is said from on high. You can measure the claims that are being made by the people in authority against the reality. And you can look at similar claims that were made before, and see what happened then. There's President Bush saying we're going to war for democracy. And then you go back through history and say, "How many times have presidents said we're going to war for democracy, and what have those wars really been about?" The history can clarify things, prepare you for dealing with the duplicities of the real world.

Is it fair to say that you retain a cautious optimism about human nature?

Cautious in the sense that I'm not positive that things are going to go well. The future is indeterminate. But after all, the future depends on what we do now. If we are pessimistic now, we are doomed in the future. If we give up at this point, then we know nothing good is going to happen. If we act on the assumption that there's a chance that something good may happen, then we have a possibility. Not a certainty, but a possibility. So I believe it's useful, it's pragmatic to be optimistic.

But not simply as an act of faith, but also because there is historical evidence for the fact that when people act, persist, get together, organize, they bring about changes. There haven't been enough changes. So you can look at that and say, not enough. True. But the fact that some changes have been made. The fact that labor, by struggling, won the eight-hour day. The fact that blacks in the South did away with the signs of segregation. The fact that women changed the consciousness of this country about sexual equality. Even though those are only beginnings, that historical experience suggests reason to think it is possible that other things may change.

It's important that people read and learn—and this goes back to John Dewey and Alfred Lord Whitehead—that the purpose of learning is to have an effect on a world in which mostly people don't have the leisure, don't have the opportunity, don't have the breathing space, don't have the physical health even, to read a book or learn. So we who can do those things have an obligation to create a world in which maybe then people can learn for fun.

If you're engaged in a movement where the future of that movement is uncertain, even if you're trying to achieve an objective which looks very, very far away, simply working for it makes life more interesting and more worthwhile. So you don't have to look for some victory in the future. The very engagement with other people in a common struggle for something that you all believe in, that is a victory in itself.